It's *Our*

Reviews

This innovative and original volume contends that Jewish educational leaders should think of their field as a species of social entrepreneurship. While drawing on concepts from business studies, the author actually reinterprets them and applies them especially to the social and cultural goals of Jewish education. While thoroughly documented and deeply informed, the book is written in a clear, crisp style meant for policy-makers and practitioners. It is jam-packed with retainable information and fruitful concepts, together with narratives of success stories and "existence proofs" rendered in a most instructive and readable style. This book is a must for all those wishing to make a real impact on the field of Jewish education in the coming century.

Professor Jonathan Cohen, Director, Melton Centre for Jewish Education, The Hebrew University of Jerusalem

Mirvis has written a noteworthy and readable book illustrating ways to apply principles of social entrepreneurship to the field of Jewish – in particular, non-Orthodox – education. The explication is accompanied by inspiring examples of innovations in Jewish education. Those dedicated to furthering modern Jewish education will find useful concepts and paradigms to help promote the potential impact of their endeavors.

Professor Malka Rappaport Hovav, Provost, Rothberg International School, The Hebrew University of Jerusalem

Jonathan Mirvis has a powerful, important social vision: to advance quality Jewish education and make it accessible. This book offers a roadmap to achieve that vision - with critical insights that go beyond conventional wisdom and harness the depth of his expansive knowledge on social entrepreneurship, disruptive innovation, and understanding what motivates people to consume. With this book as a guide, it's time to innovate and bolster Jewish education worldwide. "It's Our Challenge" is educational and inspiring. It gives insight to how we as a community can move forward together embracing change.

Michael Horn, Cofounder Clayton Christensen Institute, Coauthor "Disrupting Class"

Philanthropists who wish to move from the virtue of contributing to the social good of Klal Yisrael, to making far more impactful strategic investments in the future potential of our world-wide community, have much to gain from the insights offered.

Sir Mick Davis, Founding Partner of X2 Resources and formerly Chief Executive of Xstrata Plc. Chairman of the Board, the Jewish Leadership Council of Great Britain

A masterful tapestry of text and context, personalities as powerful change agents, innovation and investment, influence and impact. Dr. Jonathan Mirvis has taken a 360-degree view of theories from all quarters (including his own), researched the patterns and seen how they have been applied to "best practice" Jewish educational models across the globe.

This work draws out the principles for effective practice. Mirvis lays the obligation of Jewish continuity squarely on the shoulders of the gatekeepers of Jewish knowledge. Jewish education in its broadest sense here is the microcosm for analysis. All who care deeply about the perpetuation of Jewish identity through knowledge and experience should study this seminal work from cover to cover.

Viv Anstey, Director of the Midrasha Adult Education Institute,
Community activist and serial social entrepreneur,
Cape Town, South Africa

Mirvis leaves one feeling optimistic about what our community can achieve when we support passionate, inspiring, and entrepreneurial leaders who care deeply about our Jewish future.

Jeremy J. Fingerman, CEO Foundation for Jewish Camp

A refreshing and essential resource that offers funders a 21st century framework for thinking about the world of Jewish education. Mirvis has put together a tool kit that doesn't exist: stories and theory are deftly interwoven to reveal how past creativity can inform and inspire future efforts in the field. Ultimately, it can help us to be accountable in new ways for our decision making.

Lee M. Hendler, Trustee, The Joseph and Harvey Meyerhoff Family
Charitable Fund, Author, "The Year Mom Got Religion"

A thoughtful book which develops a lens through which to view the challenges which Jewish education leaders face in the advance of continuity and change. This work provides profiles of those who have found the balance, and provides guidance relating to how each of us can play a critical role in ensuring a vibrant Jewish future. "It's Our Challenge" is THE book Jewish educators will be discussing and debating for years to come.

Dr. Marc N. Kramer, Co-Executive Director, RAVSAK

An absorbing book with great insight. A compelling invitation for philanthropists, leaders, policy makers and practitioners to reassess traditional approaches to Jewish education and view them through the increasingly important lens of social entrepreneurship and innovation.

**Dr Hilton Immerman OAM,
CEO, Shalom College and The Shalom Institute. Honorary Fellow,
University of New South Wales, Australia**

What elements help ensure successful innovation? Weaving fascinating stories into the "process" narrative, Mirvis unravels this mystery in elegant steps while reminding us about the importance of community. By supporting educators pushing boundaries, we are creating a vibrant future for our Jewish community. A must read for Funders, educators and policy makers

Jonathan makes the case for investment in Jewish education and argues that providing both young and old access to Jewish thought and learning is a fundamental ingredient of renewal and vibrancy.

**Diane Troderman, educator and philanthropist, a past chair of
JESNA and PEJE, Board member of the Davidson school at JTS
and Hebrew Public (Hebrew charter schools)**

Jonathan Mirvis provides an indispensable bridge between Jewish education and social entrepreneurship. Mirvis proposes a theoretical model and offers real-world examples of how great ideas in education can be developed and up-scaled into programmes that can transform Jewish education on both local and international scales.

**Michael Wegier, Chief Executive,
United Jewish Israel Appeal (UJIA) UK**

Jonathan Mirvis gives us our first comprehensive analysis of and guide to Jewish educational entrepreneurship using the entrepreneurship and innovation literature selectively and thoughtfully. Through the lens of social entrepreneurship, this work highlights the unique challenges of Jewish education. This work gives both would-be innovators and their potential supporters a road map for embarking on an entrepreneurial journey to expand educational participation and increase its impact.

**Dr Jonathan Woocher, President,
Lippman Kanfer Foundation for Living Torah**

It's *Our* Challenge

A Social Entrepreneurship Approach to Jewish Education

Jonathan Mirvis

YOUCAXTON PUBLICATIONS

OXFORD & SHREWSBURY

To my beloved wife
Micky
עצם מעצמי ובשר מבשרי
An intrinsic part of my essence and core being

Our dearest children
Shlomo and Shira
Tami and Ronen
Dana and Eldad
Elana and Dani
Our source of pride and admiration

And adorable grandchildren
Ori, Yuval, Noam, Dvir, Yair, Alon, Roni,
Yishai, Hadas, Beri, Hadas, and Eyal

Contents

Foreword

Jonathan Mirvis has taken upon himself the arduous challenge of drawing a connection between two independent disciplines, social entrepreneurship and Jewish education. The two realms seemingly have a different history, cover different content areas and have different goals. Dr. Mirvis has mastered this challenge in a remarkable manner.

He leads the reader on a wonderful journey that interweaves three destinations: a theoretical conceptualization of social entrepreneurship that includes concrete steps for achieving social goals and realizing a social vision; the development of Jewish education, with emphasis on its aims and needs, and the contemporary challenges it faces; and personal experiences that connect these different aspects.

Today, the concept of social entrepreneurship is at the heart of social activism. Many organizations encourage their members to adopt new ways of thinking and original strategies for implementing the organizations' tasks. Workshops promising to boost social entrepreneurship abound. An overview of the concept readily reveals that it is fluid, diffuse and amorphous, serving a variety of different needs and purposes.

In taking the reader on this journey, Mirvis examines the ideological roots of "social entrepreneurship," explains its intentions and provides practical tools for the realization of a social vision and the attainment of social goals. Thus, the book offers a very important, systematic analysis of the development and use of this concept.

Mirvis analyzes the foundations of Jewish education through its various manifestations, articulates its aims and defines success in the field. He focuses on the importance of Jewish literacy, the need for Jewish education to be meaningful and the development of Jewish identity. He skillfully merges the worlds of social entrepreneurship and Jewish education, offering detailed descriptions, analyses and assessments of test cases for these two realms.

The book is intended for a wide range of readers, who will be captivated by its contents. These include those with an interest in social activism in general, and especially those seeking to take their first steps. Those who are interested in developing this field with a view to supporting individuals and groups will find analyses on the macro level as well as practical guidance on the micro level.

Mirvis guides the reader in defining the aim of the social initiative, assessing the resources available and those that might be attainable. He describes strategies for developing the initiative in such a way as to conform with its stated aims on the one hand and the reality in which it operates on the other. He discusses paradigms for identifying potential markets, appealing to noncustomers who could benefit from the initiative. He discusses the art of bridging between different resources and making use of different platforms as strategies for enhancing social initiatives.

The language flow captivates the reader from the first page to the last. This is an important contemporary book which undoubtedly will become a seminal work both for social entrepreneurs and for those engaged in the field of Jewish education.

Professor Mimi Ajzenstadt
Mildred and Benjamin Berger Professor of Criminology
Dean, Paul Baerwald School of Social Work and Social Welfare
The Hebrew University
Jerusalem, Israel

Acknowledgments

My thanks to Professor Jonathan Cohen, Director of the Melton Centre for Jewish Education at The Hebrew University of Jerusalem, for encouraging me to complete this work. Thanks also to my Melton Centre colleagues for their support in my academic endeavors.

The following people were very generous of their time, sharing with me their insights and expertise either through interviews or via written communications. I felt privileged to be party to their narratives and in awe of their achievements:

Robert Aronson , Viv Anstey, Maya Bernstein, Mem Bernstein, Mark Blazer, Dr. Jonathan Boyd, Matti Borowski, Rabbi Kenneth Brander, Dr. David Bryfman, Rabbi Richard Camras, Sandy Cardin, Professor Barry Chazan, Professor Jonathan Cohen, Professor Steven Cohen, Amy Scott Cooper, David Cygielman, Gershon Distenfeld, Peter Deutsch, Ira Dounn, Joel Einleger, Rabbi Dr. Josh Elkin, Alastair Falk, Jeremy Fingerman, Allan Finkelstein, Arthur Fried, Joe Freedman, Peter Geffen, Shoshana Boyd Gelfand, Lauren Gellman, Dr. Roberta Goodman, Andrew Gilbert, Harold Grinspoon, Mathew Grossman, Felicia Herman, Jody Hirsh, Alan Hoffmann, , Michael Horn, Dr. James Hyman, Avraham Infeld, Dr. Hilton Immerman, Simon Jacobson, Genia Janover, Richard Joel, Lila Kagedan, Dr. Marc Kramer, Nathan Lauffer, Clive Lawton, Aliza Mazor, Deborah Meyer, Simon Myerson QC, Rabbi Efraim Mintz, Rabbi Jay Henry Moses, Steve Miller, Saskia Swenson Moss, Rabbi Hershey Novack, Elliot Osrin, Rabbi Stanley Peerless, Dr. Alex Pomson, Yossi Prager, Dr. Zohar Raviv, Ana Robbins, George Rohr, Rafi Rone, Professor Leonard Saxe, Jaynie Schultz, Scott Shay, Tova Shimon, Roanna Shorofsky, Dr. Shimshon Shoshani, Jerry Silverman, Marcie Simons, Jane Slotin, Rabbi Phillip Warmflash, Naomi Korb Weiss, Farley Weiss, Michael Wegier, Reuven Werber, Rabbi Nechemya Wilhelm, Dr. Jonathan Woocher and Rabbi Joel Zaiman.

I am indebted to my Hebrew University students for their stimulating questions, critiques and valuable comments. It is a privilege to teach students who are both intellectuals and passionate about the importance of social change.

In researching the fields of Jewish education and Jewish demography I was fortunate to be assisted by Daniel Held and Nadine Bdil.

I am highly indebted to my editing team: to Moira Schneider for her work on many of the profiles, to Dr. Hilton Immerman for his keen academic eye, to Israel Sykes for his input and guidance and to Deena Nataf for her editing expertise. Their dedication and professionalism were key components in bringing this work to fruition.

A special thanks to Arthur Fried, trustee of the AVI CHAI Foundation. I discussed the ideas and proposed the conceptual framework of this book with him in early 2011. His immediate enthusiasm and encouragement were important starting points. This seminal discussion was yet another encounter with Arthur which took place at a critical tangent in my career.

Finally, my eternal gratitude to He Who created us in His own image and commanded us to inhabit the universe, and be proactive and master it.

הודו לו, ברכו שמו. כי טוב ה', לעולם חסדו, ועד דור ודור אמונתו

Jonathan Mirvis
April 2016/ Nissan 5776

Introduction

A personal introduction

I have often been fascinated by the Biblical narrative of Jacob's dream, which takes place after he flees from home from the wrath of his brother Esau.

According to the Biblical text, "And he dreamed, and behold there was a ladder firmly placed on the ground with its head reaching the heavens. And the angels of G-d were ascending and descending [the ladder]" (Genesis 28:12).

This description is intriguing. What was the message that G-d wanted to convey to Jacob as he entered an era of uncertainty?

The message, I believe, was that that Jacob was now the master of his destiny. While he was certain to face daunting challenges in the home of his uncle Laban, if he maintained a healthy outlook he would successfully navigate his future. This required that his feet should be firmly placed on the ground while his head should be reaching for the heavens.

Translating this metaphor into a life strategy is not easy. In order to keep one's feet on the ground, a person needs to be immersed in the current reality. The individual needs to understand and master the culture in which he or she operates. By contrast, in order to reach for the heavens a person needs to have a higher belief that transcends the current situation and aspires to achieve seemingly unattainable goals.

Jacob's ladder, I believe, is an invitation from the Divine to embark on a path of social entrepreneurship. In navigating the future a person should always be rooted in the present, while his or her head constantly challenges the status quo and dreams of a new reality. The social entrepreneur is forever aspiring to change the world, yet in order to succeed must engage in an ongoing negotiation between where he or she is and where he or she is aspiring to be. This process is alluded to by the angels who constantly ascend and descend the ladder.

Personally, I was privileged to be born to South African parents for whom Jacob's ladder was the prevailing paradigm. My father, Rabbi Dr. Lionel Mirvis, has had an extensive educational career, including the founding of the Hillel Jewish Day School in Benoni, South Africa, and to this day he continues to be a revered teacher and scholar. With the support of his wife, Raisel, he constantly aspires and acts to impact the Jewish world. My late mother, Freida, who passed away all too young, was a gifted educator in the area of early childhood education. During the apartheid years she was director of the Athlone Teachers' Training College in Cape Town. In this position she dedicated the last decade of her life to the advancement of early childhood education among the populations which suffered from racial discrimination.

While my parents were committed to changing different aspects of society, they shared the common belief that education is the ideal vehicle for achieving this goal.

The aspiration to "change the world" was thus part of my personal dna, and this aspiration accompanied me through my school years in South Africa and my continuing studies at yeshiva in Israel.

Prior to making my career choice, I married my future soul mate, Micky Levin, who full heartedly supported my aspirations. She too grew up in a home in which impacting the community and the world at large was a prime aspiration. Her late father Dr Shlomo Levin was a renowned Jewish educator whose international career included the establishment of The Theodore Herzl Jewish Day School in Port Elizabeth, South Africa. Sadly his promising career was cut short with his passing at a young age in the midst of his service as the Israeli consul in New York City.

Entering the field of Jewish education

Originally I thought that social changes could be achieved politically, and thus I majored in political science for my bachelor's degree. In addition I contemplated a legal career that would enable me to achieve my aspirations. However, my future career choice ultimately became the field of Jewish education.

Having studied at yeshiva and received rabbinical ordination, without any intention of entering the rabbinate, I made my passion for Jewish education the focus of my career. In making this choice I was persuaded by the late Professor Michael Rosenak and inspired by the foremost Jewish education entrepreneurs of the twentieth century, with whom I studied and for whom I worked. These giants include Avraham Infeld, the late Professor David Hartman, Professor Alice Shalvi, Rabbi Shlomo Riskin, the late Professor Seymour Fox and Alan Hoffman, who ultimately became my entrepreneurial guide and mentor.

My decision to make Jewish education my career focus became sealed in 1989 when I entered the Jerusalem Fellows program with the encouragement of my friend and colleague Dr. Howard Deitcher. After the two-year fellowship, Alan Hoffman, Director of the Melton Centre for Jewish Education at The Hebrew University of Jerusalem, offered me the position of director of the Florence Melton Adult Mini-School Institute. This position was stimulating and challenging, and I went on to fill it for over two decades. The institute's mission was centered on adult Jewish education, which had become my primary research focus, and the position itself presented exciting entrepreneurial opportunities.

Embarking on an academic career

The Melton Centre encouraged me to complete my PhD in Adult Education, which I had pursued at the University of Surrey under the United Kingdom's foremost adult education academic, Professor Peter Jarvis. Thus, parallel to my work in the Mini-School Institute,

I followed an academic career teaching graduate courses in the field of adult education at The Hebrew University.

In my attempts to grow the mini-school's core project globally, I researched the area of franchising in depth and was fortunate to be tutored by Dr. Martin Mendelsohn, who was a uk-based international legal expert in this field (Mendelsohn, 2004). This led to my development of the social franchise model, an adaptation of commercial franchising to the nonprofit sector.[1]

Specializing in social entrepreneurship

In pursuing this area of research, I discovered the new academic discipline, Social Entrepreneurship. This field, which focused on entrepreneurship as a vehicle for solving social problems, fascinated me. The late Professor Greg Dees had given the first academic course at the Harvard Business School in this field in the late 1990s, and this started a trend among business schools across the globe. I researched this area in depth, and was inspired by David Bornstein's book, *How to Change the World,* which became a standard reader for numerous academic social entrepreneurship courses (Bornstein, 2007).

In 2004 I offered my first graduate course in social entrepreneurship, and ever since, this has been my prime teaching and research focus. As the years progressed, different Hebrew University departments expressed interest in this area. Thus, today I have the privilege of teaching courses in this field to a wide range of graduate students from both Israel and overseas, in the fields of Jewish education, business administration, nonprofit management and community development.

After a few years of teaching in these different settings, I realized that there was a fundamental difference between social entrepreneurship that operates in the general setting and social entrepreneurship pursued in the realm of Jewish education. In

---

1   In 2004 I received the Kaye Innovation Award from The Hebrew University of Jerusalem for developing this model.

the former, the entrepreneur's central challenge is to develop solutions for social problems. In the realm of Jewish education, the primary challenge is to develop a market for a "product," Jewish education. Thus the literature and prevalent paradigms that were studied in the field of general social entrepreneurship were not entirely applicable to Jewish education.

A search for alternative paradigms

Troubled by this lack of congruency, I searched the literature on commercial entrepreneurship that I sensed could address the challenges we face in growing the market of Jewish education. There I discovered a wealth of literature that was pertinent to the challenges which are encountered by Jewish educators. This book is the net result of this long process of research and deliberation.

Structure of the book

The book is divided into five sections. The first comprises Chapter One. This opening chapter highlights the pioneering work of four entrepreneurs in the field of Jewish education and sets the scene for the book.

The second section comprises Chapters Two through Five, which articulate the foundational concepts that underlie the area of a social entrepreneurial approach to Jewish education. These chapters introduce and explain the concepts of social needs entrepreneurship, social vision entrepreneurship, three important approaches to Jewish education and the maximization of educational impact.

The third section, Chapters Six through Eight, focuses on growing the field of quality Jewish education. This section takes paradigms developed in the commercial realm and applies them to Jewish education.

The fourth section includes Chapters Nine through Twelve, and provides an insight into the workings of entrepreneurs. The underlying assumption is that there are four meta-strategies that could be followed. Each strategy is explored drawing on examples from different fields of entrepreneurship, with an emphasis on entrepreneurship in the Jewish education sphere.

The final section comprises Chapter Thirteen, and explores investment in educational innovation and the challenge of sustainability.

Methodology

Two components in this book are interwoven:

- Theories, paradigms and concepts which are germane to the general field of social entrepreneurship.
- The application of the theories to the realm of Jewish education primarily in the English-speaking Diaspora, with an emphasis on the non-Orthodox communities.

Research on the first component commenced at the beginning of the millennium. It comprised an analysis of social and commercial entrepreneurship literature, an analysis of case studies in these subject areas and over fifty in-depth interviews with entrepreneurs.

I have performed in-depth research on the application of the theories, paradigms and concepts to the realm of Jewish education from 2011 through to 2016 My research comprised an analysis of the Jewish education, the sociology of North American Jewry and Jewish demographics literature.

In addition, I conducted seventy-five in-depth interviews and approximately ten written communications with entrepreneurs and knowledgeable informants primarily from the United States and Israel, but also from Canada, the United Kingdom, Australia and South Africa. The interviews were recorded and the information categorized. In some situations follow-up interviews were conducted. I then chose the examples to use in the book that would best reflect the theories and paradigms.

Use of terminology: quality and high-impact programs

In our use of examples to illustrate the different theories and paradigms, we have at times described programs to be "quality" and/or "high impact." In determining whether a program is quality or high impact we have based our judgment on either outside evaluations or knowledgeable informants. Evaluation sources have been cited. If no attribution appears, the source is knowledgeable informants. Thus in the use of the terms "quality" and "high impact," there certainly may be an element of error.

Style of the Book

The first drafts of this book were written in an academic style and sent out to a number of readers whom I viewed to be the target readership. The overwhelming response to these drafts was that, while the work was informative, it was not interesting. I concluded that continued pursuit of this writing style would result in a limited readership, and thus in order to reach multiple audiences I ultimately chose a popular style of writing.

I hope this work will be of value to the wide range of stakeholders who are committed to entrepreneurship in the field of Jewish education. This includes professionals, funders, policymakers and academics, all of whom have personally adopted Jacob's paradigm, and in so doing have made improving the Jewish world their challenge.

References

Bornstein, D. (2007). *How to Change the World: Social Entrepreneurs and the Power of New Ideas.* Updated ed. New York: Oxford University Press.

Mendelsohn, M. (2004). *The Guide to Franchising.* 7th ed. London: Thomson.

Chapter One

They Made it Their Challenge

CENTRAL IDEA

EVERYONE HAS THE PREROGATIVE TO ENHANCE THE ACCESSIBILITY OF
JEWISH EDUCATION BY DESIGNING NEW MODELS.

Imagine the following scenario: You live in a certain city, and a
thousand miles away there is a place of interest. The primary way
to get there is by flying with a commercial airline. The flights are
expensive and thus only a limited number of the city's inhabitants
who are extremely committed to making the trip avail themselves
of the opportunity.

Those who have traveled to this place report on the visit's
impact on their lives. They feel personally enriched and are far
more motivated to be active in the community. However, given
the remoteness of the destination and its inaccessibility, very few
are willing to contemplate the trip.

In the city there are four determined individuals who are not
prepared to accept the status quo. They believe that too many city
dwellers are missing the experience of a lifetime and they plan
feverishly to make the destination accessible.

The first decides to found an alternative airline. He will introduce
amenities and options that the current airline does not offer. A second
decides to open a low-cost airline, thereby making flights much
more affordable. A third has an even more creative idea. He noticed
that the train passes the destination a few miles to the west. He
decides to invest in a bus service which would connect the rail with
the destination. This would enable him to utilize an existing rail

1

infrastructure which was built with state funding. A fourth decides to build hotels on the way to the place of interest in order to entice those in the city to consider making the long drive and combining the trip with a vacation.

Along with their public-spirited efforts, the activists encounter numerous obstacles. Some commercial airline officials do not understand the need for an alternative airline, claiming that there are too few air commuters to support even current aircraft capacity. Others protest the introduction of low-cost travel. They assert that the customer's overall experience will be compromised and disadvantageous.

The train and hotel entrepreneurs are harassed by vendors in the home city, who express no interest in making the destination accessible to the city dwellers. Some bring lawsuits against the initiative to make cheap rail transport accessible, while local hoteliers do everything possible to ensure that the new hotels on the way to the destination will not be licensed.

In spite of all these obstacles, the entrepreneurs forge ahead successfully, thereby ensuring far greater access for the city dwellers to the remote getaway.

The four individuals are Peter Geffen, Gershon Distenfeld, Peter Deutsch and Ana Robbins. The destination is quality, comprehensive Jewish schooling.

Peter Geffen

Peter Geffen is a Jewish education visionary. In 1967, at the age of twenty-one, he created a unique after-school high school program at New York's Park Avenue Synagogue (Conservative). Geffen, who came from a family of Conservative rabbis including both his father and uncle, had not attended a Jewish day school. Instead he obtained his Jewish education from traditional afternoon Hebrew school and Camp Ramah, the movement's network of summer camps.

Politically and socially progressive, Geffen did not believe in schools that removed Jewish children from the mainstream, and consequently never had interest in the day school movement. However, from his experience at Park Avenue Synagogue where he had built a highly successful Hebrew high school, he also knew the limits to what could be accomplished in the few hours of after-school education.[1]

When in the late 1970s the synagogue put up a new after-school building that would be standing empty for most of the day, Geffen pondered a change in his thinking. He became intrigued with the idea of replicating his successful Park Avenue model in a day school setting.

He thought of his social justice heroes, the great humanitarians Rabbi Abraham Joshua Heschel, John F. Kennedy, Robert Kennedy and the Reverend Dr. Martin Luther King, Jr. (Geffen had been a civil rights worker for Dr. King in the 1960s), and realized that they had all come from somewhat exclusive educational universes. He began asking himself whether the parochialism of the school environment was the determining factor or whether the philosophy, curriculum and orientation of the school's educational system had been the determining influence upon these men who were his personal role models.

Geffen became convinced that a differently conceived Jewish day school could also encourage and foster outer-directedness accompanied by progressive social values, and that a child going through this system could emerge like the profound, religiously committed yet broadly humanistic individuals he so admired.

The year was 1980, and Geffen's first step was to draw up a manifesto incorporating basic principles, which remains the organizing document of the school he founded to this very day. The thirty-four-year-old father sent it to fifteen friends and close

---

1   The Park Avenue Hebrew High School is discussed in detail in Chapter Five.

colleagues, inviting those interested to join him in his proposed endeavor. To broaden the appeal of the school and in keeping with his commitment to pluralism, Geffen stressed that the school would not be affiliated with any movement or organization, and would appeal to students from across the Jewish denominational spectrum and beyond.

Although the idea for the school germinated from the construction of the building at Park Avenue Synagogue, ultimately the synagogue board refused to give Geffen permission to use the facility. Thus, in the fall of 1983 (and in the face of a feasibility study showing that there would be no interest in such an institution), the Heschel School board opened the Abraham Joshua Heschel School in rented classrooms at the Stephen Wise Free Synagogue on Manhattan's Upper West Side.

In marketing the school, the board focused on parents who had a strong Jewish commitment yet had not considered Jewish day school as an option for their children. These parents were apprehensive that a Jewish education would dilute the quality of the general education they were seeking. However, they were quickly taken by the new vision. Geffen, together with the newly hired principal Michael Wolf, and president of the board Dr. Rebecca Shahmoon Shanok, explained to these parents that a high-quality, integrated curriculum of Jewish and general studies could only enrich the young and intellectually growing child. Rather than diminishing the student's academic program, it would actually enhance it! Packaging the Jewish content and Hebrew language as parts of an integrated whole began to give Heschel a competitive edge in comparison with the other outstanding public and private schools in the Manhattan area.

Likewise, Geffen believed that a high-quality general education would enrich the quality of the Jewish education, and thus Heschel developed an integrated model of education whereby each class would have two teachers present in every classroom for the entire day, one with general studies expertise and the second with Jewish studies/Hebrew language expertise.

Starting in September 1983 with twenty-eight children in two mixed age groups – pre-K and kindergarten in one group and grades one and two in the other – and operating in two classrooms, Heschel expanded year by year, adding on an additional grade annually. Two months after the school opened its doors, it was clear that significant growth was inevitable and more space would be needed. When the opportunity presented itself in April 1984, the board made a then-outrageous – or at least courageous – decision to purchase a building.

By 1990 the middle school had moved to its own, additional building, and the establishment of a high school in a dedicated building followed in 2006. In 2015 the entire school population, from preschool through high school, numbered close to one thousand.

Early on, the school succeeded in competing in the academic market to such an extent that Heschel students were among those who scored in the top ten places in the competitive examinations for entrance to the New York City's prestigious high schools. Heschel's key strength was its ability to offer high-quality, sophisticated education within a Jewish context.

The parents' ultimate vote of confidence in Heschel came with the opening of the high school. With college entrance on the doorstep, parents seek high schools that will most likely enable their children to excel academically. Many Heschel parents could afford any private high school of their choice, yet they chose Heschel. Today, Heschel is the only non-Orthodox Jewish high school in Manhattan.

In the early years Geffen served as executive director and at one point headed the middle school, but his key role was within the realm of educational visioning and philosophy. Michael Wolf led the school's day-to-day operations and the essential areas of curriculum development, teacher supervision and training, and parent relationships until 1988, when Baruch Rand succeeded him. In 1990 Roanna Shorofsky replaced Rand as head of school, and she filled the position with great accomplishment through to her retirement in

2014. Shorofsky spearheaded the growth of the entire system; under her leadership, the school grew to over eight hundred students from kindergarten through twelfth grade.

Geffen guided the school's development for over two decades to its position of international prominence as a purveyor of sophisticated and integrated secular and Jewish education, until he was appointed director of the Center for Jewish History in lower Manhattan in 2003.

In the 1990s, with the establishment of PEJE (The Project for Excellence in Jewish Education) and its mandate to create more Jewish schools across North America, Geffen was approached by highly motivated people in Austin, Texas; Columbus, Ohio; Lafayette, California; and Toronto, Ontario to help them bring the Heschel model to their communities. Today these schools represent outstanding examples of the "Heschel model."

In addition, other trans-denominational schools have established their own models of excellence in both general education and Jewish studies. These include Milken High School in Los Angeles, California; Charles E. Smith Jewish Day School in Rockville, Maryland; and Gann Academy in Waltham, Massachusetts.

Gershon Distenfeld

Gershon Distenfeld is a young senior vice president at asset management giant AllianceBernstein. He grew up in an Orthodox family and attended a yeshiva day school. Based on his personal experience he believed in the importance of day school education not only for his three children, but for the Teaneck, New Jersey, community at large.

Distenfeld was mindful of the fact that Jewish day school tuition costs had spiraled at a rate of almost double that of inflation over the past twenty-five years, making Jewish education a luxury beyond the reach of most families. While he could afford to send his own children to private schools, he was highly troubled by the cost of day school education for the average Jewish household. He considers the affordability of Jewish day schools to be *the* defining challenge of the present generation.

During the years following the 2008 recession, Distenfeld used his creative entrepreneurial skills to investigate alternative solutions, convinced that there had to be a way of doing things differently. Harnessing his passion and focus, he was at the forefront of attempts to make Jewish education sustainable, assuming a number of positions in the community.

Distenfeld started a website called "Northern New Jersey Jewish Education for Generations" (NNJ kids), a *"kehillah"* fund through which individuals were encouraged to contribute to Jewish education by helping to pay for scholarships. He wrote many op-eds in newspapers on the subject and served on the board of his children's school, all of which bolstered his reputation and credibility among his target market for the landmark initiative he would soon lead.

In early 2011 he started researching a model of "blended" education. In this model, the curriculum comprises the traditional face-to-face teaching courses with online courses which every student studies individually. Blended learning would address the issue of sustainability as well as provide a quality product that would correlate better with each student's unique learning style. Distenfeld was influenced by Harvard Business School publication, *Disrupting Class* [Christensen, Johnson and Horn, 2008], in which the world's foremost authorities on disruptive innovation expounded their theory that disruptive innovation would change the way people learn.

With the support of an AVI CHAI Foundation grant, Distenfeld hired one of the best blended learning consultants in the field and recruited talented teachers who underwent a considerable amount of training to become cutting-edge educators. In 2012, Yeshivat He'Atid opened its doors in Teaneck, New Jersey, with tuition fees at $9,000. This fee was 40 percent less than those of other day schools in the area! Costs were cut because there are fewer teachers (whose salaries generally make up 85 percent of a school's expenses). Nevertheless, there is more meaningful interaction between teacher and student.

The traditional day schools were initially very upset. They also claimed there was no way Distenfeld would be able to cut costs. Nevertheless, he forged ahead, enduring intense political pressure in the form of threats and (false) accusations by his "competitors," who claimed he was destroying the existing schools. But being a free market adherent, he was unfazed. And once he started to succeed, others followed, claiming not only that they were also employing blended learning, but in fact had always done so!

By the academic year 2015–2016, Yeshivat He'Atid was offering pre-kindergarten through third grade, with plans to add one grade per year; among the pupils is Distenfeld's youngest child. The use of the blended model in this age group means much more project-based work and regular assessments on a real-time basis, while enabling children to learn in different styles and at different paces. The teacher, who is more of a facilitator, knows where each child is holding academically and can address his or her needs in real time. This model is not unique to Yeshivat He'Atid. It has been successfully adopted in a number of charter schools across the United States for many years.

Distenfeld's ideal, as expressed in the school's mission statement, is that Yeshivat He'Atid will serve as a model for twenty-first century Jewish education that is innovative and economically sustainable [Yeshivat He'Atid]. He is proud that the school is thriving, that parents are delighted and that the results speak for themselves.

In addition to Yeshivat He'Atid, Yeshiva High Tech, an Orthodox high school in Los Angeles, has chosen a similar path. Its tuition fees in 2015 were $12,000 per annum and it too follows the blended learning model. Hopefully, this format will be replicated in many more settings in the future.

While the blended learning model has evolved in the Orthodox sector, it has great promise for the non-Orthodox market as well. Parents who believe in a quality secular education along with a sound Jewish education are often forced to choose between outstanding public schools where there is no tuition and Jewish day schools whose tuition is in line with that of secular private schools. High tuition private schooling is beyond the reach of many of these parents. Thus, given their current choices, they must forgo a comprehensive Jewish education for their children – even though they believe in its importance.

However, if these parents were offered an affordable, excellent Jewish day school, they might well be enticed to enroll their children in it.

Peter Deutsch

In 2001, Peter Deutsch, a Democratic congressman in Florida from 1993 to 2005, was approached by members of the Greek American community in South Florida to assist them in their endeavor to establish the Archimedean Academy as a charter school. This group's motivation was their desire to preserve their Greek cultural identity [Shulzke, 2012].

In assisting with this initiative, Deutsch was struck by the similarities between the aspirations of the Greek community in the United States, which was struggling to maintain its heritage, and the parallel aspirations of the Jewish community. The Archimedes Academy, which opened in Miami in 2002, offers a demanding curriculum. It focuses on mathematics and modern Greek, using an immersion model in which students learn in Greek two and a half hours a day. In 2012 it was reported that the school had 950 students and a waiting list of one thousand [Shulzke, 2012].

Deutsch witnessed the tremendous success of the Archimedean Academy in offering a superior education. This inspired him with the notion that charter schools could serve a similar purpose in the

Jewish community. His idea was to establish a network of Hebrew charter schools that would attract a large Jewish student body and would focus on Hebrew language and Hebrew culture.

The charter school concept, originally developed by Ray Budde in 1989, has become widespread in the United States. By 2011, 4.2 percent of students who attended public schools were enrolled in charter schools [National Center for Educational Statistics, 2014]. This concept envisaged autonomous schools that receive public funding, on condition that they have no religious affiliation and there is no selection of students. Deutsch championed this concept and established the Ben Gamla Charter School in Hollywood, Florida, in 2007.

Deutsch's motivation was not personal, as his children attended a Jewish day school. He was a champion of public causes. A law school graduate, he was elected to Congress in 1993 at the young age of 35. He was driven by his deep commitment to the future of the Jewish people. Raised in a Reform home, Deutsch was on a personal journey toward increased Jewish commitment and was deeply troubled by the growing number of Jewish children who were enrolled in public schools and were receiving only the bare rudiments of a Jewish education. He felt that a Hebrew charter school supplemented by a strong after-school Jewish studies component could address this challenge.

Deutsch encountered major opposition to his initiative. He was attacked by those who were ideologically opposed to the concept of a Hebrew culture charter school, claiming it was a violation of separation of church and state in public education. Furthermore, the Jewish day schools in the area felt threatened by this new concept, as did the congregational supplementary schools. In its first week of operation, the Broward County school board ordered Ben Gamla to suspend Hebrew lessons because its curriculum referred to a website that mentioned religion. Nevertheless, Deutsch tenaciously carried on, and by 2013 over two thousand students were enrolled in four Ben Gamla schools in the South Florida area.

In the K–8 classes the students study Hebrew and Hebrew culture during school hours and are offered a robust Jewish studies program in the after-school hours. An estimated 50 percent of the Jewish students participate in the latter. On the high school level, Jewish studies programs are offered during a special "release-time" at an adjacent facility and these optional classes are well attended by the Jewish students.

While the precise number of Jewish students among Ben Gamla's student body is not known, knowledgeable informants estimate that 85 percent of the school's population is Jewish [Heilman, 2013].

In addition to the Ben Gamla schools in Florida, the Hebrew Charter Schools Center was operating six schools on the West Coast and in the Northeast as of 2014. Among these schools, the percentage of Jewish students was reported to be considerably lower than that of Ben Gamla [Nussbaum Cohen, 2013].

Deutsch's entrepreneurial endeavor holds great potential for offering Jewish education to those populations who have never previously considered comprehensive Jewish education to be an option.

Ana Robbins

Ana Robbins grew up in a traditional, committed Jewish family in Atlanta, Georgia. She attended public elementary school, Hebrew school three afternoons a week and JCC camps. In ninth grade, she was part of the first intake at the New Atlanta (now Doris and Alex Weber) Jewish Community High School, an experience that made a significant impact on her future.

Following a fourteen-month stint in Israel during which she studied at an Israeli high school, Robbins returned to Atlanta, working as an intern at the Israeli consulate general. Later she continued her education, majoring in Jewish Studies and Middle Eastern Studies at Emory University. After graduation, she was employed as a researcher and teaching assistant at the university, in between backpacking around the world.

Since her college days, Robbins had made a reasonable living teaching Hebrew school, but had been frustrated by the lack of support and guidance provided by the administration. Not being a professional educator, she had only a limited idea of requisite expectations, but nevertheless continued to teach afternoon school for a number of years.

When Robbins was in her mid-twenties, parents in the neighborhood asked her to organize something "cool" for their children to do after school. By then she had a good idea of what *not* to do.

Meeting once a week in a garage, the program started with six children; the numbers rapidly grew to thirty, and then sixty. This explosive and unanticipated growth prompted the organizing of a series of focus groups in 2011 to determine the needs of Robbins's constituents. The responses of the parents in the focus groups were quite unexpected. They requested a daily Hebrew after-school program, and Robbins rose to the challenge. She took the radical decision to offer a five-day, twenty-hour-a-week program. Her decision ran counter to the decision many synagogue supplementary schools had made to reduce their programs from three days a week to two, and from two to one.

Robbins prepared herself for this new challenge. As a graduate of PresenTense and ROI, two Jewish leadership and entrepreneurial initiatives, she clearly understood the issues she would be facing as a social entrepreneur. She visited the Kesher School in Newton, Massachusetts, which had implemented such a program since 1992, and was particularly impressed with their strong Judaic and Hebrew program.

Robbins thus founded Jewish Kids Group (JKG), an independent school that offered both a once-a-week and a five-day-a-week program.

Fifty percent of families being served by JKG were unaffiliated. Of those who did belong to a temple, half chose to send their kids to JKG (in addition to their synagogue's Sunday Hebrew school) because of its quality Jewish education. Many of the parent body mentioned that as children they were taken "kicking and screaming" to Hebrew school three times a week, and that they were delighted their children would have a positive Jewish educational experience.

The attraction of a five-day-a-week Hebrew after-school program should not be seen as evidence of a deep interest in Jewish education. In families in which both parents work outside the home, a problem arises as school finishes at two-thirty, while parents can pick up their children only after work, at six. Consequently, there is a great demand for after-school programs to fill these hours, and consequently they have proliferated. Robbins's creative innovation was developing a Hebrew after-school program with a focus on Jewish educational experiences.

The JKG Afterschool Community is in the league of specialist music and art after-school programs. Robbins has created a boutique niche in the field, providing all the services of a premium after-school program in addition to a full experiential Hebrew school curriculum – all in a camp-like environment [JKG]. It is critical to parents that children come home with homework finished and checked by an adult, but the school also has to fit in Hebrew and Israel education, and give dedicated time to building Jewish friendships – all critical factors for enhancing a child's Jewish identity.

While expensive at $4,900 (for the 2016–2017 academic year) a year per child for the five-day-a-week program – which does not include optional transportation from the child's school – tuition is still competitive in the marketplace of after-school programs. This amount, however, does not cover the full cost of the program, and Robbins must fundraise. Robbins employs professional educators, and her high-quality faculty assures JKG of a competitive edge.

In her desire is to replicate her Hebrew after-school model, Robbins became one of the pioneering members of the Nitzan Network, which supports the renewal of Jewish learning after school by sharing resources and practices [Nitzan Network]. It currently has nine affiliated after-school programs across North America [Nitzan Network]

Programs such as the JKG Afterschool Community offer an attractive and sustainable model for experiential Jewish education. If this model were to be adopted by temples and Jewish community centers in North America, children who attend supplementary Hebrew schools once or twice a week could be attracted to a rich and intensive Jewish educational experience five days a week.

In the Footsteps of Rabbi Yochanan ben Zakai

The four innovators I have described are part of an elite core of mission-driven individuals who are committed to Jewish education, believe in its importance for the Jewish future and have developed new Jewish educational models.[2] This area is a major challenge in the United States today, given the preclusion of state funding for religious education, and as a result the number of children in the United States who receive a quality formal Jewish education is proportionally much lower than that of other sizable Diaspora Jewish communities. Peter Geffen, Gershon Distenfeld, Peter Deutsch and Ana Robbins are all walking in the footsteps of a hero who changed Jewish history and ensured its future, Rabbi Yochanan ben Zakai.

Rabbi Yochanan ben Zakai: A Social Entrepreneur Who Met the Challenge of a Changing Era

In the year 70 CE the Jewish people faced their greatest challenge in Jewish history. The Roman army was besieging Jerusalem and the destruction of the second Temple was imminent. At that time the Temple in Jerusalem was *the* focus of Judaism, *the* place where the Jewish religion was practiced, via the Temple service. This required pilgrimage to Jerusalem and the offering of sacrifices. The Temple was the place where Jews prayed and celebrated, and the whole enterprise was threatened with catastrophe.

---

2   These four models are discussed in detail in Chapter Seven.

Rabbi Yochanan ben Zakai, a sage who lived in Jerusalem, understood the dangers facing the Jewish people and begged the Jewish military leaders to surrender to Rome. The zealots, who ruled the city, believed in fighting to the bitter end, and proscribed any activity that could be a hint of surrender. They thus forbade all citizens of Jerusalem to leave the city.

Realizing that the situation was calamitous, Rabbi Yochanan was desperate to escape. Together with his nephew Aba Sikra, who was the head of the zealots, Rabbi Yochanan devised a scheme whereby he feigned illness and then "passed away." Since the zealot sentries permitted the dead to be carried out of the city for burial, Rabbi Yochanan ben Zakai's "body" would be allowed to exit the gates. Clearly, the plan carried extreme risk.

After a successful escape fraught with last-minute danger and drama, Rabbi Yochanan reached the Roman camp. He greeted the Roman general Vespasian with "Hail Caesar!" Vespasian rebuked him for this inappropriate salutation. Thereafter followed a lengthy interchange between Rabbi Yochanan and Vespasian, in the midst of which a messenger from Rome entered, proclaiming that all should rise before Vespasian; Caesar had died and the powers in Rome had decided to appoint Vespasian in his stead.

Vespasian was taken by Rabbi Yochanan's foresight. He told the sage to make a request, which he promised to fulfill. Rabbi Yochanan asked that Vespasian grant him "Yavneh and its Sages" – i.e., to grant him the right to build a center of Jewish learning in Yavneh which would attract multiple Sages. On hearing Rabbi Yochanan's request, the Sages who had accompanied him rebuked him for this modest request; he could have asked Vespasian to save Jerusalem from destruction! [Bavli Gittin.]

It is important to analyze Rabbi Yochanan's request, as the future of Judaism and of the Jewish people was in the balance.

The Temple, the focus of Jewish ritual practice, was about to be destroyed. It was the locus of public worship, the place where the Jews felt the Divine presence. The sacrificial rituals were at the heart of Judaism, and the thrice-yearly pilgrimages to the Temple were an integral part of the celebration of the three festivals, Pesach, Shavuot and Sukkot. Not only was the Temple to be destroyed, Judaism as it was practiced was about to become devoid of its focal contents.

The battle for Jerusalem was part of the Jewish rebellion against Rome. Since 6 CE Rome had ruled over the area with various degrees of severity. The destruction of Jerusalem would lead to a tightening of Rome's rule of the area. The interest of Rome and only of Rome would be primary. The future of the Jewish people was at stake!

In the wake of these existential dangers, Rabbi Yochanan had a number of options. Political pragmatism seems to have made a request to save the Temple a non-option, yet other options existed that could have met the existential threats. One would be to request Jewish autonomy, thereby ensuring the future of the Jewish people in the Holy Land. Another, given the imminent destruction of the Temple, would be to request permission to build alternative houses of worship.

Yet Rabbi Yochanan decided in favor of neither of the above. He requested neither Jewish autonomy nor permission to build edifices that would be the locus of public worship. Instead, he asked for Yavneh and its Sages. He believed that the future of the Jewish people lay in the nurturing of its social and intellectual capital! The development of a center of Jewish learning would be the key to the future.

Common Threads

While the achievements and impact of Rabbi Yochanan's endeavors are of a completely different magnitude, they share common threads with the four initiatives described above. This is reflected in each of the four activists themselves, who possess:

- A strong belief in the importance of Jewish education and its necessity for the future of the Jewish people.
- A high level of social responsibility. A deep commitment to the Jewish community at large.
- A deep commitment to making quality Jewish education accessible to larger audiences. Each one developed models that are both scalable and sustainable.
- A readiness to personally step forward. Whereas many of us share similar sentiments, we will channel our insights into what we believe *others* should be doing. These individuals felt compelled to come forward and lead the initiatives themselves.
- A "sixth sense" for spotting the opportunity. While others may not have identified it or realized its potential, they grabbed it and moved into action.
- The courage to "put themselves on the line" and move forward, despite the risks involved. While the story of Rabbi Yochanan presents an extreme case of personal risk, all faced threats and dangers, and moved forward courageously.
- A high level of ingenuity and political acumen. They all used their natural instincts to navigate the treacherous paths.
- The ability to operate in multiple time frames. In order to succeed, they all dealt with both immediate and long-term challenges simultaneously. They realized that decisions taken today would have a bearing on the challenges at hand as well as on those in the future.

In scrutinizing these common threads, we have a picture of social entrepreneurship at its best. Social entrepreneurship is the utilization of entrepreneurial strategies for the attainment of social value, i.e., value which is in the interests of society.

In the next two chapters we will discuss the concept of social entrepreneurship in detail. In Chapter Two we will address the concept in general; in Chapter Three we will explore its application to the field of Jewish education.

References

Christensen, C. M., C. W. Johnson and M. B. Horn (2008). *Disrupting Class: How Disruptive Innovation Will Change the Way the World Learns.* New York: McGraw-Hill.

Heilman, U. (2013, July 1). "Jewish Public Schools? Hebrew Charter Franchises Offer Radically Different Models." JTA. Retrieved Septmeber 18, 2015. http://www.jta.org/2013/07/01/life-religion/jewish-public-schools-hebrew-charter-franchises-offer-radically-different-models.

JKG (n.d.). "JKG Afterschool Cummunity." Retrieved September 16, 2015. http://www.jewishkidsgroups.com/jkg-afterschool-community.html.

National Center for Educational Statistics (2014, April). "Charter School Enrollment." Retrieved April 6, 2015. https://nces.ed.gov/programs/coe/indicator_cgb.asp.

Nitzan Network (n.d.). "Affiliated Programs." Retrieved September 20, 2015. http://www.nitzan.org/affiliated-programs.html.

Nitzan Network (n.d.). "What We Do." Retrieved September 20, 2015. http://www.nitzan.org/.

Nussbaum Cohen, D. (2013, September 12). *Haaretz.* Retrieved September 20, 2015. http://www.haaretz.com/jewish-world/jewish-world-features/.premium-1.546804.

Shulzke, E. (2012, September 10). "Hebrew Charter School Founder Looks to 'Mormon School.'" Retrieved March 26, 2015, from Deseret News. http://www.deseretnews.com/article/765603214/Hebrew-charter-school-founder-looks-to-Mormon-model.html?pg=all./

Talmud Bavli, *Gittin* 56a–56b.

Yeshivat He'Atid (n.d.). "Mission Statement." Retrieved September 16, 2016. http://www.yeshivatheatid.org/mission-statement/.

Chapter Two

An Introduction to Social Entrepreneurship

CENTRAL IDEA

THE STRATEGIC GOAL OF SOCIAL ENTREPRENEURSHIP IS TO CREATE AND ENHANCE SOCIAL VALUE.

Muhammad Yunus is an economist who grew up in East Pakistan and taught at Middle State Tennessee University in the United States. He returned home in 1971 after Bangladesh became an independent country, separating from Pakistan. In 1974 Bangladesh suffered a major famine, bringing suffering to millions of destitute people. Yunus wanted to find ways to alleviate this poverty and undertook a series of visits to poor villages.

In a village called Jobra, Yunus encountered a situation in which the poor were being exploited in their efforts to eke out a living [Yunus, 2008]. He noticed a woman who made beautiful bamboo stools, and yet she herself could not benefit financially from her talent. The root cause of her problem was her inability to secure a bank loan to finance the raw materials, a plight shared by millions of others who were poor. She was dependent on a local moneylender who not only lent her money at an exorbitantly high level of interest, he also forced her to sell him her work at a price which he determined. Upon exploring the situation further, Yunus counted a total of forty-two people in the village who had each borrowed a total of twenty-seven dollars from the moneylender. Yunus immediately decided to lend the appropriate sum in order to free the villagers from exploitation.

When his loans were due for repayment, Yunus was struck by the fact that borrowers almost universally made their payments on time.

This contradicted the prevalent belief that the poor were unworthy borrowers and loans to them would run a high risk of default. Yunus extended his loans to other villages, having identified the borrowers with the help of volunteers. There too he was impressed by the high percentage of on-time repayment. Armed with his proven insights, Yunus approached a bank to create a microcredit system. He was rebuffed, however, with the claim that the poor in his "pilot project" returned their loans only because of a personal commitment to him and his volunteers.

Frustrated by this impasse, Yunus created a bank specifically designed for the purpose of microcredit loans to the poor, which operated as a for-profit organization. This bank, the Grameen Bank, has played a major role in alleviating poverty in Bangladesh. It has enabled millions of people who had no access to credit from regular banks to receive credit and operate their small businesses.

Muhammad Yunus was awarded the Nobel Peace Prize in 2006 jointly with the Grameen Bank that he founded. The award was made *"for their efforts to create economic and social development from below"* ["The Nobel Peace Prize 2006," 2006].

Yunus is accepted as *the* outstanding example of social entrepreneurship.

Entrepreneurship

We will begin with an understanding of the concept "entrepreneurship." In the twentieth century, the Bavarian economist Joseph Schumpeter described entrepreneurs as innovators who drive the creative instructive process. According to Schumpeter, entrepreneurs are the change agents in the economy. They strive to serve new markets, create new ways of doing things and move the economy forward [Dees, 2001].

The activities of an entrepreneur, as described by Schumpeter, are anchored in a free, capitalist economy that empowers individuals to take advantage of opportunities in order to create value. Capitalism encourages the individual to better his or her personal plight without dependence on central authorities. The entrepreneur takes responsibility for changing his or her reality, and is often totally obsessed with achieving this goal.

An Operative Definition of Entrepreneurship

Our operative definition will echo that of Schumpeter by incorporating into our definition two of the aspects of entrepreneurship that Schumpeter identified:

- **Taking responsibility for changing the reality and being obsessed with achieving this goal.**
- **Changing the reality through innovation, i.e., by creating new ways for achieving one's goals.**

For our purpose, "entrepreneurship" is therefore the dedication to changing a given reality, be it economic or social, by the use of innovative methods and technologies. This is achieved by the development of high-impact initiatives, either within an existing organization or by establishing a new organization for this purpose.

The Development of Social Entrepreneurship

Social entrepreneurship is the harnessing of entrepreneurship for the attainment or enhancement of social value. Social entrepreneurship requires defining a root problem or challenge and developing a number of strategic options for a solution or for meeting the challenge. All social entrepreneurship should ideally commence with a diagnosis of the current situation and a general idea regarding the preferred direction to be followed in the quest for a solution.

Social entrepreneurship is a fast-growing practice comprising "change makers" who relentlessly pursue social change. As defined above, the underlying assumptions are that individuals should be encouraged to take responsibility for changing their social reality, and that this goal is achievable through passion, dedication, commitment and innovation.

With the growth of global capitalism, which has been accelerated since the collapse of the Berlin Wall in 1989, we have witnessed two factors contributing to the widening gap between rich and poor. The first is the opportunity gaps which have developed between the "haves" and the "have nots." The free market system tends to favor those who already have. For example, those who have will enjoy access to a better education, ensuring they start their careers one step ahead. Furthermore, through their social networks they will be able to secure better jobs. Those at the bottom of the ladder are likely to remain there, even if they possess superior natural talents and abilities.

A second factor is the retreat of governments, both central and local, from welfare commitments to the less fortunate. Many governments are under pressure to balance their budgets, and for many the preferred options may be to cut their welfare budgets and renege on their welfare responsibilities to the underprivileged.

The governments of many underdeveloped countries simply do not have the resources to meet the needs of their citizens. Thus here too, there is a major void that calls out for social initiatives.

In general, the field of social entrepreneurship is comprised of attempts to counterbalance the inequality caused by the capitalist system and to give the underprivileged the opportunity to live lives in which their basic needs are met. Social entrepreneurship may address many social problems, such as struggles against disease, poverty, lack of education, lack of equal opportunity, discrimination and environmental pollution.

Social entrepreneurship made its entry into academia fairly recently. The first MBA course in this subject is attributed to the late Professor Greg Dees, who taught it at Harvard Business School in 1994 [Fulton, 2006]. Today, courses on social entrepreneurship are offered at business schools throughout the world. In the area of research, leading centers have been established such as the Center for Social Innovation at Stanford University and the Skoll Centre for Social Entrepreneurship at Oxford.

Social Value

Social value is the "currency" of social entrepreneurship. It refers to the creation of "social goods," i.e., goods and services that will benefit society. These are usually in the fields of medicine, education, social welfare including human rights, and ecology. Social value ensures a happier and more fulfilling existence for individuals and for society.

In light of the above, we could say that social impact is a key manifestation of social value, and thus social ventures are evaluated in terms of their yield of social value. If there is a high yield, they are deemed "profitable"; if there is no yield, the venture is deemed to be "bankrupt."

The complexity of the term "social value"

Using the commercial terminology of "profit" and "bankrupt" to describe social ventures creates a level of comparison between social and commercial values. However, serious differences between the two concepts should be borne in mind, particularly when the context is educational and the focus is on generating educational value.

As Young [Young, 2006] points out, commercial value is objective and quantifiable. Accepted accounting procedures exist for calculating profit and loss; following them enables those involved to assess the final health of the endeavor. On the other hand, social value is subjective and often not quantifiable. Its definition is often a cultural construct, and consequently there may be differing opinions regarding what is defined as "valuable." Examples of this complexity are art and music. In both areas there are cultural opinions regarding their value and appropriateness.

The Social Entrepreneur

The role of the entrepreneur, i.e., an individual who is passionate, dedicated, creative and mission-driven [Dees, 2001], lies at the heart of social entrepreneurship. According to Dees, social entrepreneurs play the role of change agents in the social sector by adopting a mission to create and sustain social value (not just private value), recognizing and relentlessly pursuing new opportunities to serve that mission, engaging in a process of continuous innovation, adaptation and learning, acting boldly without being limited by resources currently in hand and exhibiting heightened accountability to the constituencies served and for the outcomes created.

While commercial entrepreneurs are far more celebrated for their achievements than social entrepreneurs, the role of social entrepreneurs in impacting society should not be underestimated. For instance, the impact of both Florence Nightingale and Robert Owen is legendary. Likewise outstanding is Uri Lupolianski, the recipient of the 1993 Israel Prize, who established Yad Sarah, a national Israeli organization that lends out, at no cost, medical equipment to all. The range of items is comprehensive, ranging from cribs to wheelchairs, and the Israeli rehabilitation system is designed on the assumption that patients will have free access to the vital equipment Yad Sarah provides.

Social Enterprise

Since social entrepreneurship is dedicated to meeting the needs of the less fortunate, there is little expectation that the social endeavor will be able to recover its costs on a fee-for-service basis. Therefore, most social entrepreneurial endeavors rely on either philanthropic or government funding in order to operate financially.

However, there is a growing tendency among social entrepreneurs to reduce their dependence on these outside sources of income. Some are ideologically motivated; they feel that receiving funding from outside sources may compromise their mission. Beholden to these funders, they might not be able to implement a program that is in the best interests of the beneficiaries. Others, however, are practically motivated. They feel that reliance on philanthropy and government is too risky in the current economic climate, and thus prefer to be self-reliant. These endeavors are defined as social enterprises and are often registered as for-profit companies.

The Grameen Bank mentioned earlier is an outstanding example of a social enterprise. Following its success, founder Yunus extended the idea of social enterprise for serving underserved populations to other industries such as mobile networks [Yunus, 2008].

The Key Difference between Commercial and Social Entrepreneurships

The key difference between commercial entrepreneurship and social entrepreneurship lies in the core mission.

In commercial entrepreneurship, the core mission and goal of the entrepreneurial endeavor is to generate financial profit. The commercial entrepreneur may achieve this using a number of strategies that may include developing a new business model or a new product. For the commercial entrepreneur, success or failure is determined by the financial bottom line. Thus, if a commercial entrepreneur develops an innovative product or service that could potentially contribute to the welfare of society – a revolutionary drug, for example – the product or service might be discontinued if it is not profitable.

Implications of the differences in core missions

Access to investment funding

Within the commercial world there is a system that supports start-ups, commencing with angel funding and followed by funding from venture capitalists. Since the goal of a commercial entrepreneur is for his or her venture to become profitable in the future, investors have an incentive to invest in it. Furthermore, commercial entrepreneurs have access to loans given on the assumption that they will be able to pay them back in the future.

Social entrepreneurs, on the other hand, are far more pressed for funding. They have no systematic access to foundation support, and often have to tailor their project to fit in with the mission and interests of the foundation from which they are seeking funds. In

25

the event that the social entrepreneurial start-up has no assets, it will face great difficulty in securing loans.

The financial objective

The commercial entrepreneur aspires to make a profit while the social entrepreneur aspires to reach sustainability. In aspiring to achieve his or her goal, the commercial entrepreneur needs to cover overhead before realizing profit. By contrast, the social entrepreneur's highest priority is to maximize social value, and he or she needs money to cover costs. In the event that there is a surplus, a social entrepreneur may well choose to invest this amount in an activity that will generate additional social value.

The possibility of an "exit"

Successful commercial start-ups are able to work toward an exit that will not only enrich the entrepreneurs but may also free them from their initial financial responsibilities. By contrast, social entrepreneurs, who are dependent on philanthropic support for sustainability, have no exit. Unless they are adopted by the government or a foundation they will always be in start-up mode, continually searching for investments to sustain their endeavor.

Competition and cooperation

In the free-market system, commercial entrepreneurs in the same industry are natural competitors with one another in their quest to maximize profit. In the social arena, social entrepreneurs are natural strategic allies in their quest to enhance or create social value. Therefore, if a specific social value is achieved by a parallel organization, all who are committed to this social goal should feel a sense of achievement.

Ownership

Commercial entrepreneurs who found companies and register them in their names are the legal owners of their companies, unless they decide to sell. In the event that the company goes public, they may continue to retain a share of the business even if they have no formal connection with the running of the company.

Social entrepreneurs who operate nonprofit organizations have no ownership or "shares" in their organization. Their appointment to a professional position is contingent upon the agreement of a board of directors. In the event that the board decides on a change, the social entrepreneur can be dismissed and detached from the organization that he or she founded.

Use of commercial language in social settings

There are those who are uncomfortable with the use of commercial language to describe work in the social arena. They draw a clear distinction between endeavors with a clear profit motive and those in which there is a social value motive. This group will insist on referring to those who offer social services as doctors, educators and the like, and to those who receive these services as patients or students.

Social entrepreneurs tend not to share this reticence, believing that the application of commercial language to the social field in no way detracts from its social value. Therefore, they will refer to students as "clients" and "customers," and to teaching as a "delivery system." In this book we will use social and commercial language interchangeably, although in no way is it our intention to blur the distinction between those motivated by financial profit and those who strive to create social value.

Dual commercial and social entrepreneurship

In general, there is a demarcation between commercial and social entrepreneurs, the former committed to the accumulation of financial profit and the latter to the production of social value. However, there are those who choose a dual career. It is prevalent among entrepreneurs who succeeded in the commercial world to pursue a second career of social entrepreneurship.

A shining example of this is British entrepreneur Sir Ronald Cohen. He was the founding partner and former chairman of Apax Partners, which went on to become Britain's largest venture capital firm. Later he entered the field of social investment and is today the chairman of both the Portland Trust and Bridges Ventures, as well as director of Social Finance UK [Apax Partners]. In his social entrepreneurial role Sir Ronald is having a global impact as he aspires to develop financial mechanisms that will channel private investments to social endeavors.

What is less prevalent is to find highly successful social entrepreneurs who have commenced a second career in commercial entrepreneurship. The story of Sivan Ya'ari, who started off as a social entrepreneur and moved into commercial entrepreneurship, is therefore quite unique.

Sivan Ya'ari

Sivan Ya'ari was born in Israel. Her family moved to France when she was twelve years old [Epoch Times, 2012]. She returned to Israel in her late teens, and following her military service went to the United States in 1999 to study English.

During her undergraduate studies, Ya'ari applied for a summer job at Jordache Jeans. Given her mastery of French she was sent to Madagascar, a French-speaking country in Africa. Her job was to manage quality assurance at the local Jordache plant.

Her visit to Madagascar, which was her first to Africa, proved to be a seminal experience. She was exposed to poverty and suffering unlike anything she had ever encountered, and witnessed similar conditions on subsequent trips to Kenya and Botswana. What she saw made her determined to do what she could to alleviate the situation [Ya'ari, 2016].

Ya'ari realized that an underlying cause of this dire situation was the lack of electricity, a problem which was common to Africa at large. Without electricity the villagers were doomed to a fight for survival, as they consequently had no access to refrigerators, running water and all other amenities that rely on power.

Ya'ari recalled the ubiquitous solar panels in Israel, and during her graduate studies in International Energy Management and Policy at Columbia University established contact with Israeli companies for the purpose of supplying solar panels to African villages. Ya'ari and her friends in the master's degree program raised funds for a prototype which was installed under her watch in a village in Tanzania in 2007.

In 2008, Ya'ari established an organization which later became known as Innovation: Africa. As of 2016, Innovation: Africa has supplied electricity to approximately one million people in Africa using Israeli technology [Innovation: Africa]. *It has brought power to 104 villages in seven countries. In recognition for its major impact, the organization was awarded the United Nations Innovation Award in 2013.*

In addition to enabling villages to have electricity, Ya'ari is now determined to deal with the challenge of running water, and has succeeded in this area as well.

A few years ago Ya'ari returned to Israel from the United States with her husband and three children. In addition to being the CEO of Innovation: Africa, she has opened a commercial venture: a chain of women's beauty parlors in Israel's periphery towns, which provide both a service to the public and employment for local residents [Mako, 2016].

Social Entrepreneurship and Jewish Education

In Chapter One, we discussed the endeavors of Peter Geffen, Gershon Distenfeld, Peter Deutsch and Ana Robbins, and concluded that they fall into the category of social entrepreneurship. Now that we have fleshed out this concept, we shall revisit this conclusion. Just how well does their work fit in to the category of social entrepreneurship? This issue will be the focus of the next chapter.

References

Apax Partners (n.d.). "Sir Ronald Cohen." Retrieved March 1, 2016. http://www.apax.com/contact-us/offices/london/sir-ronald-cohen

Bornstein, D. (2007). *How to Change the World: Social Entrepreneurs and the Power of New Ideas.* Updated ed. New York: Oxford University Press.

Dees, G. (2001, May 30). "The Meaning of 'Social Entrepreneurship.'" Stanford Business School Center for Social Innovation. Retrieved August 12, 2013. http://www.caseatduke.org/documents/dees_sedef.pdf.

Epoch Times (2012, August 3). "Meira et Hachashecha." Hebrew. Retrieved March 6, 2016. http://www.epochtimes.co.il/et/9974.

Fulton, K. (2006, February). "The Past, Present, and Future of Social Entrepreneurship: A Conversation with Greg Dees." Duke Fuqua School of Business–CASE. Retrieved August 13, 2013. http://www.caseatduke.org/documents/deesinterview.pdf.

Green, A. (n.d.). " The Story of Moses Montefiore." jtrails.org.uk. Retrieved November 18, 2013. http://www.jtrails.org.uk/trails/Ramsgate/articles/c-673/the-story-of-moses-montefiore/.

The Harold Grinspoon Foundation (n.d.). "PJ Library." Retrieved August 22, 2013. http://www.hgf.org/what-we-do/flagship-programs/the-pj-library.aspx.

Holtz, B. (2011, August 26). "How One Man Shaped American Jewish Education." *The Forward.*

Innovation: Africa. (n.d.). "Our Team." Retrieved March 16, 2016. http://innovationafrica.org.

Mako (2016, March 5). "Hatzeirah HaYisraelit Hameira et Afrika." Hebrew. Retrieved March 6, 2016. http://www.mako.co.il/news-israel/local-q1_2016/Article-c2a5aad23384351004.htm.

Marcus, B., and A. Blank (2001). *Built from Scratch: How a Couple of Regular Guys Grew The Home Depot from Nothing to $30 Billion.* Reprint ed. Crown Business.

"The Nobel Peace Prize 2006" (2006). www.nobelprize.org. Retrieved August 19, 2013. http://www.nobelprize.org/nobel_prizes/peace/laureates/2006/.

Silverman, Jerry (former CEO, Foundation for Jewish Camp), in discussion with the author, May 17, 2012.

Ya'ari, S. (2016, February 23). "Africa: Is Good, Good Enough?" Tedex Tel Aviv University. Retrieved March 6, 2016. https://www.youtube.com/watch?v=tfgAexR5Z2w.

Young, R. (2006). "For What it is Worth: Social Value and the Future of Social Entrepreneurship." In A. Nichols, *Social Entrepreneurship: New models of Sustainable Social Change.* Oxford: Oxford University Press, 56–73.

Yunus, M. (2008). *Creating a World without Poverty: Social Business and the Future of Capitalism.* 1st ed. New York: PublicAffairs.

Chapter Three

Social Vision Entrepreneurship

CENTRAL IDEAS

SOCIAL ENTREPRENEURS ARE GENERALLY DIVIDED INTO THOSE WHO PRIMARILY FOCUS ON "SOCIAL NEED" AND THOSE WHO ARE MAINLY CONCERNED WITH WHAT HAS BEEN CALLED "SOCIAL VISION."

JEWISH EDUCATION WILL BE VIEWED WITHIN THE CONTEXT OF THE LATTER.

Is the Social Entrepreneur Addressing a Social Need or Implementing a Social Vision?

This anecdote serves to illustrate the difference.

In 2002, during the second Intifada in Israel, I worked feverishly to raise funds for a new initiative that would provide Jewish learning opportunities for secular Israeli adults. I set up a meeting with a particular philanthropist who had come to Israel and I passionately explained the importance of promoting text study among the target population.

The philanthropist listened to my monologue and responded with a description of his afternoon experience. His previous appointment comprised a visit to children maimed by terrorist bus bombings in Jerusalem. During the visit, he was solicited by a welfare organization that took extra care of these children and their families. He challenged me by asking: "Given the immediate urgency of the needs of the victims and their families, which cause – text study or helping victims – would I personally support?"

This question highlights an important distinction between two types of social entrepreneurship. Clearly my initiative was an example of "social vision" and that of the welfare organization was a case of "social need."

Social Needs Entrepreneurship

Many social entrepreneurs feel challenged to respond to critical human needs that are ignored or poorly responded to by their society. Inequality, unemployment, poor-quality education, disease and suffering are very much part of our world. There are large populations across the globe that do not enjoy the equality, privileges and lifestyle to which many of us in industrialized societies are accustomed. They lack access to quality education, advanced medical services and employment opportunities. For them, life is an ongoing struggle for survival. Such populations have attracted the attention of many social entrepreneurs who are dedicated to improving their quality of life. We have called this type of entrepreneurship "social needs" entrepreneurship.

The central challenge of social needs entrepreneurship

The social needs entrepreneur empathizes with the disadvantaged and as a result is constantly pursuing solutions that will alleviate the hardships of and add value to those for whom life is a struggle. The entrepreneur is dedicated to providing sustainable and affordable products and services that will have major social impact.

From this perspective, the entrepreneur's major challenge is to develop a "solution," with the built-in assumption that its availability will generate a high level of demand for the product or service. Since social need products and services directly respond to unmet market needs, large numbers of "customers" are likely to come forward to access these newly accessible solutions.

This was the situation when Muhammad Yunus, whom we discussed in the previous chapter, developed the Grameen Bank. Millions of citizens in Bangladesh had no access to regular bank credit, which concerned him deeply. He realized that the solution needed to be an economically viable yet easily accessible system of microcredit. In developing the system, he knew that there would be no shortage of customers.

Social Vision Entrepreneurship

The second type of social entrepreneurship is motivated by the social vision of the entrepreneur and his or her aspiration to implement it. The vision is embedded in ideology and the motivation for spreading it is ideological. As such, this entrepreneur will invest major efforts in convincing others of the virtues of the ideology.

Since implementing a social vision is central to this entrepreneur, we will call it "social vision entrepreneurship." As opposed to the needs entrepreneur who responds to the plight of the disadvantaged, the central focus of the vision entrepreneur is the value system of the surrounding society.

The two opposing campaigns led by social entrepreneurs that relate to abortion policy are examples of social vision entrepreneurship. The issue is clearly one of values. Those entrepreneurs who establish pro-choice endeavors do so because they believe that abortions are morally justifiable. Likewise, those who establish pro-life entrepreneurial endeavors believe that abortions are immoral.

The central challenges of social vision entrepreneurship

In order to implement their vision, social vision entrepreneurs must convince the given society that the vision is worth pursuing. Their major challenge is therefore to nurture "buy in" for the social vision. They focus on marketing their vision, with major market share support being critical for the realization of the social vision.

The implications of this major difference in challenges between the two types of social entrepreneurs are far-reaching and affect the essence of the entrepreneurial activity. The needs entrepreneur has a natural potential customer base that seeks solutions to their problems. Thus he or she will invest major resources in understanding the source of the problem and developing solutions that are both practical and sustainable.

The social vision entrepreneur has a "solution" which he or she believes will enrich the lives of members of society but does not have a natural customer base. He or she will make a major investment in trying to convince the potential marker of the virtues of the social vision.

Is a Given Endeavor Social Need or Social Vision?

At first glance, the distinctions between needs entrepreneurship and vision entrepreneurship seem to be clear. However, when one examines entrepreneurial endeavors in the field it is often difficult to differentiate between the two. This blurring is evident in entrepreneurial endeavors in the area of social welfare that are sometimes motivated by the dissemination of social vision. For example, it is probable that the welfare endeavors of church missionaries in Africa are a gateway for spreading the gospel, and therefore they would be called social visionaries.

Let us examine an example that is far closer to home: the Jewish Community Center (JCC). Is the mission of the JCC to serve its constituents and seek solutions to their social needs, or is the mission to strengthen Jewish identity, which is clearly a social vision? This question has important implications for both policy and funding. If the focus is on serving the community's needs, in those centers where there are a large number of non-Jewish members, meeting the members' needs will be the highest priority and there will be a minority of activities with a rich Jewish content. If on the other hand the core mission is to disseminate a Jewish vision, the center will focus on its Jewish constituency and make a major investment in high-impact Jewish programming. Most likely it will view meeting the needs of the general population as an important component of its financial model, as opposed to its being part of the core mission.

The Endgame of Social Vision Entrepreneurship

All goal-seeking entrepreneurs like to have a benchmark of their success. In the commercial world, each entrepreneur determines his or her endgame and at that point will aspire to do an exit.

What should be the final goal of the vision entrepreneur? It is most likely the attainment of maximum buy in of the target market. Success will be achieved when the vision becomes a social need. When the target population makes the value system its priority and is prepared to make a sacrifice for the vision, the social vision entrepreneur will have accomplished the goal.

Is Jewish Education a Manifestation of Social Needs or Social Vision Entrepreneurship?

Is Jewish education primarily a manifestation of needs entrepreneurship or of vision entrepreneurship? Is our challenge to find educational solutions for a market in need or is our challenge to disseminate a social vision? In pursuing this question, it is important to explain what we mean by the term "Jewish education."

Defining Jewish education

Lawrence Cremin, an influential American educational historian, offered this definition of the concept "education":

> Education is the deliberate, systematic, and sustained effort to transmit, evoke, or acquire knowledge, attitudes, skills, values, or sensibilities, and any learning that results from the effort, direct or indirect, intended or unintended. [Cremin, 2007]

According to this definition, education does not just "happen." It is deliberate, systematic and sustained. In defining Jewish education, I will employ Cremin's definition of education in general. And in keeping with my social entrepreneurial perspective which focuses on the importance of creating social value, I will address expected outcomes as well. Accordingly, the definition of Jewish education adopted in this book is as follows:

The deliberate, systematic and sustained effort to transmit or evoke Jewish knowledge, attitudes, skills and sensibilities, with the aspiration that these efforts will either create high impact or be the first steps toward high impact.

I have thus narrowed the definition of Jewish education to include only those efforts whose goals are to impact the students. My adoption of this definition is informed by the following:

- A strong belief that Jewish education is a critical vehicle for ensuring that our future generations will make informed Jewish choices regarding their lifestyles, and that it is in our interests that they do so.
- The belief that this vehicle will be successful only if it is highly impactful.

The Jewish educational endeavors described in Chapter One were chosen because they are highly impactful, or are certainly gateways to effective outcomes. With this in mind, let us look at the field with a view to assessing whether Jewish education manifests itself as a social vision or as a social need.

In Orthodox circles, high-impact Jewish education tends to be a community need. Many Orthodox parents who face difficult financial choices will prefer to lower their standards of living in order send their children to Jewish day schools, which are costly. This choice may be the preferred option even if parents are offered a high-quality, free public school education which eclipses the secular education given by the local Jewish day school.

Particularly in the United States among those who are not Orthodox, the situation is quite different. Many parents will opt for religious and Hebrew instruction for their children during the pre-bar and -bat mitzvah years, but will not invest in high-impact, comprehensive formal Jewish education for their children. Others who do believe in high-impact Jewish education and will send their children to summer overnight camps that excel in providing quality Jewish educational experiences. A smaller group will enroll their children in Jewish day schools through the eighth grade, and an even smaller minority will opt for a Jewish (day) high school.

Thus, for an overwhelming majority of those who do not define themselves as Orthodox, high-impact Jewish education is not a need. Entrepreneurs who create these type of educational experiences targeted at the non-Orthodox population should be viewed as social vision entrepreneurs.

Accordingly, in this book we will regard Jewish education as a social vision, and we will look at the dissemination of high-impact Jewish gateways and experiences. We will focus on strategies for achieving major market share, and will highlight entrepreneurial endeavors that have excelled in the realm of educational impact.

A Search for Paradigms

With regard to the social vision approach to Jewish education, there seems to be a dearth of relevant literature. Almost all of the growing literature on social entrepreneurship, from Bornstein's important work, *How to Change the World* [Bornstein, 2007], to the acclaimed Amazon best-seller, *The Promise of a Pencil*, by young Jewish social entrepreneur Adam Braun [Braun, 2015], focus on social needs entrepreneurship. All discuss the creative, sustainable solutions developed through social entrepreneurship to benefit large-scale populations in need.

These works are of limited value, however, concerning our quest to find strategies for disseminating social vision. Indeed, they highlight inspiring examples of social entrepreneurship and its impact on people, while illustrating the art of navigating the nonprofit world and funding opportunities. However, they do not relate to the "how," which is critical to our success: how to reach out to potential populations and encourage them to buy in to our vision. How do we design educational formats which offer high impact and which are accessible and inviting, to those who are indifferent?

To my knowledge, little has been written on the subject, and the search for paradigms continues. Nevertheless, the literature on commercial entrepreneurship, despite its being a completely different realm with radically different objectives, can be a major resource.

The Mutual Challenge of Social Vision Entrepreneurship and Commercial Entrepreneurship

Commercial entrepreneurship is strikingly similar to social vision entrepreneurship. Both have products or processes (goods or services) that they would like to market to a world that may be indifferent. In both situations they need to succeed in highly competitive environments. In the commercial world the customer has multiple options, and the commercial entrepreneur is successful only if the customer chooses the goods or services he or she has to offer and makes a purchase.

Similarly, in social vision entrepreneurship the target market has multiple options relating to values and lifestyle, and the social vision entrepreneur is successful only if his or her desired values are chosen.

In the field of Jewish education we have a tangible example. When parents choose schools for their children they have multiple options. The social vision entrepreneur will do everything possible to market an option in which there is a high-impact Jewish educational component, with full knowledge that parents have other options.

In this book we will draw on the rich literature relating to consumerism. We will draw on paradigms which relate to consumer choices, and harness these insights in order to succeed in implementing our vision. We will continue to use consumer terminology; participants will often be referred to as customers, and those who "buy in" will be referred to as consumers.

40

Yet we must never lose sight of the fact that we are engaged in a realm which is far more elevated and existentially important than a commercial transaction. In the latter the aspiration is to accrue financial benefits, while in the former we are dedicating ourselves to the sacred task of Jewish education.

Commercial Entrepreneurs Who Establish High-Impact Jewish Educational Endeavors

Over the past forty years, the field of Jewish education has benefited enormously from the initiatives of commercial entrepreneurs who have established new high-impact endeavors. In the post-Second World War era, Jewish philanthropists responded to the ideas of educational entrepreneurs and offered support as tacit, passive investors. However, from the 1980s onward, commercial entrepreneurs spearheaded the endeavors themselves, providing leadership and mentoring together with financial support.

In 1980 Florence Melton, the inventor of foam rubber slippers and founder of RG Barry, conceived the idea of a curriculum-based, adult Jewish literacy project. After being turned down by several US-based universities, she convinced The Hebrew University of Jerusalem to take it on. This became known as The Florence Melton Adult Mini-School.

In 1984 Leslie Wexner, founder of The Limited, conceived the idea of a lay leadership program with rigorous Jewish content. This was the beginning of the Wexner Heritage Program.

In 1996, after being convinced that an Israel educational experience could have a major influence on the Jewish identity of the participants, Charles Bronfman and Michael Steinhardt spearheaded the founding of Taglit–Birthright. More recently, Harold Grinspoon conceived of and led the development of PJ Library, a project which reaches out monthly to hundreds of thousands of young parents and their children across the globe.

One could attribute the widespread success and major impact of these endeavors to the funding they received from their generous benefactors. However, numerous Jewish educational initiatives that received major funding never got off the ground, while others that did materialize never achieved the impact of the initiatives mentioned above.

It is my contention that the success of these initiatives was primarily due to the active leadership roles played by the entrepreneurs. They understood the secret of developing a winning product, one that would speak to and attract a population previously considered indifferent. They translated the perceptions they had developed so successfully in the commercial world into the realm of social vision-driven Jewish education – to the benefit of us all.[1]

A commercial entrepreneur who embarked on a similar path is Devin Schain. In 2011 he founded Shalom Learning, an exciting and sophisticated online pre-bar mitzvah program.

Devin Schain
Devin Schain's entrepreneurial endeavors began when he launched On Campus Marketing (OCM) as a sophomore at the University of Pennsylvania about thirty years ago and grew it over the next decade by building endorsed partnerships with more than 1,100 colleges and universities. After selling OCM for $18 million, in 2009 he started Educational Direct, an online student loan consolidator, thereby

---

1   I attribute this insight to the late Professor Seymour Fox. In 1990, when I participated in a seminar as a Jerusalem Fellow, Professor Fox extolled the virtues of involving commercial entrepreneurs in Jewish education. I was abhorred by this and asked why he thought those whose expertise was accumulating wealth could have any insights regarding Jewish education. His response made a lasting impression on me: "Successful commercial entrepreneurs are experts in the understanding of the human psyche, of cultural norms and of society at large. These insights are crucial for our success in Jewish education."

building on his expertise in direct marketing within higher education. The company, leveraging technology and the underutilized assets of education partners, quickly became a category leader, growing from start-up to a valuation of $375 million in three years. In 2012 Devin cofounded Access Health [Campus Direct].

Devin is a dedicated philanthropist, actively involved with the Jewish Federation of Greater Washington, Hillel International, and United Synagogues of Conservative Judaism.

The founding of Shalom Learning was precipitated by a discussion he had in 2010 with his rabbi, who told him he could not officiate at his children's bnei mitzvah because they did not attend the synagogue's Hebrew school. Schain was stunned, blurting out, "That is the most anti-consumer response I have ever heard!"

When the rabbi conceded that numbers at the school had dropped because "the model is challenged; parents are busy," Schain decided then and there that there had to be another way.

He recalls: "My Dad hated Hebrew school; I hated Hebrew school – why does it have to be a rite of passage that children hate Hebrew school?"

Being the educational technology entrepreneur that he is, Schain set about finding a solution. He called Andrew Rosen, cofounder of Blackboard, an online learning management system, suggesting that the two of them create a blended model of Jewish education using Blackboard's technology and Schain's marketing expertise.

Meeting with their rabbis, they suggested augmenting what was already on offer at the Hebrew school. They saw that the curriculum was "antiquated," and got to work.

"We brought in some professional, world-class Jewish educators and we created a values-based education curriculum. We have three pillars – technology, Jewish values curriculum and teacher training," he stated.

Shalom Learning started with a pilot class of seven students at Schain's synagogue in 2011. Two years later, the numbers had risen to 312 kids and twenty-one synagogues in Toronto, Montreal,

Baltimore, Washington, DC, New York, Detroit, Miami, Chicago and California.

"We have taken a nineteenth-century and older curriculum, twentieth-century teachers and twenty-first century students, and we've integrated them with a great curriculum, great teachers and great technology," he said.

"I hope that Shalom Learning will be my legacy. We are making a difference with parents, students, synagogues – we're teaching kids to really enjoy and like Judaism." The nonprofit initiative's pluralistic curriculum is "relevant, engaging, fun and affordable.

"If I can make a Jewish student more engaged, irrespective of whether he's unaffiliated or Orthodox – that to me is a win."

It is predominantly synagogues that pay for use of the model, although the Jewish Community Centers and Federations do so as well. It is also available directly to consumers.

Schain is now considering offering free online, live Shalom Learning to children in the fourth to sixth grades who receive no formal Jewish education. Those who complete the three years will be offered a subsidized educational trip to Israel, including a bar or bat mitzvah.

"We're partnering with synagogues but we're also going direct where synagogues cannot be successful, in rural areas and with mixed-faith marriages when they don't want to step in a synagogue, but they're not averse to their kid getting bar or bat mitzvahed. Why shouldn't we provide them that opportunity?"

The Sustainability Challenges of Vision Entrepreneurship

Thus far, we have discussed at length the challenge of Jewish education when viewed through the prism of social vision entrepreneurship, with specific reference to connecting with those who would not consider high-impact Jewish education to be a priority. A second challenge of no small magnitude is that of sustainability.

44

At the beginning of this chapter I described my encounter with a potential philanthropist who turned down support for my social vision endeavor due to the burning priority of a venture that responded to social needs. This highlights only one of the challenges social vision entrepreneurship can expect to encounter – competition for financial resources with social needs-based programs.

However, there is an even greater challenge which relates to the financial capabilities of the potential students. Many prospective participants can afford to cover the full costs of tuition, and if so, why offer them discount prices? Furthermore, who is responsible for picking up the tab? This issue hits at the core of social vision entrepreneurship: who is responsible for supporting the endeavor?

To respond to this question I will showcase the sustainability achievement of the United Herzlia Schools in Cape Town, South Africa – my alma mater.

Herzlia School is a cross-community school founded in 1940. Today it comprises a network of private Jewish day schools from pre-K through the twelfth grade. There are three primary schools, a middle school and a high school. In 2015 there were 1,850 Jewish children in the entire Herzlia system, comprising 80 percent of the Jewish children in the community.

In addition to Herzlia, there is now a small Orthodox school in Cape Town, the Phyllis Jowell School, as well as a new Torah high school. Together these schools contribute an additional 10 percent. Thus, in 2015 about 90 percent of the children in Cape Town's Jewish community were enrolled in a Jewish day school.

The Cape Town Jewish community comprises South Africa's second largest Jewish population. In the 1970s and 1980s the Jewish community numbered about 25,000, and due to emigration, in 2015 numbered approximately 16,000. Many families are members of the Orthodox synagogues but do not lead halachically observant lifestyles. Traditionally the number of *shomrei Shabbat* (those who are Shabbat observant) in Cape Town has never been more than 10 percent.

The 80–90 percent market share that Herzlia has steadily maintained is no mean feat. It is probably the highest per-community rate worldwide among Jewish communities whose members on a whole do not live halachic lifestyles. This has been achieved in the face of fierce competition. There are outstanding state and private schools that welcome Jewish children, meaning that parents enroll their children at Herzlia out of choice.

An extraordinary aspect of the school's achievements is its ability to sustain itself. The South African economy has been in turmoil for decades. Toward the end of the Apartheid era, sanctions hurt, and after the abolition of Apartheid major investments to advance those who had suffered discrimination exacted a major economic price. The local currency, the rand, had parity with the US dollar in 1981. In January 2016, the rate of exchange had fallen to 6.25 cents.

Yet with all the economic turmoil that has affected countless families, United Herzlia Schools has continued to flourish. It continues to welcome each and every Jewish child in the community and to maintain its market share.

A Cape Town Jewish community leader who contributed significantly to this economic "miracle" is Eliot Osrin.

Eliot Osrin

Growing up in the early 1940s in Mossel Bay, a small South African coastal town, Eliot Osrin was the only Jewish boy at his school and knew "absolutely nothing" about Judaism. After moving to Cape Town, he reluctantly sent his first child to a Jewish kindergarten, but when the little boy came back singing Hebrew songs, Osrin was hooked.

Having initially dismissed the idea of his children attending a "ghetto" school, he and his wife Myra ended up sending all three to Herzlia, the city's community private Jewish day school, which ran from kindergarten through the twelfth grade. Eliot has been involved with the school in various leadership capacities for close to fifty years.

Osrin, a prominent lawyer-turned-businessman, believed in the importance of day school education both for his children and for the community at large. After he assumed a communal leadership position in the early seventies, he wanted to advance the school. He set off in search of a customer base, persuading parents at the well-attended, excellent Jewish early childhood centers to send their children on to Herzlia.

Osrin embraced the ethos of community responsibility for Jewish day school education and contributed significantly to the sustainability of a community-wide day school system that continues to this very day. He achieved this by solidifying the two major sources of community income: the endowment fund and the annual campaign. He made major efforts to grow the endowment fund, and placed Jewish day school education at the center of the annual community campaign. While parents pay school fees of approximately $5000 per annum,[2] 35 percent of the students receive either partial or full scholarships. The widespread community support has ensured that parents of all social strata feel comfortable sending their children to the school.

The importance of Jewish education at Herzlia has led not only to graduates who have continued to live as strongly identifying Jews and have become prominent members of society both locally and abroad. Another outstanding achievement is the quality of faculty that the school has nurtured. Many members of the school administration and faculty have gone on to lead Jewish day schools in the United States, Canada, Australia and New Zealand, as well as in other cities in South Africa.

Herzlia's sustainable model has endured throughout the political changes and economic challenges the country has faced. The school has always been and continues to be strong academically, invariably

---

2   Fees are paid in local currency; thus this sum in US dollars is dependent on the exchange rate.

*featuring in the Cape's annual "top ten" based on school-leaving
examination results.*

There are three crucial factors which come to the fore when
analyzing the story of United Herzlia Schools, all of which have
implications for sustainability:

1. Outstanding leadership. Social vision organizations need
   outstanding leadership in order to prosper. These leaders
   need to be dedicated to the cause and must have a long-term
   view of the situation.
2. An ethos of community responsibility for social vision. Those
   who are committed to the social vision need to assume
   responsibility for supporting it. In Cape Town, Jewish day
   school education was and continues to be affordable to all
   because the Jewish community believes Jewish education is
   its responsibility. Tuition flexibility and sensitivity is possible
   only because there is a large endowment, developed over the
   years, to support and welcome those who are less fortunate.
   This endowment, as well as the annual campaign, is supported
   by many who are no longer connected to the school yet feel
   compelled by the community vision to contribute.
3. The evolution of Jewish day school education from a social
   vision to a social need has taken root in the minds of many
   parents. Those who have graduated from the system do not
   need to be convinced of its importance for their children.
   Whereas for their parents Jewish day school education was
   merely an option, for them it is a priority. Thus, the 80 percent
   market share is the culmination of decades of successful work
   on the part of the social visionaries.

It has been proven that those who have had a quality day school
experience will seek a similar experience for their children. Herzlia

graduates who have immigrated to the United States, Canada, the United Kingdom, Australia and New Zealand have become leaders of their day school communities, reflecting the impact and success of their own Jewish education.

References

Bornstein, D. (2007). *How to Change the World: Social Entrepreneurs and the Power of New Ideas.* Updated ed. New York: Oxford University Press.

Braun, A. (2015). *The Promise of a Pencil: How an Ordinary Person Can Create Extraordinary Change.* New York: Scribner.

Campus Direct (n.d.). "Leadership." Retrieved March 6, 2016. http://www. campusdirect.com/leadership.html.

Cremin, L. (2007, November 7). "Educative Institutions." Pocket Knowledge. Retrieved April 2014. http://pocketknowledge.tc.columbia.edu/home.php/ viewfile/26567.

Chapter Four

How Do We Define Educational Success?

CENTRAL IDEA

SUCCESS IN EDUCATION IS THE ATTAINMENT OF THE EDUCATIONAL VALUE
WE ARE ASPIRING TO ACHIEVE.

THREE APPROACHES DOMINATE THE FIELD OF JEWISH EDUCATION: THE
LITERACY APPROACH, THE RELEVANCY APPROACH, AND THE IDENTITY
AND CONTINUITY APPROACH.

Recently a student organized an educational event and we met soon afterwards to discuss it. Both the large turnout and the positive feedback from the participants excited him. He discussed with me the contents of the program and asked me to "rate" its success. As a teacher, I naturally asked the student for his evaluation. The student felt a little uncomfortable. He realized that the participants' active engagement and enjoyment were necessary factors; however, these alone were not sufficient. If the goal of the event was entertainment, both participation and audience satisfaction would be necessary and sufficient. However, in educational endeavors we expect educational impact as well.

This issue requires further elaboration; what do we mean by "educational success," or in social entrepreneurial terms, what is the educational value we are trying to achieve?

This question is of major significance. The social entrepreneurial perspective pushes us to focus our efforts on creating and sustaining social value. Thus both for the entrepreneur and for the other stakeholders in an educational endeavor, a clear definition of educational value is crucial.

Three Approaches to Jewish Educational Value

Within the realm of Jewish education, it is possible to differentiate between three dominant approaches in defining educational value. These approaches differ in their goals, and hence also in their definitions of success. Since each approach aims to achieve different outcomes, they vary in terms of the educational strategies they employ.

The three approaches are literacy, relevancy and meaning, and identity and continuity.

Literacy

According to the literacy approach, the goal of the educational endeavor is to ensure that the participants will be able to participate in the "Great Conversation." Participation in the great conversation is an ideal of liberal arts education, as articulated by Robert Hutchins [Hutchins, 1954].

The great conversation

Hutchins maintains that throughout the generations there has been an ongoing discussion about ideas that are pertinent to all humanity and which have universal interest. Transmitted from generation to generation, these ideas relate to the human spirit in all its complexities and to the challenge of living a meaningful life. Every generation analyzes and interprets the ideas of the preceding ones. Intergenerational debates as well as debates between contemporaries take place. Some ideas are discarded, while others provide inspiration for the creation of new ideas. From Hutchins' perspective, the great conversation is based on the works of western culture, ranging from the Bible and Homer to William James and Jean Paul Sartre.

An educated person is defined as one who is able to participate in the great conversation, and the goal of education is to enable this participation. Mortimer Adler, Hutchins' colleague at the University of Chicago and co-proponent of liberal education, believed that since the crux of education is intellectual in nature, authentic education can take place only when the student reaches maturity. From his perspective, small children are too young to be educated, and therefore the importance of education at an early age is to whet the appetites of the young to ensure that they will be inquisitive and eager learners when they grow up [Adler, 1977].

Liberal education within a Jewish context

Within the context of Jewish education, a liberal education would refer to knowledge of classical Jewish literature (as opposed to Western literature), and participation in the great conversation would refer to the Jewish conversation (as opposed to the Western conversation). In order to participate fully in this conversation, it is crucial that Jews be "literate."

In referring to literacy, it is important to differentiate between textual literacy and cultural literacy.

Textual literacy

Textual literacy calls for a knowledge and understanding of Jewish texts in their original languages, and requires an understanding of Bible, Talmud, rabbinic literature, Jewish philosophy and contemporary Jewish literature. Textual literacy thus requires a mastery of Hebrew and Aramaic as well as text analysis skills. All of this enables the student to study, analyze and interpret texts independently, and to fully participate in the great conversation.

The importance of textual literacy came to the fore following the destruction of the second Temple in 70 CE. As mentioned in Chapter One, Rabbi Yochanan ben Zakai played an important role in the transformation of Judaism, which faced an uncertain future at that time. The transformation comprised a change of emphasis from a religion centered around Temple worship and sacrificial ritual to a religion focused on text study.

While synagogues were the locus of prayer, it was the *beit midrash*, or public study hall, that replaced the *Beit HaMikdash*, the Temple, as the "heart" of Judaism. Existentially, there was a transition in how Jews experienced a sense of connection with the Divine Presence. During the time of the Temple one felt the Divine Presence when he or she was physically at the Temple. In post-Temple times a Jew felt God's Presence by studying His word as revealed in the biblical and rabbinic literature, generally referred to as "Torah study."

This transition is validated by multiple comparisons within rabbinic literature between Temple service and Torah study, and major efforts were made to elevate the importance of Torah study over the importance of Temple service.[1]

An important by-product of this transformation was that it enabled Judaism to survive and flourish in every geographical area. Whereas a focus on Temple worship required annual pilgrimages to Jerusalem and emphasized sacrificial ritual which could be performed only in the Temple, Torah could be studied anywhere. Thus the devout practice of Judaism became possible independent of place.

Moreover, this transformation ensured that Judaism would always grapple with the present while also transmitting its past. In placing an emphasis on text study and interpretation, study in the *beit midrash* would always provide a contemporary meeting place between the learners and the Divine word. Given the changing cultures and social contexts, *beit midrash* study provided the text with its future vitality. If there is a major difficulty with prevailing interpretations the learner is invited to provide his or her interpretation, with a large measure of admiration given for new, creative interpretations, called *chiddushim* in traditional parlance.

Among those who believe in the revelation at Sinai, textual literacy is important because it is the text that conveys the contents of the

---

1   According to the Mishna in tractate *Horayot*, precedence due a Kohen or Levite based on their lineage is important only if it goes hand in hand with Torah knowledge. If one individual has a deep knowledge of Torah but no lineage and another has lineage but no Torah knowledge, the first is deemed to be of a higher status.

revelation. Among others the motivation for adopting a textual literacy approach may be as follows:

- To ensure that the chain of the great conversation continues to this very day. Since this conversation is a major focus of Judaism, this is crucial.
- To enable all sectors of the Jewish people to contribute to and shape the conversation. Ultimately, Judaism maintains its vitality through its ability to be relevant to diverse populations that reside in disparate eras and settings. In order to achieve this, active contributions to the conversation are required from all sectors of the Jewish people.
- To develop a cadre of educators. A growing field requires learned personnel, and thus investing in textual literacy is vitally important.

Educational institutions that have adopted the textual literacy approach

The textual literacy approach is *the* approach that dominates traditional Orthodox male education. The study of text and its interpretation is the focus of study at yeshiva high schools, post-high school yeshivot and kollels. In these institutions the study of and proficiency in Talmud is an important strategic goal.

Within Modern Orthodox circles, the literacy approach has been adopted also by a number of women's learning institutions. In New York, Drisha is renowned for its focus on text study and in Israel, Matan, Midreshet Lindenbaum and the Midrasha in Migdal Oz have a strong focus on textual literacy. Among the egalitarian institutions, Mechon Hadar in New York, and the Pardes Institute and the Conservative Yeshiva in Israel, have all made their mark in this field.

55

Cultural literacy

Cultural literacy, which is grounded in the works of E. D. Hirsch [Hirsch, 1988], calls for an understanding of culture in its broadest sense. Within a Jewish context this would refer to a mastery of Jewish culture. The cultural conversation is much broader than the conversation that focuses on text. It includes everything connected to Jewish community and the Jewish people, including culture, history, religion, Israel and Jewish peoplehood.

Proponents of cultural literacy point to its importance for the growth and strength of Jewish communities. The Jewish people were able to survive in exile without the support of a centralized, national authority thanks to their ability to establish Jewish communities wherever they lived. Jewish communities establish and maintain institutions of all types, ranging from spiritual to welfare. To do so they require the support and involvement of those in the community who are both passionate and culturally literate. Jewish cultural literacy empowers the members of the community to assume leadership roles and to become the local visionaries.

It is with this in mind that formal structured programs in cultural literacy were instituted, primarily among adults. An outstanding example is the Wexner Heritage Program which since its inception in 1985 has made a remarkable impact on young leaders in North America.

The Wexner Heritage Program

The Wexner Heritage Program had its genesis in philanthropist Leslie Wexner's fundamental belief that the quality of leadership determines the outcome of group endeavors, and that it was therefore critically important that Jewish lay leaders be intelligent, educated and informed [The Wexner Heritage Program].

The program was piloted in September 1985 in Columbus, Ohio, under the leadership of Rabbi Herb Friedman, the former CEO of the National United Jewish Appeal. Within a short time, it was rolled out to four cities in the Midwest: Detroit, Minneapolis, Pittsburgh, and Milwaukee. Rabbi Jay Moses has headed the program since 2003, and in its thirty years of operation it has graduated close to two thousand alumni across thirty-three cities in North America.

The program runs over a two-year period, with twenty select participants meeting biweekly for four hours during the school year, thirty-six sessions in total. In the summer the fellows participate in retreats, including one in Israel. Wexner is a highly intense experience for very busy people. It requires a significant commitment of time and energy from each participant.

An outstanding feature of the program is the quality of the faculty. Top scholars with excellent communication skills are drawn from across the globe and brought in to teach. The intellectual stimulation is thus of the highest level.

The study experience incorporates pillars of literacy, including exploration of the fundamental texts, Jewish history, Jewish thought, Jewish practice, Israel and contemporary leadership issues, all taught by Wexner's world-class faculty.

Since the program's inception there has always been a heavy emphasis on Jewish history in addition to Bible, rabbinic literature, liturgy and modern Jewish thought. Over the past thirty years there has been an increasing emphasis on issues relating to leadership, which now constitutes 20 percent of the program. In addition to acquiring concrete leadership skills, participants learn about the key issues facing the Jewish people today in both the Diaspora and Israel.

The desired outcome of the Wexner program is for lay leaders to take increasing responsibility for making change in Jewish life, whether by creating new organizations or by helping current structures to innovate and adapt to changing circumstances in order to better meet the needs of the community.

The program's success has always been driven by the prestige factor, with only one of every two or three applicants being accepted.

In the world of Jewish education, it is one of the few non-degree programs with a rigid selection process.[2]

Communal professionals, lay leaders and Wexner alumni nominate applicants based on their promise as future leaders. Diversity of the cohort is an important factor, as it enables participants to see the bigger (Jewish) picture and to be more accepting of the different choices others make.

In earlier years one of the big issues under discussion was Jewish day schools, and Wexner prides itself on the fact that it helped give birth to twenty such institutions.

By linking text study to leadership, the program empowers participants to view contemporary issues through the lens of Jewish history and tradition, thereby enabling them to take a proactive role in writing their own generation's chapter.

Important parameters for the enhancement of a Jewish literacy program

Programs that aim to promote Jewish literacy require the following parameters in order to succeed:

- Participants must be intellectually mature. In order to participate in the great conversation, students need to need to be able to grapple with texts and with ideas. The literacy approach is therefore most suited to educational frameworks whose participants are of high school age and older.
- The faculty needs expertise in both subject matter and communication skills. This approach requires faculty who are able to draw on their mastery in a manner that will interest the students. While educators may be proponents of the literacy approach, they cannot automatically assume that their students are similarly motivated. Thus, they need to make

---

2 Another is the Bronfman Fellows for high school seniors.

concerted efforts to ensure that the students comprehend and enjoy the lessons.

- The curriculum needs to be both comprehensive and engaging. A comprehensive curriculum ensure a focus on literacy. Because it is crucial that students be actively engaged, texts that evoke engagement should be chosen.

- Awareness that being Jewishly literate is a long-term objective and requires a long-term commitment. New concepts and ideas that are introduced need to be reinforced over time, and each lesson should be viewed as a building block of the next.

Relevancy and Meaning

The goal of the relevancy and meaning approach is to enable the individual to fulfill his or her personal potential. This approach is reflected in Lamm's "individuation" approach [Lamm, 1986] to education, which places the individual at the center of the educational enterprise and attaches importance to each individual's quest to realize his or her full potential. Each individual is encouraged to make his or her choices, and the role of the educational system to facilitate these choices.

The ideal teachers are those whose who can empower the students to embark on their journey of choice. They will be masters of facilitation and excel in their abilities to empathize with their students. They will be acutely sensitive to the specific needs and interests of each and every individual. As opposed to the liberal educators, who focus on the commonality of humankind, these educators focus on the uniqueness of each individual and strive to enable him or her to reach their full potential.

In this setting, the curriculum will be tailor made to students' interests and needs. The search for relevancy and meaning will be a focal aspect of each educational encounter, and the curriculum will fail if it is not relevant to the students.

In school settings, where there is an administrative need for uniformity and standardization, individuation provides a major challenge. However, this approach is highly feasible in informal and adult education. In both settings there is broad flexibility with regard to curriculum and types of educational experiences, enabling empathetic educators to take full advantage of them.

Within the realm of Jewish education, the proponents of individuation education may be motivated ideologically and/or practically [Woocher, 2012]. Those who are motivated ideologically believe that the individual should be at the heart of the educational enterprise and the role of Jewish education should be further a student's self-development. They value the importance of choice and deem it important that educational settings should both empower and exemplify this.

Educators who endorse individuation education from a practical perspective feel that it is, simply put, attractive to prospective students. In a market where there is strong competition for the attention, time and financial resources of the students, educational programs must be relevant and meaningful. Accordingly, individuation education that focuses on the individual's needs may give the educational endeavor a competitive edge.

An outstanding example of an individuation Jewish educational endeavor is "Rosh Chodesh: It's a Girl Thing!"

Rosh Chodesh: It's a Girl Thing!

Rosh Chodesh: It's a Girl Thing! was created and launched in 2002 by Kolot: the Center for Jewish Women's and Gender Studies at the Reconstructionist Rabbinical College (RRC), when Deborah Meyer was the center's codirector. The program aimed to provide girls from sixth through twelfth grades with educational activities that empowered them to express their Judaism in ways that were meaningful to them.

From the start, the program was pilot-tested in partnership with Jewish institutions – congregations, JCCs, schools, camps, etc. – of all denominations. It proved to be extremely popular among teenage *girls, many of whom were not enrolled in any Jewish educational program at all.*

The program grew so quickly that it soon became apparent that it required an independent organization as its platform. In a truly generous move, RRC gave the new organization the intellectual property, and under the leadership of the original founder Deborah Meyer and board chair Sally Gottesman, Moving Traditions was established in 2005.

Since then Rosh Chodesh: It's a Girl Thing! has experienced momentous growth both in content and in participants. Three additional years of curricular resources were developed, for a total of five years of material. By 2014, a total of fourteen thousand girls had participated, the majority for two to three years, and the organization has trained more than one thousand Jewish women to facilitate the groups.

Moving Traditions has also researched, tested and launched a program for eighth through twelfth grade boys called Shevet Achim: The Brotherhood, which was launched in 2011. By 2014, 1,800 boys had participated in the program and some two hundred men had been trained to lead the groups.

Important parameters for the enhancement of relevancy and meaning

- Students must be allowed to choose the programs and contents they believe address their needs. Choosing empowers students and enables them to be a genuine partner in the educational process.
- The faculty needs to be highly empathetic and show a deep understanding of the student and his or her needs. In "reading" the students, the faculty will be able to design programs that meet these needs.
- The curriculum needs to be built around issues that are of deep concern to the student. Jewish ideas and texts should be selected in terms of their relevancy.

- Multiple methodologies should be contemplated, and the choices should be made in accordance with students' preferences. For example, students who express themselves through art and dance should be given the prerogative to grow Jewishly in these areas, with Jewish themes interwoven in these educational methodologies.

Identity and Continuity

Proponents of this approach are deeply committed to social continuity. They are concerned that future generations will neither treasure nor safeguard the prevailing values of the society, and believe that education should facilitate continuity.

In keeping with the educational ideas professed by French sociologist Emile Durkheim [Durkheim, 1956], the focus of education should be on socialization. This process requires that students be encouraged to internalize certain cultural values and to identify with traditional culture and its norms. The goal of this approach is therefore identity reinforcement, or alternatively, when the individual's identity is distant from traditional culture, identity transformation.

In order to stimulate the affirmation of certain values or the adoption of new values by the students, educators need to lead by example. They should be passionate about the values they articulate, inspiring students to follow in their footsteps.

In this approach success is a function of behavioral and attitudinal outcomes. If these are in line with the ideological goals of the educational endeavor, the educational process is deemed successful.

Within the Jewish realm, identity and continuity education is considered important in the context of Judaism, the Jewish people and Israel. In educational settings in which identity strengthening is a prime goal, educational themes will touch on all three, with the primary goal of nurturing values and affinity.

The Importance of Intensive Social Experiences with Emotional and Intellectual Components

A principal methodology in identity and continuity education is the design of high-impact emotional experiences that ideally should ensure the following:

- The experiences should be intensive. Identity education requires that the students evaluate and reevaluate their current value system. Intensive educational experiences are important catalysts for this personal evaluation process.
- The experiences should comprise emotional and intellectual components. The emotional components should "touch the soul" to ensure students are able to connect with the proposed values. The intellectual components should ensure that students are able to evaluate and critically analyze the proposed values and ideals.
- The educational experiences should be social in nature. Socialization is not only an embracing of values, it is an embracing of community. Social interaction provides camaraderie and support for those engaged in the educational process.

An example of an integrated educational endeavor designed to impact identity and continuity is the teen trips to Poland.

March of the Living

In 1983, the first delegation of teens from Israel went to Poland on an educational seminar to mark forty years since the Warsaw Ghetto uprising. The impact of this trip and those that followed culminated in the establishment of the first March of the Living program by former Israeli minister of finance Avraham Hirschson. Since then hundreds of thousands of teens from Israel and the Diaspora have embarked on educational trips to Poland in their junior or senior year of high school. Today the trip to Poland is officially sanctioned by the Israel Ministry of Education. In addition, Israel Defense Force officers visit Poland as part of their training program, as do numerous post-high school and adult groups.

The visits are generally preceded by an intense period of study of the history of both the Jewish people in Europe and the Holocaust.

Itineraries vary. In general, they commence with a visit to those areas in which there was a rich cultural and spiritual Jewish life in Poland, and end with a visit to the extermination camps.

March of the Living groups are scheduled to coincide with Holocaust Memorial Day, which takes place a week after Passover, and their trip ends with a visit to Israel coinciding with Israel Memorial Day for the Fallen Soldiers and Yom Ha'atzma'ut, Israel Independence Day.

An important component of the trip is accompaniment by a Holocaust survivor, who gives a living testimony to the atrocities perpetrated by the Nazis.

As one can imagine, these trips have a profound educational impact on the participants. In a study of Los Angeles teens in 2009 who participated in the March of the Living, Tobin Belzer [Belzer, 2009] found the impact to include the following in the areas of attitudes and behavior:

Attitudes
- Both students who had been to Israel and students who had not been to Israel reported increased attachment to the State of Israel.
- Some felt a strong sense of Jewish identity and pride.
- Many felt a greater appreciation for their lives in general.

Behavior
- The trip motivated many students to consider involvement in Jewish student life during college.

- Some became interested in taking college courses in Jewish and Israeli studies.
- A small number of participants decided to increase their religious practice.
- Many felt motivated to return to Israel.

It is fair to assume that while there are probably varying intensities of impact from group to group, the trip to Poland coupled with the trip to Israel provides an outstanding educational opportunity for strengthening Jewish identity and Jewish continuity.

Important parameters for the enhancement of identity and continuity programs

There are several parameters which, if fulfilled, will enhance programs aimed to strengthen Jewish identity and continuity. First, the ideal ages of participants are teens and young adults, as members of these age groups are exploring and affirming their identities. Second, the focus of the program should be experiential, and it is crucial that the experiences reflect the ethos of the desired value system. Third, educators should personally embrace the desired value system; their passion and commitment is a crucial vehicle for the education of the participants. Fourth, the families of the participants need to be supportive for the program to be effective. Thus, thought should be given to parent programs as well.

Which Direction to Go?

In defining success, the educational entrepreneur will need to decide which outcome he or she strives to achieve: literacy, meaning and relevancy, or enhancement of Jewish identity.

All three approaches are critical. The literacy approach is critical because we need to have intellectually informed and empowered members of the Jewish people. The relevancy and meaning approach is critical in order to enable future generations to take ownership of their

65

Judaism; for many, relevance and meaning may be a precondition for taking on ownership. Finally, the identity and continuity approach is critical because we have a moral commitment to transmit the values we inherited to future generations.

Given the importance of all three approaches, entrepreneurs may attach significance to all of them, but choose one as primary and the others as secondary. This was the direction chosen by Rosh Chodesh: It's a Girl's Thing! As described, their primary approach was individuation, i.e., that of relevancy and meaning. However, in addition to focusing on what it means to be a teen in today's world, the program also enhances Jewish identity and community through both their social models and the topics of identity that they discuss. There are discussions that allude to Jewish literacy as well.

Whichever approach is adopted, it is crucial that the expected outcome be realistic and of value. How do we ensure this? That is the subject of the next chapter.

References

Adler, M. (1977). *Reforming Education.* Boulder: Western Press.

Belzer, T. (2009). *2009 March of The Living – Los Angeles Delagation. Report One: Ethnography of the Journey.* Jim Joseph Foundation.

Durkheim, E. (1956). *Education and Sociology.* Glencoe, IL: The Free Press.

Hirsch, E. D. (1988). *Cultural Literacy: What Every American Needs to Know.* New York: Vintage Books.

Hutchins, R. (1954). *The Great Books.* New York: Simon and Schuster.

Lamm, Z. (1986). "Ideologies and Educational Thought." In B. Tal, *Psychology and Counseling in Education.* Hebrew. Jerusalem: Ministry of Education.

The Wexner Heritge Program (n.d.). "About The Wexner Heritage Program." Retrieved September 8, 2015. http://www.wexnerfoundation.org/programs/wexner-heritage-program/about/.

Woocher, J. (2012). "Reinventing Jewish Education for the 21st Century." *Journal of Jewish Education*: 182–226.

Chapter Five

Maximizing the Possibility of Success

CENTRAL IDEA

IN ORDER FOR THEM TO SUCCEED, EDUCATIONAL ENDEAVORS NEED TO BE
BUILT ON THE FOLLOWING FOUR FOUNDATIONS:

- A CLEARLY DEFINED ARTICULATION OF THE EDUCATIONAL VALUE IT ASPIRES
  TO ACHIEVE
- A PLAUSIBLE THEORY OF CHANGE
- A POSITIVE RETURN ON INVESTMENT
- A STRATEGY FOR SUSTAINABILITY

I invite you to assume you are a philanthropist who funds projects that enhance the Jewish identity of teens. On your table, you find two proposals that seek your support. While you may be inclined to support both, you are able to fund only one. Which proposal would you fund, and what are the criteria you should use for making this decision?

The two proposals are as follows:

A three-week summer camp

This camp will provide an opportunity for unengaged Jewish teens to spend three weeks in the summer in a low-barrier Jewish environment. The program will focus on hiking and outdoor sports interwoven with Jewish experiences.

A club for teens

This club will organize weekly social events targeting unengaged Jewish teens. The events will be of a general social and intellectual nature, with a focus on providing a Jewish context.

In reviewing these two proposals, we see that there are striking similarities between them. They both target the unengaged teens and they both provide programs of general content within a Jewish context. In addition, they both strive to enhance the Jewish identity of the participants and offer high-impact educational experiences. However, they sharply differ in terms of the time commitment they require from the participants and the time allocation and intensity of the educational interactions. The teen camp offers an intense educational experience over three weeks that requires the participants to participate for the entire period, while the club offers weekly programs of two-hour duration that require only ad hoc participation.

Assume your hypothetical foundation's policy is to limit investments to those projects that have a reasonable chance of success, thereby securing the maximum educational value for its investment. Therefore, in order to make an informed decision on which proposal to support, you will need to grapple with the following four issues:

- What is the educational value that each endeavor aspires to achieve?

Since "educational value" is the strategic goal of educational entrepreneurship, it is important to be able to articulate the type of educational value we are interested in achieving. Is it Jewish literacy, relevancy and meaning, and/or the strengthening of Jewish identity?

- What are the chances of each endeavor's achieving its desired educational value?

This question focuses on the plausibility of each program achieving its desired outcomes. If the chances of achieving the desired educational value are higher in one of the proposals, this would be good reason to accept it.

- Will the success of each endeavor be cost-effective? What will be the return on investment (ROI)?

This question relates to the correlation between the resources invested and results attained. If the success of an endeavor requires a minor investment and the desired outcomes are far in excess of comparative programs, this would give the program priority for funding.

- Will each endeavor be financially sustainable over of period of time?

A program with potential for longevity may give it the funding edge because the investment sought will also indirectly impact those who will benefit in the future.

1. Desired Educational Value

As described, both endeavors aspire to achieve the same category of value, i.e., the strengthening of Jewish identity. We will expect each proposal to articulate what it means when it refers to strengthening Jewish identity. Are the proposals referring to Jewish peoplehood, Jewish religion, connection with Israel or all three?

In general, it seems that both proposals are operating in the same area of educational value and therefore we will be able to compare their relative strengths and weaknesses

2. Chances of Achieving Success

In order to predict the chances of each endeavor's achieving success, it is important to understand each one's theory of change.

Theory of change

When we embark on a process of social intervention, we want our efforts to influence members of the target market. What steps do we need to follow in order to evoke the desired response? We must develop a plan of action, and for this we need a theory of change. A theory of change is the crucial underpinning of all social endeavors and, in this context, of educational endeavors. It should always underlie the planned interventions of all social entrepreneurs.

The macro theory of change

When we embark on an endeavor we will face multiple constraints, ranging from time, budget and resource constraints to participant availability and motivation. When analyzing these constraints, we will find that some are nonnegotiable and therefore beyond our control, while others will be within our sphere of influence. Those factors beyond our control are "givens" and will have to be factored in to all plans of action. This is in sharp contrast to those we can endeavor to influence.

An educational entrepreneur's first step should always be to develop a plausible macro theory of change. A macro theory articulates that certain strategies will evoke a desired response, given two important assumptions: That the strategies will be operating within the constraints of the "givens," and that the entrepreneur will be able to influence the other factors in the best possible manner, thereby ensuring success.

What are the macro theories of the two proposals?

In the first proposal, the following factors are not negotiable:

- The camp is a three-week long social and educational endeavor.
- It is an overnight camp.
- It takes place in the summer.

The macro theory of the summer camp would then be as follows:

If a three-week, overnight summer camp were offered to teens and marketed effectively they would enroll. Furthermore, if the program offers rich and compelling Jewish content, it will strengthen the Jewish identity of the participants.

In the teen club proposal, the nonnegotiable factors are as follows:

- The club will offer educational and social activities for teens.
- Participants will be invited to participate on an ad hoc basis.

The macro theory of change of the club would be as follows:

Establishing and effectively marketing an accessible clubhouse for teens which offers ongoing activities will lead to their participation. Furthermore, if there is rich and compelling programming with Jewish content, the teens' participation will lead to a strengthening of their Jewish identity.

The macro theory of changes identifies two central challenges the social vision entrepreneur encounters: the recruitment of the target population and the implementation of an impactful educational process.

The plausibility of the macro theory
What are the chances that the planned activity will lead to the desired outcome? This is certainly a crucial question. In planning

an educational endeavor, the macro theory assumes its best possible implementation.

If the macro theory is implausible the endeavor will be doomed to failure, no matter how hard the entrepreneur tries to succeed. An example of weak macro theory was a proposal for a traveling Jewish museum, which I was invited to evaluate. Those submitting the proposal envisaged that it would visit distant Jewish communities for a week or two. Their theory was that the presence of the museum would stimulate the observance of Jewish customs and precepts among the target population.

While there was a strong possibility that the museum could have a positive impact on the local Jewish community, I was skeptical that the museum could achieve the long-range goal of stimulating the observance of Jewish customs and/or precepts. The latter would require a far more intensive educational interaction in order to succeed. Based on the feedback, those who submitted the proposal changed their macro theory and projected outcomes far more in line with a museum experience, and this proposal was accepted.

Expert evaluation of a macro theory is of prime importance. A mistaken evaluation can lead to a waste of precious resources, a demoralization of the faculty and a loss of faith by other key stakeholders.

Both proposals described above, the summer camp and the clubhouse, have a strong macro theory. With regard to the camp, the assumption that an intense social and educational experience will lead to an enhancement of Jewish identity is strongly grounded in research. This was highlighted by Saxe and Sales in their groundbreaking research on Jewish summer camps [AVI CHAI Foundation, 2004].

Similarly, there is strong evidence that shows that a Jewish club with compelling social and educational programming will succeed in enhancing Jewish identity. This has been underscored by Professor Steven Cohen, who maintains that there is a clear correlation between the maintenance of Jewish social networks and the strengthening of Jewish identity [Ledger_Admin, 2013].

The micro theory of change

When we discussed the macro theory of change we differentiated between the fixed, nonnegotiable factors and those that the entrepreneur is able to influence.

As stated, all macro theories assume that "the entrepreneur will be able to influence the other factors in the best possible manner, thereby ensuring success." In order to set about doing this, the entrepreneur will need a second theory of intervention which we will call the "micro theory."

The micro theory informs the entrepreneur in his or her choices, including the following (if they are not "givens"):

- Staffing: What staff attributes are required in order to succeed? Do staff need to be subject matter experts or skilled in educational facilitation, or both?
- Program content and process: Which content areas should be covered, and what educational methods should be applied? Should teaching be frontal or interactive, cognitive or experiential?
- Budget (assuming the entrepreneur has budgetary responsibility): What amounts of money are required for which purposes?

A micro theory of change would be articulated as follows:

If X (type and number) faculty were hired in order to implement Y (content and methodology) program with Z financial support, the educational endeavor would be successful.

The micro theory thus relates to the detailed plan of action [Bradach, 2003] and it is the different micro theories and their implementation that differentiate the brilliant and creative entrepreneurs from the rest. These resourceful entrepreneurs possess the art of selecting and inspiring their staff and a keen sense of how to develop compelling programming.

Distinguishing between macro and micro theories of change
Distinguishing between macro and micro theories of change is not only important for the planning of educational endeavors, it is useful as well for both identifying entrepreneurial opportunities and analyzing failure.

Identifying entrepreneurial opportunities
In the realm of social entrepreneurship, strong macro theories of change present important opportunities for entrepreneurial endeavors. It is this sense of entrepreneurial opportunity that has driven a number of philanthropists to invest in the growth of Jewish camping, which they believe has a strong macro theory of change.

Similarly, our focus on blended-learning day schools, Hebrew charter schools and Hebrew after-schools was driven by their strong macro theories of change. All three environments offer parents added value. The blended-learning day school offers quality day school education at affordable cost, Hebrew charter schools offer a quasi-private education for free and Hebrew after-schools offer parents a quality solution for after-school care. Furthermore, all three models offer large amounts of quality time[1] for serious, comprehensive Jewish education. Thus, if their programs are run in the best possible manner, there is a high chance of educational success. This is why we believe in the importance of developing and growing these three models.

Analyzing failure
A second important by-product of differentiation between the macro and micro theories of change is that it allows for problem diagnosis in the event of failure.

If an educational endeavor is not successful, one of the first questions to ask is whether the problem lies with the macro theory or the micro theory. If there is a problem with the macro theory it

---

1   "Quality time" is time which is conducive to educational activity.

may be counterproductive to continue with the endeavor, since the nonnegotiable factors do not encourage success. However, if there is a problem with the micro theory, the entrepreneur could continue to experiment in the hope that a successful strategy will be found.

Factors that contribute to a strong theory of change

A number of factors contribute to a strong theory of change, and entrepreneurs should do everything possible to harness them.

First, the setting should support the educational goals. If the facility is a "given," it is crucial to align the goals of the endeavor with the educational experiences that can be designed within the setting. In formal settings, it may be far easier to organize formal educational experiences that facilitate literacy. Similarly, informal settings may be far more conducive to experiential learning that facilitates socialization.

Second, the endeavor should take place during "cheap"[2] quality time. When a potential participant expresses interest in participating in an educational endeavor, yet ultimately decides not to enroll, the reason will often be that "I would love to participate but don't have the time." This reflects the familiar predicament in which multiple activities compete for our time, forcing us to make choices. When there is a great deal of competition for our time, our time is "expensive." When there is little competition for our time, it is "cheap."

For an educational endeavor to be successful, it needs to take place during quality time, a time in which students are alert and able to concentrate. When educational activities for adults are scheduled in "cheap" but non-quality evening time, participants who work a long day may not be alert, which diminishes the endeavor's chances of success. The entrepreneur's challenge is thus to find cheap time which is also quality time.

---

2   "Cheap time" is time that is available, and for which the educators do not face fierce competition.

A third factor that contributes to a strong theory of change is if the educational activity offers added value. Since we can assume that prospective participants have multiple educational options outside the Jewish realm, if the Jewish educational activity offers added educational and/or existential value that is perceived by the participant, the theory of change becomes strengthened.

The fourth factor is the social component. Study in social groups often creates positive dynamics that go beyond the original intentions of the entrepreneur. A friend who recently participated in an organized study tour related to me his excitement with the unexpected group dynamic that enriched the group experience.

Can a strong micro theory counterbalance a weak macro theory? In our discussion we have assumed that a strong macro theory is a prerequisite for success. While this assumption is generally sound, is it possible to offset a weak macro theory with a very strong micro theory? This question is extremely important for those entrepreneurs who lack an alternative. They must choose between establishing an endeavor with a weak theory of change or establishing nothing at all.

This was the challenge that Peter Geffen faced when he became the founding principal of Park Avenue Synagogue's Hebrew high school in 1967. All Hebrew high schools have a weak macro theory of change. They take place in "expensive" time and must compete with the abundance of activities offered to teens after school. Having studied formally in the morning, teens do not readily seek supplementary study. Geffen thus faced an arduous task.

The Park Avenue Hebrew High School

In 1967, twenty-one-year-old Peter Geffen was hired by the Park Avenue Synagogue in New York, flagship of the Conservative movement, to create a post-bar mitzvah age after-school program.

The community was desperate. This was the 1960s, and young youth workers were looked upon as messianic figures who could save the young people that communities were losing. Geffen was given carte blanche with regard to both budget and curriculum.

The Park Avenue Synagogue High School after-school program operated in its original format for eighteen years. It served as a political action center against the war in Vietnam, offered summer programs and took the first group of Jewish youth into the Arab world, meeting with Sadat in 1978. In the late 1980s the program initiated a food distribution scheme for the poor, and to this day the needy still queue outside the synagogue on Friday afternoon for food donations.

Geffen explained the program's success: "We were taking a radical approach educationally, Jewishly, politically – all the things that serve an adolescent perfectly." The fact that kids wanted to come after school and were eager to spend the summer with their Hebrew school teacher ensured that none of the other distractions for teens derailed the project.

In a further departure from the norm, attendance at the school was not restricted to members of the congregation. During its heyday, hundreds of kids enrolled, including non-Jewish friends and Jewish walk-ins, many of whom had never had any prior Jewish education.

The entire faculty were young, and programs revolved around high-level classes. Young, dynamic doctoral students who were budding scholars were employed rather than traditional Hebrew school teachers. The environment was intellectual, and from the intellectual came both political and social engagement.

Geffen's manipulation of discretionary elements resulted in a strong micro theory of change that counterbalanced the weak macro theory. Nevertheless, the program remained one-of-a-kind and eventually was itself transformed by the synagogue to fit a more conservative educational model.[3]

---

3   Peter Geffen established The Heschel School, mentioned in Chapter One, following his tenure at Park Avenue Synagogue.

While Geffen did succeed in offsetting a weak macro theory of change, it is preferable to establish endeavors that have a strong macro theory. As both of our proposed endeavors have a strong macro theory of change, the next stage would be to validate their micro theories of change. Whom do they intend to hire and what will be the nature of the programming?

If both proposals are deemed sound following this analysis, judgment of these theories will have to be made in terms of their expected return on investment.

3. Cost-effectiveness

In assessing the cost-effectiveness of each endeavor it is important to assess the expected return on investment (ROI) with the goal that the return be maximal.

Maximizing ROI

In establishing an educational enterprise, it is crucial that there be an aspiration to maximize the return on investment (ROI). The formula for calculating ROI in the commercial realm is straightforward; it comprises the financial gain accrued from the investment minus the initial investment [Investopedia].

Mathematically this would be presented as follows:

$$\textit{Current value of investment} - \textit{Initial Investment} = \textit{ROI}$$

Calculating ROI in the educational arena is far more complex. In a commercial investment, the entire formula is financial. One invests finances with the expectation of accruing financial profit. In the educational realm, however, one invests resources and time with the expectation of accruing educational impact.

The ROI formula in the educational realm

Similar to commercial ROI, educational ROI is a function of input and output.

On the input side of educational ROI, in addition to the financial investment, we must also factor in the *human resource investment* and the *time investment*, the latter of which here means the length of time required for the educational endeavor to deliver the impact.

With educational ROI the objective is to minimize human and financial resources as well as the time needed for the educational process. All three variables are at a premium, and this informs the aspiration to minimize them. From an accounting perspective there may be an overlap between human and financial resources, but they are not completely interchangeable. There are human resources given gratis, while there are financial resources that relate to other areas such as logistics and therefore need to be calculated independently.

On the output side, the objective is to enhance educational value. In reality, we aspire to impact upon as many people as possible, in a manner that will be of major personal significance to the "clients" and will produce long-lasting effects. Therefore, in evaluating accrued educational value we factor in the *number of beneficiaries*, the *depth of impact* of the educational endeavor and the *length of impact*.

We now have six variables to factor in to educational ROI: financial, human resource, time, number of beneficiaries, depth of impact and length of impact. Mathematically, the educational ROI would present the six variables, as follows:

$$\frac{\textit{number of beneficiaries x (length of impact + depth of impact)}}{\textit{financial resources + human resources + time}}$$

This formula applies only to the primary impact of the educational endeavor; stakeholders in education should be cognizant of education's secondary impact as well. For example, the education of leaders impacts on their social peers and the education of parents impacts on their families. Thus, in evaluating the total educational impact, one should factor in the secondary impact in addition to the primary impact.

Before we move ahead and apply the ROI formula within the educational setting, we face two major challenges: the complexity of evaluating educational impact and the different currencies of the formula.

Complexity of evaluating educational impact

Evaluating educational impact is extremely difficult, and includes the following complexities:

- Which outcomes reflect the desired impact? Are they cognitive, attitudinal or behavioral? How does one measure length and depth of impact?
- At what point in time should impact be evaluated? I have often encountered parents who spoke of the delayed impact of childhood educational experiences. It was only when the children themselves became parents that they truly appreciated what they had learned and how important it was for life.
- It is difficult to determine *the* decisive educational experience that impacts the student. Educational experiences take place in a range of contexts, including the home, the school, the synagogue, the community and overnight camp. They also take place during different life stages, including early childhood, teen and young adult. Moreover, is a person a product of his or her home, school or larger environment? Schools often take ownership of their graduates' achievements, asserting a correlation between the success of the graduates and the quality of the school's educational program. Is there solid proof for this assertion?

Existence of different currencies in the formula

All six variables have their own "currencies." In the commercial realm there is one currency on both the input and the output sides, i.e., money. In the educational realm we are dealing with apples and oranges. In order for the formula to be applied usefully we need to assign numerical equivalents to each variable in order to reduce them to a single "currency." This requires that all stakeholders agree on the relative importance of each variable. For instance, they need to decide on the importance of financial resources versus time and the importance of the number of beneficiaries versus length and depth of impact.

The importance of determining ROI

While the process of evaluating the ROI of an educational endeavor may be daunting, it is critical for strategic planning and investment. Given the paucity of resources and the urgency of educational investment, we need a formula and metrics that will enable us to evaluate our current endeavors and plan future ones.

Evaluating ROI of our two proposals

In evaluating the two proposals outlined in the beginning of this chapter in terms of their ROI, one would have to quantify each variable. On the input side, estimation should be made of the financial and human resource costs of each proposal. While the camp proposal has a finite time investment, i.e., three weeks, in the club proposal there is a question regarding how entrepreneurs envision the length of client participation.

On the output side, the camp proposal would probably impact upon far fewer participants than the club. However, the length and depth of impact would probably be far greater for the camp than for the club. Thus, quantification of the variables is required in order to reach a comprehensive conclusion regarding which proposal to support

4. Financial Sustainability

Entrepreneurs who apply for grants in order to fund their endeavors need to convince philanthropists that their organization has a realistic sustainability strategy. Donors would like their contribution to strengthen the organization's capacity to serve participants in the future as well.

Financial sustainability is a major challenge facing all nonprofit organizations, especially in their early stages.[4] In addition to building a strategy for enhancing educational value, those involved in social endeavors also need to develop a long-term financial strategy.

Developing a strategy for financial sustainability

A key element of a sustainability strategy is diversifying income sources and maximizing each source. The three major sources of income for all nonprofits are government, which may outsource work to the nonprofit sector; the philanthropic sector and earned income.

Overdependence on any one of these sources may lead to highly unfavorable results. This was clearly demonstrated in the 2008 recession when nonprofit organizations that were totally dependent on philanthropic funding were severely challenged. During this period, many well-established Jewish educational organizations were unable to weather the financial storm and went out of business.

In the United States, separation between church and state renders most Jewish educational organizations ineligible for any government funding. Thus the two sources that serve as a major focus are philanthropic dollars and earned income.

We will not discuss the art of fundraising in this book. Instead we will focus on methods for increasing earned income, which may provide a far more predictable source of income than fundraising.

Increasing earned income

The primary source for earned income is the participants. However, in order to encourage as many participants as possible to avail themselves of the program we may be unable to raise fees beyond the proposed level. The following are avenues for earning income which apply particularly to the teen club and overnight camp proposals:

---

4   This issue will be discussed in detail in Chapter Thirteen.

- In both situations there is a high probability that the physical facilities are dormant for a portion of the week. Is it possible to rent them out?
- If the programs provide kosher food, is it possible to offer this service to the wider Jewish community?
- If the endeavors employ accounting staff, can they do the accounts of other organizations as well?
- Is the faculty able to offer seminars to the wider public on a fee-for-service basis?

Making the Choice

While we have outlined the criteria for making a choice between the teen club proposal and the overnight camp proposal, ultimately the decision will depend on the details. On the surface, if either of these proposals would be supported, the Jewish community would benefit immensely.

References

The AVI CHAI Foundation (2004). *2004 Annual Report.*

Bradach, D. (Spring 2003). "The Challenge of Replicating Social Systems." *Stanford Social Innovation Review*: 19–25.

Investopedia (n.d.). "Return On Investment – ROI." Retrieved August 10, 2014. http://www.investopedia.com/terms/r/returnoninvestment.asp.

Ledger_Admin (2013, February 25). "Conversation with…Dr. Steven M. Cohen." Connecticut Jewish Ledger. http://www.jewishledger.com/2013/02/conversation-with-dr-steven-m-cohen/.

Chapter Six

Extending the Market Boundaries

Central Ideas

Growth and enhanced impact of Jewish education are dependent on identifying uncontested market space to attract participants, uncontested time to capture the participants' attention, recruitment of quality personnel and financial support from untapped philanthropic resources. If these spaces are occupied, it is important to extend their boundaries into uncontested areas.

Recently I made a presentation regarding the importance of both developing an array of quality Jewish educational experiences that have a plausible theory of change and maximizing our ROI by increasing the number of participants and the impact.

An educator in the audience responded to my remarks. After complimenting my passion and expressing that he was equally committed to the vision I had articulated, he delivered the "punch line." He urged me to "come down to earth."

This man was an educator in an organization that was certainly offering quality Jewish education. However, the organization was facing enormous challenges on three fronts:

- Class sizes were small and they were unable to recruit large numbers of students. They had worked hard to grow their school but their efforts had been unsuccessful.
- Quality faculty was hard to attract. The institution was not in the New York area, and finding dynamic and committed Jewish educators was proving to be a major challenge.

- The institution was under financial pressure. It was becoming more and more difficult to raise funds, and as a result the organization had to raise tuition fees. This move made it even more difficult to attract new students.

The educator concluded: "How are we to grow the field given these formidable challenges?"

The Challenges of Attracting Participants, Personnel and "Pennies"

The question asked by this man highlights the difficulties we face as we aspire to grow the field of Jewish education and heighten its impact. In effect, we are operating in three markets, one primary and two secondary which enable the primary to function.

The primary market is the participants. They are the focus of our endeavors, and without their presence and attention Jewish educational organizations would be redundant. As discussed in the previous chapter, all educational programs should be evaluated in terms of their ROI, which relates to the number of participants and the impact of the educational endeavor. Given the voluntary nature of Jewish education we are in constant competition for our students' time and attention.

One secondary market is personnel. Quality personnel is critical to the success of most educational endeavors. While it may be possible to increasingly rely on technology for liberal arts education, in individuation education and socialization education the role of the educators is paramount. Success in individuation education requires faculty who are attuned to the unique attributes of each learner, while socialization requires faculty who are inspiring role models.

In today's open society outstanding people have multiple career options, and in our quest to attract talented personnel to Jewish education we face stiff competition.

The other secondary market is the "pennies," the financial resources that support the organizations and their endeavors. All organizations require dependable sources of income to enable them to grow with confidence. Long-term planning and the hiring of quality personnel are only possible if there is financial security. While for-profit companies rely on earned income, in the Jewish educational realm very few participants are able and/or prepared to pay the cost of tuition. Consequently, educational endeavors must rely heavily on fundraising, which pits them "against" others who are competing for the same monies.

In all three areas, educational entrepreneurs face stiff competition!

In responding to the question posed above by my colleague I would like to draw on a commercial insight, and to portray how educational organizations have successfully used it, wittingly or unwittingly, when facing the challenges of growth.

Blue Oceans and Red Oceans

Kim and Mauborgne [2004] researched multiple corporations that succeeded in increasing their market space. They identified two approaches for achieving growth. The first is the conventional approach of capturing existing markets and the second looks to develop new markets. Those who choose to compete in existing markets will engage in battle with the existing market incumbents, and in order to succeed they may need to employ extreme and aggressive measures. In the face of this "attack," the current market incumbents will do all they can to foil the efforts of the new players who are "invading" their market, and may respond with equally aggressive tactics. Thus Kim and Mauborgne coined existing, contested markets "red oceans," calling to mind "bloody" waters resulting from the bitter battles between those vying for market share.

In red oceans, there is an "I win, you lose," zero-sum game dynamic. Competition is fierce since growth of one's customer base will be at the expense of other companies. Competitors will do everything possible to both protect their customer base and attack others in order to attract new customers.

An alternative approach is to develop entirely new markets for one's products. Those who choose this approach have the luxury of avoiding competition and consequently operate in relatively tranquil conditions, which Kim and Mauborgne term "blue oceans." The researchers found that this second approach was an important vehicle for driving growth among multiple leading companies.

In blue oceans, wins are not at another's expense. This makes it possible for companies to focus on growth without having to worry about defending their customer base. Blue oceans are therefore highly attractive for businesses that wish to grow their markets.

An example of a red ocean is the mobile phone carrier market in Israel. Ten companies (five with networks and five with "virtual networks") compete for a population of eight million-plus citizens. Since most people in Israel are connected to mobile networks (except for toddlers and perhaps those on the most senior end), this market will continue to be a zero-sum game, and a company that seeks to grow will succeed only if it entices current mobile carrier customers to leave their current carrier and join them. Competition is therefore rife, and each company works fiercely to convince potential customers to transfer to their network. This has caused mobile carrier prices to plunge, with one company now offering a comprehensive phone and data plan both in Israel and overseas for those who travel for as little as ILS 99 (about $26) per month [Perez, 2014].

An example of a blue ocean is the 3D printing industry. Three-dimensional printing technology enables the common household to "print" plastic gadgets and toys. Instead of purchasing expensive, durable products on the open market, 3D printing enables the household to manufacture products at a cost far lower than the current market price. At the time of this writing very few households have 3D printers, resulting in this being a virgin market.

Early entrants into this market will thus have the opportunity for high growth. They have the potential to dominate the market from a position of strength. However, in the future, in the same way the smartphone and tablet markets commenced as blue oceans and are fast becoming red oceans, this market will probably move in the same direction in the not-too-distant future.

The educator who posed the question thus assumed that in the participant, personnel and pennies markets we are functioning in red oceans, where we have few participants, a paucity of quality personnel and a lack of funding. He intimated that if we attempt to grow these markets, it will be at the expense of those in the field who are already facing major challenges.

Is this assumption correct, and if so, how should we respond?

Answering this question depends on how we relate to the boundaries of the market. If we define the boundaries in terms of the *existing* market, quality Jewish education is indeed operating in a red ocean. There are a limited number of students, limited personnel and limited financial resources. However, if we explore the *potential* market, the picture is radically different.[1]

Extending Market Boundaries in Jewish Education

With regard to potential markets in the areas of student recruitment, quality programming time and finances, the boundaries can be extended exponentially. In the pre-bar mitzvah years, although there is a sizable population of American children who have quality Jewish educational experiences during the year, there is certainly ample room for extending the boundaries. In the high school population the number of young people who enjoy quality Jewish educational experiences is far smaller, so by extending

---

[1] Kim and Mauborgne developed a strategy for redefining the market boundaries which they published in a book, *Blue Ocean Strategy* (Watertown, MA: Harvard Business Publishing, 2005). We highly recommended this book.

the boundaries we will be able to create a major blue ocean of new customers.

Similarly, in the area of the "pennies," only a small percentage of philanthropic dollars contributed by Jews is given to Jewish causes. In their research on the giving patterns of mega-wealthy Jews, Tobin and Weinberg [2007] found that in the years 2001–2003, only 5 percent of contributions given by Jews in excess of $10 million was to Jewish causes. Even assuming that smaller gifts are more likely to go to Jewish causes, it is clear that the boundaries of giving could be extended greatly.

It will be possible to extend the boundaries of the potential market only if there is a large group of noncustomers. If the field comprises only customers, as in the cell phone market in Israel described above, there will be little room for maneuver and a red ocean will prevail.

With this in mind, the personnel market presents a far more complex challenge. There appears to be a shortage of trained professionals capable of creating and running high-impact Jewish educational experiences. This market appears to have narrow potential for growth, as only a limited number of high-quality individuals are prepared to dedicate their lives to Jewish education within the non-Orthodox sector. In such a small universe, highly creative strategies are needed.

Developing a Blue Ocean Product which Generates Participant Growth

In order to attract participants it is important to develop a product or process that is unique and will thus extend the market boundaries. This product or process will operate in a blue ocean if it brings added value to the participant. It will attract participants if it offers features and/or experiences unavailable in the general marketplace, thereby creating and growing a unique market niche.

An outstanding example of this type of offering is illustrated by the recent growth of BBYO (Bnei Brith Youth Organization).

BBYO is a nondenominational youth organization. Founded by the B'nai B'rith Organization in 1923, BBYO became independent in 2002. In 2004 Matthew Grossman became its CEO, and today it is the fastest growing Jewish youth organization in North America. Under Grossman's leadership BBYO more than tripled the number of participants in its programs, from twelve thousand in 2004 to over forty thousand in 2014. Participants are spread among forty regions, with a total of 550 chapters.

BBYO: a safe social space in a Jewish context[2]

Matthew Grossman came to BBYO from the Hillel Foundation, where he had served under two outstanding CEOs, Richard Joel and Avraham Infeld. These two inspiring leaders, whom we will discuss in detail later on,[3] proved to be excellent mentors for Grossman as he took on BBYO's transformation. He saw the potential in this organization for large-scale growth, and was able to transform it without compromising its core values.

BBYO's expansive growth can be attributed to the following:

1. It focuses on providing a safe social environment. In today's competitive educational world in which teens compete for coveted places in college, teens have a "blue ocean" need for safe social environments. In their transition from children to young adults, teens often need a safe and supportive, nonjudgmental context in which they can just "be themselves." For many, a nonjudgmental, peer-led environment may be critically important as a counterbalance to the demanding and competitive schooling experience.

---

2   This section is based on a phone interview with Mathew Grossman, September 29, 2013.

3   Richard Joel's tenure at the Hillel Foundation is discussed in detail in Chapter Twelve. Avraham Infeld's tenure at MELITZ is discussed below.

BBYO chapters are divided along gender lines, Aleph Zadik Aleph (AZA) chapters for boys and the B'nai B'rith Girls (BBG). This enables each gender to develop in environments that meet their needs and sensitivities, and is a competitive advantage in an era in which most social teenage environments are coeducational.

While the chapters are divided according to gender, the social activities, conventions and camps are coeducational.

2. It fosters leadership and social responsibility. As a peer-led organization, BBYO members assume responsibility for organizing their chapter's programming, recruitment and budgeting. The programs are often oriented toward social justice, enhancing awareness of the larger environment. Members learn leadership "on the job," and those who are highly talented run for regional and international BBYO positions. The Panim el Panim seminars offer members the opportunity to meet and lobby members of Congress, to learn from Israel advocacy experts and to engage in service projects aiding those in need in Washington, DC.

3. It provides a "Jewish space." In their high school years, teens who do not attend Jewish day schools appreciate the opportunity to have a Jewish space that will enable them to nurture their Jewish identity. In their post-bar/bat mitzvah years, there is often no contact with a local synagogue or any other Jewish organization. Existentially, many teens feel a Jewish connection is important. Thus, as a Jewish organization, BBYO has a competitive advantage over general youth organizations.

In addition, there is strong support from the parents, who approve of their children being in a Jewish environment and who believe that there their children will be safe. This is of crucial importance in an era in which teens are tempted by myriad environments which may not be safe.

4. It is a multifaceted organization. At its core, BBYO is a fraternity with a well-organized structure. It is also a club that offers social activities to both members and non-members. It offers its members shabbatonim (weekend seminars) and summer sleepover camps, giving the organization a camping dimension as well.

5. It counts recruitment and growth as core values. There is a research-based assumption [Israel Policy Forum, 2013] *that Jewish social networks are an important factor in choices relating to Jewish identity, and this has inspired BBYO to aggressively pursue new members on all levels.*

In developing itself along these lines, BBYO has differentiated itself from the other social options available to teens. As such, it has embarked on a blue ocean growth trajectory, focused on enhancing the quality of the organization and its impact.

Identifying and Creating Blue Ocean Opportunities for Educational Programming and Experiences

Attracting participants to an educational activity is a necessary first step, but it is not sufficient for the delivery of impact. Educational entrepreneurs often encounter two major red ocean challenges.

One challenge educators face is participants being physically present in an educational encounter while their focus is elsewhere. With smartphones and tablets present in the classroom, students may be tempted to communicate with their friends via social media as opposed to engaging with those who are physically present with them in the classroom. In a university setting this has become a major challenge for lecturers, and no doubt this challenge is felt in other settings as well.

This situation creates a red ocean whereby the educator is forced to compete for the attention of the participant even when the participant is seated in close proximity.

A second challenge educators face is competition with other activities that take place in the same setting. In Jewish high schools, for example, those who teach the upper grades will often have to compete for time in the school's schedule. All faculty will want to ensure that their subject receives priority in the allocation of quality time, and this might create stiff competition for the Judaic subjects.

Furthermore, those in the Judaic faculty who are teaching juniors and seniors find themselves competing for the students' attention even if the teachers succeeded in being allocated quality time for their subjects. In the junior and senior years of high school, students may be vested in ensuring their acceptance to the college of their choice. They will focus on excelling in those subjects that will be important for getting accepted to the prospective college, and if the Judaic subjects are not viewed as important the students will not be vested in them. Consequently there is a phenomenon in certain Jewish high schools where in the eleventh and twelfth grades the students will receive only a smattering of formal Jewish education!

Given these serious challenges, the research on Jewish summer camps undertaken at Brandeis University's Maurice and Marilyn Cohen Center for Modern Jewish Studies was a watershed.

Jewish summer camps: blue ocean opportunities for experiential, high-impact Jewish educational programming

In the year 2000, The AVI CHAI Foundation commissioned the Cohen Center for Modern Jewish Studies, headed by Professor Len Saxe, to undertake a study of Jewish summer camps in the United States. Professor Saxe and Amy Sales carried out in-depth research of eighteen Jewish summer camps [AVI CHAI Foundation, 2004]. In this study Saxe and Sales describe how successful Jewish summer camps utilize the informal, experiential setting for high-impact Jewish educational experiences, and offer multiple examples of how the camp setting is conducive for these experiences.

Saxe and Sales describe the potential educational impact which exists when Jewish practice and ritual are woven into the camp routine. They describe the impact of the use of Hebrew in the design of camp signs and symbols, and the power of Jewish song and Jewish art. They even refer to the sports field as an opportunity for an Israeli experience.

Creative and knowledgeable counselors are able to transform mundane discussions into educational interactions. The passion and commitment of these counselors is often contagious, and as a result campers are impacted in multiple ways.

Jewish summer camps thus have the potential to offer comprehensive, holistic Jewish experiences which can be interwoven naturally into the camp routine.

Foundation for Jewish Camp: investing in a field with blue ocean educational opportunities

The educational potential of overnight camps which came across in the Cohen Center study was not surprising for Elisa Bildner and her husband, Robert, who established Foundation for Jewish Camp (FJC) in 1998.

The Bildners were passionate about serving the Jewish community, and they provided seed money for a public foundation that would grow Jewish camping. As stated on the FJC website, "Through Wexner's leadership program for Jewish volunteers, the two (Elisa and Robert) studied the bigger picture of Jewish life in North America. What they found was a great need for more and better informal education opportunities for Jewish children, specifically overnight camp. Camps were not high on the agenda of the Jewish community, and as a result, suffered from lack of attention and funding" [Foundation for Jewish Camp].

In 2004, the board of directors of Foundation for Jewish Camp appointed Jerry Silverman as CEO. Under his leadership, overnight Jewish camps have become a major force in Jewish education.

Jerry Silverman's strategy for strengthening and growing Jewish overnight camps[4]

Jerry Silverman came from outside the Jewish professional field. While he had a background as a committed lay leader, his previous career was in the commercial world. A decade before his appointment he served in executive positions at the Stride Rite Corporation of Boston, and previously held several senior executive positions at Levi Strauss & Co. in San Francisco [Huffington Post].

Silverman was passionate about Jewish camping even before he became CEO. *As a father of five, he saw the impact Jewish camping had on his children. His commitment to the mission was rooted existentially.*

On entering the position, Silverman understood that in order to attract new customers, Jewish camping would have to compete successfully in the open marketplace. Jewish children and teens had a menu of multiple and exciting options from which they could choose in designing their summer activities. Parents were sensitive to the social and educational offerings at hand, and often made their choices with a critical eye. In order to attract these noncustomers Silverman would have to convince them of the advantages and quality of Jewish overnight camping.

*He developed a strategy compris*ing the following components:

1. *Investment in the senior leadership of the camps. Silverman was convinced that the pathway to building the "industry" was through superior executive training, and this became his starting point.*

2. *Strong focus on raising the quality of the camps. New customers would be attracted to Jewish camping only if it could compete favorably in the open market, and thus development of quality*

---

4   This section is based on a phone interview with Jerry Silverman, May 8, 2012.

product became a high priority. To ensure maintenance of standards, camps would need outstanding leadership; thus the direct linkage between the investment in senior leadership and quality enhancement.

3. *Aggressive pursuit of new customers. Families who had never sent a child to a Jewish overnight camp were offered a $1000 voucher toward their camp tuition.*

4. *A bunks-and-beds incentive plan for enlarging the capacity of the camps and enabling them to enroll more campers.*

5. *Offering of incentives to organizations to open Jewish specialty camps that would compete with general specialty camps, ranging from sports to ecology, which existed in the open market.*

6. *Raising of awareness in the general Jewish community regarding the educational impact of camping and its importance.*

As a result of embarking on this strategy, FJC facilitated a dramatic growth of the field of Jewish camping. In 2004, roughly 53,000 campers attended overnight camps. By 2009, this figure had jumped to 75,000.

In 2009, Silverman was appointed CEO of what became known as the Jewish Federations of North America. He was succeeded at FJC by another "outside" appointment, Jerry Fingerman, who also came from the commercial sector. Under Fingerman, the FJC continues to play a major role in growing the field of Jewish camping, fulfilling the vision of Elisa and Robert Bildner.

The successful strategy adopted by Jerry Silverman is a paradigm for the development of a field that has a high level of educational potential. The FJC avoided becoming a player in the Jewish overnight camping space or entering other areas of Jewish camping such as day camps and overseas camps. Instead, it chose to work with and nurture the general field of Jewish overnight camping, investing heavily in human resource development and improving quality. It encouraged new and veteran entrepreneurs to be bold and innovate, and rewarded success by investing in enhanced capacity.

Extending the Boundaries of the Pennies Market

Many of those involved in trying to sustain quality Jewish educational endeavors will identify with the question posed at the beginning of this chapter regarding the tough competition for limited financial resources. Only a small number of foundations support these endeavors, and if one of these decides to support new initiatives it may be at the expense of the existing ones. Is it possible to extend the boundaries of the "pennies" and attract new blue ocean funds?[5]

An organization that excelled in this realm is Taglit–Birthright Israel. This "gold standard" nonprofit has, since its first trip in the winter of 1999, attracted 500,000 noncustomers from sixty-six countries to a quality Jewish educational experience [*Annual Report*, 2015]. Its success is a product of multiple factors which should be studied in depth in schools of education and management across the globe. Taglit–Birthright Israel's ability to attract blue ocean funding is one of the critical factors in its success.

Taglit–Birthright Israel

Taglit–Birthright Israel was established in 1999 as a response to the 1990 Jewish population survey that reflected a growing trend of intermarriage among young Jews and a declining Jewish community [Getz, 2011].

---

5   In Chapter Thirteen new sources for funding are discussed in detail.

Originally proposed by Dr. Yossi Beilin, a former Israeli cabinet minister in the Rabin government, it was Charles Bronfman and Michael Steinhardt who pioneered the initiative [Saxe and Chazan, 2008]. *They were convinced of the power of an Israel educational experience to enhance and solidify Jewish identity, and believed that every Jewish, college-age young adult should have the privilege of this experience.*

With this assumption, they commenced a program of action that would bring tens of thousands of college students to Israel annually. In order to conceptualize this idea, a team comprising Bronfman and Steinhardt, together with Jeff Solomon from the Andrea and Charles Bronfman Philanthropies and Rabbi Irving (Yitz) Greenberg from the newly established Steinhardt Foundation for Jewish Life, spearheaded discussions with experts in the field, which eventually brought the program to life.

In building the first prototype, which was launched in 1999, the following key elements were incorporated:

1. *The program would comprise a ten-day educational trip to Israel.*

2. *The participants would be in the 18–26 age group.*

3. *The trips would only be for those who had never participated in a previous educational experience in Israel. Thus, effectively, it was the noncustomers who were earmarked.*

4. *The participants would receive the trip gratis, as a gift from the Jewish people. This trip would be their "birthright."*

5. *The objective of the program would be to strengthen the Jewish identity of Jews who wished to build their future in the Diaspora.*

6. *The outcomes of the trip would be evaluated on an ongoing basis by an academic institution.*

Taglit–Birthright Israel has proven to be highly successful in accomplishing its objectives. The following are the key findings in an evaluation report carried out by a team led by Professor Len Saxe of the Cohen Center for Modern Jewish Studies at Brandeis University in 2014:[6]

- *"As of 2013, 45 percent of JFP (Jewish Futures Project) panelists are married and another 15 percent are living with a significant other. Among those who are currently married, Taglit participants are much more likely than nonparticipants to be married to a Jew. Overall, the likelihood of in-marriage for participants is 72 percent, while for nonparticipants the likelihood is 51 percent. This finding is consistent with previous waves of the study."*

- *"Particularly striking is that among participants whose parents are intermarried, the probability of in-marriage is 55 percent, compared to 22 percent for those nonparticipants who are children of intermarried parents. For participants whose parents are in-married, the probability of in-marriage is 75 percent, compared to 60 percent for nonparticipants."*

- *"Overall, just under 30 percent of JFP panelists have at least one child. Parents who are married to Jews are more likely to raise children Jewish. In addition, they are more likely to have a brit milah (Jewish ritual circumcision) or Jewish naming ceremony for their children, celebrate Shabbat and Jewish holidays, be members of a synagogue and attend religious services, send their children to Jewish day care or preschool, and participate in the PJ Library.*

---

6   The findings are from data collected in 2013 for the fourth wave of the Jewish Futures Project (JFP), a panel study of individuals who applied to Taglit–Birthright between 2001 and 2006.

Because Taglit increases the likelihood of marrying a Jew, participation in the program leads to higher levels of engagement."[7]

Bronfman and Steinhardt realized the full financial implications of their idea. If it would reach fruition and 44,000 young people would be provided with free trips to Israel, on the assumption that the cost would be $3000 per participant the total annual cost would be $130 million!

They devised the following funding formula to cover these costs

- Major philanthropists would shoulder a third of the cost.
- The Israeli government would be asked to cover a third of the cost.
- Local Jewish Federations would cover the remainder.

Analysis of Taglit–Birthright Israel's strategy reveals that it anticipated raising at least two thirds of its funding from blue ocean sources, while having to compete with funds allocated by the local Federations.

The first "blue ocean" was to be expected. Bronfman and Steinhardt were major philanthropists and there was an expectation that they would contribute generously to the project. However, the second blue ocean, i.e., funding from the Israeli government, was an audacious idea, totally out of the box. Up to this point the Israeli government had supported only educational activities related to *aliyah* (immigration to Israel), so Birthright's request for funding ran contrary to prevailing policy.

An important principle of Taglit–Birthright was that the program was not to actively encourage *aliyah* but rather to strengthen the Jewish identity of Jews who choose to reside in the Diaspora. An

---

7   The operational aspects of Taglit–Birthright Israel are discussed in Chapter Twelve.

Israeli government that supported Taglit–Birthright could be accused of using the taxpayers' money to strengthen the concept of living in the Diaspora. Nevertheless, Prime Minister Binyamin Netanyahu supported the idea in his first term of office in the late 1990s, and Prime Minister Ehud Barak implemented it during his term.

Both prime ministers realized the strategic importance of a strong Diaspora for the future of the State of Israel. Both realized that the support of successive United States administrations for Israel might be related to the support of the American Jewish community for Israel. Thus it was in Israel's long-term interest that the Diaspora community remain strong and their support for Israel remain firm.

With acceptance of this principle Taglit–Birthright has enjoyed support from the Israeli government since its inception, with a promise of increased support in the future. Monies come from the Prime Minister's Office budget and as a result are not prone to the political pressures that take place in the other ministries. Thus, the commitment is grounded in an "absolute" blue ocean.

The blue ocean that existed with regard to the third of the funding from philanthropists continues to this very day despite the original funders having taken a back seat. The Birthright Israel Foundation, which was established in order to raise the philanthropic dollars, has had outstanding success in attracting new funding to this Jewish educational project. While the project is blessed with the support of mega-philanthropist Sheldon Adelson, it has successfully secured the support of a large community of donors on all levels [*Annual Report*, 2015].

Attracting New Personnel: Transcending the Limits of a Red Ocean

All attempts to implement high-impact programs in the Diaspora in the non-Orthodox world are likely to face a serious personnel challenge. In this realm we face a red ocean with seemingly very firm boundaries.

While we have academic programs in both North America and Israel that offer personnel training, enrollment in these programs is extremely limited, leading to a shortfall of trained, quality personnel.

One response to this challenge is to ensure that Jewish education offers a career track with compensation packages commensurate with what is being offered in other professions. A second may be to provide job security for those who are successful. However, while these adjustments to the profession are necessary, they are not sufficient. The area of career choice is a red ocean, and if we are to attract quality individuals to Jewish education we will require additional motivating factors.

Attracting high-quality, passionate individuals to Jewish education

With regard to motivating talented individuals to choose a career in Jewish education the following come to mind:

- If idealistic young people experience meaningful roles as educators in their formative years, there is a possibility that they will choose to continue in this field.
- If students have inspirational learning experiences they may be motivated to ensure that others are able to have similar experiences.

The impact of a meaningful educator role in the formative years

An interesting Israeli phenomenon might serve as a paradigm for meeting our challenge.

Social workers, despite their academic training, are among the most poorly paid professionals in the country. Since the welfare system serves the weaker sectors of the community, their industry is unable to advocate for them. As a consequence their trade union is weak, and all who enter the field are cognizant of this situation.

Nevertheless, students compete for acceptance to the various schools of social work. At The Hebrew University of Jerusalem, for example, acceptance requirements at the School of Social Work are extremely high, and the students are exceptionally talented.

This paradox was the subject of a master's thesis I recently supervised. The researcher interviewed a number of social work students in order to understand why they were so motivated to become social workers, despite the low compensation levels that prevail in the field. One of his findings was that many of those who studied social work were impacted by their years of service in the military and National Service.[8]

Most social workers are female, and in the course of their service they were given responsibility for dealing with social issues. Those in the military dealt with soldiers from "youth at risk" backgrounds, while those in National Service ran many of the welfare organizations. These experiences highly influenced the career choices of the young women, convincing them to dedicate their future to the welfare of society.

This phenomenon illustrates the impact of a series of meaningful experiences on future career decisions. Therefore, an important first step in attracting talented young people to the field of Jewish education is to enable them to have meaningful experiences as educators during their formative years. From this perspective, experiential education, which is the focus of both Jewish camping and Jewish youth organizations, is not only important for attracting and impacting participants, it is important as well for providing meaningful educator experiences to teens and college students who serve as counselors.

---

8   Young men and women who are exempt from military service can opt for National Service. Some opt for one year of service, while others serve for two years. The overwhelming majority of those who serve in the National Service programs are Orthodox women, who are exempt from military service.

An organization that has attracted highly talented personnel and which succeeded in motivating them to become committed to Jewish education is MELITZ, under the helm of Avraham Infeld.

Avraham Infeld makes MELITZ an incubator for talented Jewish educators

What do David Dishon, founding principal of Hartman Boy's High School; Dani Danieli, founding director of Beit AVI CHAI; Yonatan Ariel, founding director of Makom; Derek Perlman, founding Director of Yahalom; and I all have in common? We all worked for Avraham Infeld at MELITZ: *Machon leChiunch Yehudi Tzioni* (Institute for Zionist Jewish Education).

Avraham Infeld

Avraham Infeld was born in South Africa in 1943. His father, Zvi Infeld, was an ardent secular Zionist and secretary general of the South African Zionist Federation. His mother, Olga, was an educator, and taught my siblings at the King David Jewish Day School in Johannesburg. Both had a profound influence on their son.

Infeld opted for a religious lifestyle at a young age, and in 1959 studied at Yeshivat Kerem b'Yavneh in Israel. Having made aliyah, his illustrious career includes a shlichut (mission) to England on behalf of the Jewish Agency, founding MELITZ, serving as president of Hillel International and the Chais Family Foundation, and taking on the unique role of roving ambassador for Limmud International. Today, Infeld is accepted not only as the "Roving Ambassador of Limmud" but also as the ambassador for Jewish education and particularly Jewish informal education, an area he professionalized when he served as the director of MELITZ from 1970 until 2002.

All those who have studied and worked with Infeld, young students and adults, professionals and lay leaders, hold him in the highest regard. His sincerity and passion for the Jewish people and for social justice, along with his unassuming nature and inclination to both physically and spiritually embrace those with whom he is in regular contact, have made him an icon in the Jewish educational world.

My personal association with Infeld dates back to the late 1950s, when he participated in a weekly class given by my father at our home in South Africa. In 1978, after I married and was living in Israel, he offered me a position at MELITZ.

Working for Infeld was a seminal period in my life, as it put me on course to be a Jewish educator. At the time, my career ambitions were elsewhere. I chose to study political science and public administration at university and saw my future in this area. As mentioned, I was not the only one whose decision to enter Jewish education was impacted by their work at MELITZ. Over a period of thirty years, hundreds of others were impacted as well.

The magic of MELITZ

In its first two decades, MELITZ was contracted by the Israel Ministry of Education to run sleepover seminars for senior high school students. These seminars took place over three days and focused on strengthening the students' Jewish identity.

MELITZ attracted a wide range of high-level graduate students to facilitate these seminars and ran high-quality orientations for the faculty. The orientations were stimulating and exciting events. Facilitators came from a wide range of ideological backgrounds, and much collegiality and mutual respect prevailed throughout. The common ideal of strengthening Jewish identity broke down the barriers between the secular and the religious facilitators, and lifetime friendships were forged.

The centerpiece of the MELITZ seminars was the discussions with the students, which impacted both the students and the faculty. The students often expressed their excitement at participating in an educational encounter in which they were not being evaluated. They loved being "themselves," feeling free to form and articulate their own opinions.

In these encounters with the students, the faculty became acquainted with the Israeli educational system first hand. They were pained by the knowledge gaps between those living in the center of Israel and those from the periphery, the frustrations of the students from Sephardic backgrounds and the feeling that the Israeli educational system was "broken." Inspired by Infeld, the facilitators felt empowered to become change makers. With a certain level of innocence the facilitators continued to work with the schools and their faculty after the seminars, and began to understand the power of being agents of change. In this way, many facilitators who worked for MELITZ en route to other careers became committed to education, and the magic of MELITZ transformed their lives.

The Importance of Inspirational Learning Experiences

In Chapter Four we highlighted the Wexner Heritage Program as an outstanding example of an endeavor that focuses on the teaching of Jewish literacy. The program was designed to develop Jewish lay leadership, and it comprises thirty-six four-hour sessions spread over two years in which high-level text study is pursued.

As opposed to other leadership programs which focus primarily on the art and science of leadership, Wexner chose to focus primarily on intellectual pursuit. The theory of change behind this highly successful leadership program is that engagement in stimulating study of Judaism can be a powerful motivation for commitment to Jewish education.

In discussion with Wexner graduates who went on to help found Jewish day schools or who labored to transform their children's supplementary schools, I discovered the power of their Wexner learning experience. They explained that as children they had a poor Jewish educational experience, and their outstanding intellectual experience at Wexner transformed their understanding of the power of Jewish education. On graduating from Wexner they decided to dedicate themselves to ensuring that many more young Jews would be able to enjoy high-impact, quality Jewish educational experiences.

Engaging people in stimulating study of Judaism in their formative years as a motivating factor for future Jewish leadership highlights its importance. High school students who have such experiences may be motivated to pursue high-level studies in this field on a graduate and post-graduate level, and ultimately to become Jewish educators.

§

In response to the question posed at the beginning of the chapter, we see that superficially it may appear that Jewish educational endeavors operate in "red oceans." However, it is possible to navigate to "blue oceans" if we either extend the current boundaries of the market or invest in the development of new sources.

References

The AVI CHAI Foundation (2004). *2004 Annual Report.*

The Birthright Foundation (2015). *2015 Annual Report.*

Blue Ocean Strategy Moves (n.d.). "Ralph Lauren." Retrieved August 22, 2015. https://www.blueoceanstrategy.com/bos-moves/ralph-lauren/.

Foundation for Jewish Camp (n.d.). "Our History." Retrieved August 12, 2015. http://www.jewishcamp.org/our-history.

Getz, P. (Fall 2011). "The Birthright Challenge." *Jewish Review of Books.*

The Huffington Post (n.d.). "Jerry Silverman." Retrieved August 13, 2015. http://www.huffingtonpost.com/jerry-silverman/.

Israel Policy Forum (2013, October 22). "Briefing with Prof. Steven M. Cohen." Retrieved August 20, 2015. http://www.israelpolicyforum.org/news/briefing-prof-steven-m-cohen.

Kim, W. C., and R. Mauborgne (2004, October). "Blue Ocean Strategy." *Harvard Business Review*: 1–9.

Kim, W. C., and R. Mauborgne (2005). *Blue Ocean Strategy: How to Create Uncontested Market Space and Make Competition Irrelevant.* Watertown, MA: Harvard Business Publishing.

Leff, G. (2013, January). "Getting Another Airline to Give You Status Based on the Status You Hold with Your Current Carrier." View from the Wing. Retrieved August 3, 2015. http://viewfromthewing.boardingarea. com/2013/01/07/getting-another-airline-to-give-you-status-based-on-the-status-you-hold-with-your-current-carrier/.

Maurice and Marilyn Cohen Center for Modern Jewish Studies (n.d.). Brandeis University. Retrieved February 2, 2016. https://www.brandeis. edu/cmjs/noteworthy/jewish_futures_taglit_2013.html.

Perez, G. (2014, September 9). "Golan Telecom Launches NIS 99 Monthly Overseas Package. *Globes*. Retrieved August 3, 2015. http://www.globes.co.il/ en/article-golan-telecom-launches-nis-99-monthly-intl-package-1000970189.

Saxe, L., and B. Chazan, B. (2008). *Ten Days of Birthright Israel: A Journey in Young Adult Identity.* Boston: Brandeis University Press.

Tobin, G. K., and A. K. Weinberg (2007). *Mega-Gifts in Jewish Philanthropy: Giving Patterns, 2001–2003.* San Francisco: Institue for Jewish Community Research.

Chapter Seven

Sustaining Innovation and Disruptive Innovation

CENTRAL IDEA

INVESTMENT IN SUSTAINING INNOVATION AND DISRUPTIVE INNOVATION IS CRUCIAL FOR THE DEVELOPMENT OF JEWISH EDUCATION.

I was recently approached by the head of a philanthropic foundation who was troubled by the diminishing market share of non-Orthodox students who attend Jewish day schools in the United States. He was a big believer in comprehensive, formal Jewish education and asked me to help him decide how to invest in order to grow the field. His question inspired both Chapter One and this chapter.

The Different Groups that Comprise the Market Universe

In all vision-driven educational endeavors, and specifically in comprehensive formal Jewish education, the market can be demarcated as follows:

- *The consumers.* This group comprises those who enroll their children in Jewish day schools for ideological reasons. These parents believe deeply in the importance of a comprehensive formal Jewish education, and consequently they will make major financial sacrifices to ensure that their children receive this type of education.

In the event that the Jewish education provided by the school in their locale is not up to standard, these parents will seek out alternative schools which, in extreme circumstances, may require their children to commute long distances.

- *The customers*. This group comprises those for whom Jewish day school education is the preferred option, as it meets their priorities. These parents choose day schools because the schools offer an academic and social mix which the parents are seeking. They are not ideologically driven, and therefore if an alternative private or even public school would offer a better academic and social mix, they could be tempted to transfer their children to that school.

- *The overshot customers*. This group comprises families who are either former customers or potential customers of comprehensive formal Jewish education. Parents in this group agree that a comprehensive Jewish education is worthwhile, and, given ideal circumstances, they would enroll their children in the Jewish day schools in their locale. Indeed, some of these parents have enrolled their older children in the system in past years, while others would like to contemplate this option.

Nevertheless, the rising costs of day school education coupled with diminishing or static family incomes have rendered day school tuition unaffordable for these middle class families, many of whom are also reluctant to ask for tuition relief. Their decision to withdraw their children from the system is often made with a sense of regret.

A second group of overshot customers are those who are prepared to contemplate day school Jewish education but feel the school in their locale does not cater to their sensitivities. They do not define themselves as religious in any sense, and they experience tension between their liberal ethos and the ethos of the school. The latent expectations of the school have overshot these parents, who have therefore resigned themselves to sending their children to either an alternative private school or to a public school.

- *The noncustomers.* This large group comprises those families for whom comprehensive Jewish education is a theoretical possibility, but which has probably never been considered. They do not contemplate Jewish day schooling either for ideological reasons, i.e., they believe in educating their children in general systems as opposed to sectarian ones, or for practical reasons, i.e., they have an excellent public school in their locale.

- *The never-will-be-customers.* This group is nominally part of the market, but under no circumstances whatsoever will they participate in comprehensive formal Jewish educational endeavors. In some situations their stance is ideologically motivated, while in others it is driven by a deep mistrust of parochial education.

Based on this breakdown, the challenges for growing the market appear to be as follows:

- How do we retain our current market of both consumers and customers?
- How we attract our overshot customers?
- How do we attract the noncustomers?

Clayton Christensen, professor of business administration at the Harvard Business School, is a leading economic theorist who has researched attempts to connect with overshot customers and noncustomers. His work on disruptive innovation has impacted not only the commercial world but the worlds of health and education as well.

Disruptive Innovation Theory

Christensen [Christensen, 1997] developed the theory of "disruptive innovation" in his groundbreaking research into the rise and decline of successful companies. In attempting to understand the success of new technologies and their impact on traditional companies, he discovered the power of "disruptive innovation" and its potential for disrupting the traditional markets.

An important aspect of Christensen's work is his focus on the large segments of the population who lack access to products and services. In their efforts to maximize profits, established companies gravitate toward meeting the needs of their high-end, demanding customers, thereby overlooking the noncustomers, who are at the lower end.

In his early works, Christensen [Christensen, 1997; Christensen and Raynor, 2003] focuses on the profit possibilities open to companies that try to capture the noncustomer markets. In his later works [Christensen, Grossman and Hwang, 2008; Christensen, Horn and Johnson, 2008] he focuses on the social value that could be attained if the providers of health care and education would maximize their efforts to enable the noncustomers, i.e., those who do not enjoy the benefits of health care and quality education, to enjoy these amenities. While ideally quality health care and education should be accessible to all, trends in these fields resemble commercial markets in that those who hold the resources focus on the high end of the population. Consequently, there is a neglect of large segments of the population who by default remain noncustomers.

The core concepts in the disruptive innovation theory are "sustaining innovation" and "disruptive innovation," and these will be explained within the context of the disruptive innovation process[1] [Christensen, 1997; Christensen and Raynor, 2003].

---

1 In his works Christensen discusses the "disruptive innovation model," which requires a discussion that goes beyond what is germane to our chapter. We have extracted three key elements from this model and refer to them as the "disruptive innovation process."

The disruptive innovation process

The disruptive innovation process comprises the following three key factors, which relate to technological and other types of advances that are made in the development of products and services as well as to the ability of customers to utilize, or in Christensen's terminology "absorb," these advances.

- *The rate at which customers are able to absorb improvements in products and services.*

In every market there is a varied group of customers who can absorb and are willing to pay for the improvements of products and services developed by innovative organizations. While customers at the high end of the market place a high value on change, the majority of the market has little use for major technology improvements and will pay only for a slight improvement.

An example of this phenomenon is car engines. Today car manufacturers produce cars that have the capacity to travel at speeds which are far beyond the needs of the average driver. Most drivers will never travel at the highest speeds and would probably far prefer to purchase cars that are cheaper and have less horsepower, as they are unable to absorb the technological advances in the development of faster cars.

- *The innovative strategy adopted by established companies.*

Established companies, in order to retain their high-end paying customers and to attract new high-end paying customers, tend to invest in advanced and costly innovations in order to manufacture products and develop services for the top end of the market. They believe that their financial success and future profits depends upon ensuring the allegiances of these high-end customers. In investing their resources in high-end innovations, companies remain firmly focused on their existing market. They are keenly attuned to this market's needs.

This focus can have two negative consequences. The first is that these companies overshoot a portion of their market, i.e., the lower end, and develop products and services that go beyond the needs of this sector (how many of us use more than 20 percent of the capacities of our laptops or smartphones?). In this situation, these lower-end-market customers might decide that the product or service offered is beyond their needs and their financial reach, leading them to search for a less sophisticated product or service.

A second consequence of this innovation strategy is that noncustomers,[2] i.e., those who are considered to be outside of the market, are completely overlooked. As potential small purchasers only, members of this group are considered to be irrelevant for the future of the company, and their needs are not even on the company's radar.

• *The distinction between sustaining innovations and disruptive innovations.*

Christensen terms the innovation strategy adopted by the established companies "sustaining innovations." The improvements made by these companies are either incremental or breakthrough. As stated above, in targeting the high end of the market they hope to hold on to their current clientele and attract new high-end customers, which will generate even higher profits.

New companies will find it difficult to compete head-to-head with established companies for the high-end market. These companies, conscious of their lack of technological capabilities, experience and brand recognition, may well prefer to focus on the overshot customers

---

2   Christenson uses the term "nonconsumers." However, given our categorization of the market, we will use the term "noncustomers."

and noncustomers. In contrast to the high-end customers who demand high-quality products and services, these potential customers demand accessible, affordable, "good enough" products and services which new companies are suited to develop. Christensen uses the term "disruptive innovation" to describe the development of accessible and good enough products and services. They are disruptive in that they "attack" the market from the bottom and as such have a disrupting effect on the market as a whole.

According to Christensen [Christensen and Raynor, 2003], in head-to-head competition with sustaining innovations, it is usually the established companies that triumph. However, if new companies commence with disruptive innovations, not only do they succeed in taking immediate root among the noncustomers and overshot customers, they will eventually threaten the established companies as well. In his research, Christensen found that initially the established companies paid little attention to the disruptive innovations, deeming them to be of poor quality with minimal capabilities. However, as time progressed, the disruptive innovations improved their technologies and moved up the trajectory – ultimately threatening the market leaders [Christensen and Raynor, 2003].

Response of the noncustomers to disruptive innovation

The conscious decision on the part of the established companies to focus on the existing market and to ignore the noncustomers creates a gap in the market that enables disruptive innovators to gain market share. Disruptive innovators identify large sections of the potential market that are not being addressed by the current suppliers or manufacturers. These noncustomers might not have the financial capacity or sense of priority to purchase the products or services currently offered. However, they may be willing to pay a small amount for a less sophisticated product or service, given that the scaled-down version may be their only option. New entrants to the market who sense the vacuum are able to develop simple and accessible products and services, thereby gaining a foothold attracting these noncustomers. Faced with the new competition, the market leaders generally ignore them, considering them not serious or labeling their products and services as being of poor quality. Thus they do not confront the disruptive innovators head-on. Ultimately, the existing companies flee in the face of the competition and the disruptive innovators take hold.

Disruptive Innovation in the Commercial World

In his book, *The Innovator's Dilemma*, Christensen [Christensen, 1997] regarded innovative technologies as the central disruptive force. However, in his later work, *The Innovator's Solution* [Christensen and Raynor, 2003], he expands the concept to include innovative new business models with lower profit margins that open new markets. An example of a new growth industry that combines both new technologies and a new business model is self-publishing.

Self-publishing

According to Bowker [Bowker, 2012], the official ISBN Agency for the United States and its territories, the self-publishing market in the United States grew 287 percent between 2006 and 2012, reaching a total of 235,000 print and ebook titles. In comparative terms, self-publishing accounted for 43 percent of the entire publishing market in 2011. While desktop publishing technology has been accessible for a number of years, print-on-demand (POD) technology and a new disruptive business model has enabled self-publishing to embark on its major growth trajectory.

Self-publishing's tremendous growth reflects its ability to attract the large number of noncustomer authors who have successfully accessed the market.

Self-publishing differs radically from traditional publishing. In traditional publishing the publishers decide what is to be published, take the financial risk and are responsible for the publishing process.

They own the copyright of the published document and are responsible for its distribution and sales. In self-publishing, the author can publish without any constraints. He or she takes the financial risk and is responsible for the marketing and dissemination of the work. Using one of the self-publishing companies such as CreateSpace, Lulu and Lightning Source, the author uploads the manuscript to the publisher's computers and is not dependent on a middleman for this process.

In the POD model, the books are printed as they are ordered and paid for by the consumers. Distribution is done online by the publishers as well as by Amazon, and there is no problem of inventory or unsold stock. The author owns the copyright and is thus able to publish updated editions of the book without having to convince the publisher of the need to do so.

As a classic disruptor, self-publishing has taken root and is threatening the future of the traditional publishing houses.

Sustaining and Disruptive Innovation Are Significant for Growth of Industries

While Christensen's insights are of major importance with regard to strategies for capturing market share, they are no less profound for the success of an industry as a whole.

All industries need investments in both sustaining innovation and disruptive innovation. Industries as a whole will grow if there are major investments in innovations that maintain standards of excellence and cater to the needs of highly demanding customers. Sustaining innovation requires major investments in research and development, and the demanding, high-end customers are the financial source of these investments.

High-end product and service innovations attract the investments needed to drive the industry forward. They give the industry a level of cache which may radiate on the lower ends of the market as well. High-end customers will not compromise standards and quality, and ultimately the industry as a whole will benefit.

The key to an industry's growth, however, is disruptive innovation. Disruptive innovation opens the industry to new customers, and while each customer may make only a small contribution to the profits, the volume of the market will engender them.

Furthermore, disruptive innovations, as they become increasingly sophisticated, ultimately influence the high end of the market as well. Thus while in the short term disruptive innovations serve only those at the lower end of the market, in the long term they serve the higher end as well.

An example of this phenomenon is the commercial air travel industry.

The dual importance of sustaining and disruptive innovation in the commercial air travel industry

In the commercial airline industry, corporate travel is a major source of income. These high-end, demanding customers might travel business or first class, purchasing tickets at premium prices. These travelers are pampered with pre-boarding lounges, luxury seating and onboard amenities. In order to ensure that these top paying customers do not migrate to other airlines or to an alternative industry such as private jet charter companies, the commercial airlines invest in sustaining innovation.

Private jet charter companies such as Executive Jet Management, owned by Net Jets [Executive Jet Management], offer executives the option of one-off travel on a private jet without having to lease the entire aircraft. Important advantages of private jet charter travel are punctuality and flexibility. They are punctual since they are chartered for specific flights, and if the entire flight is chartered it can be dovetailed to one's timetable.

In order to address the competition, commercial airlines make extreme efforts at being punctual, while offering frequent departures on popular routes such as New York to Los Angeles and New York to Washington, DC. And while coach passengers do not enjoy the luxuries poured on the business and first class passengers, they do enjoy the punctuality and regularity of the flights. Thus, the industry as a whole benefits from investment in sustaining innovation.

Likewise, disruptive innovation with regard to online reservations has benefited the commercial air travel industry as a whole. Priceline, Orbitz, Expedia and others have enabled passengers to shop for discount fares. Noncustomers who usually prefer cheaper train or bus travel are enticed to consider air travel given the possibility of highly discounted fares for empty airline seats. Prior to the phenomenon of online reservations prospective passengers needed the services of travel agents, who may have been incentivized to sell high-price airline tickets. This disruptive innovation has benefited not only those who are on the fringes of the market, even corporate customers are now able to "shop online" and acquire business class seats at discount prices.

The dual importance of sustaining and disruptive innovation applies to Jewish education as well.

Investment in Sustaining Innovation: Jewish Private Schooling

Returning to the concerned philanthropist whose dilemma opens the chapter, the optimal investment strategy seems to be a diverse one. With regard to Jewish education, it is important to invest in sustaining innovation to nurture the demanding customers and keep them within the system by focusing on the high end of the market. In doing so we will overshoot some customers, and it is crucial we establish schools that will meet their needs. In addition, we need to build new options for the noncustomers in order to attract them. The options need to be low barrier to ensure that those who do not consider comprehensive Jewish education a priority will nevertheless consider it to be a viable option.

On the higher end of the market in Jewish education it is possible to differentiate between two types of demanding customers:

- Parents who demand an outstanding, comprehensive Jewish education and are willing to make major sacrifices in order to ensure their children receive it.
- Parents who demand private schooling on the highest level and have the financial resources to pay to for it.[3]

The first group is critical for the future of the entire Jewish education "industry" and for the future leadership of Jewish communities. The students from this passionate and committed group will hopefully become the scholars, educators and spiritual leaders of tomorrow. From their ranks will grow the spiritual and cultural backbone of strong and vibrant Jewish communities.

Consumers in this group will probably demand advanced text study and highly knowledgeable faculty. They will challenge the system to make increasing investments in the quality and level of the Jewish subjects, and ultimately these improvements will benefit the system as a whole.

The second group comprises affluent, committed families who are the building blocks of a sophisticated lay leadership. They can afford exclusive private schooling for their children and are not willing to compromise on the importance of multiple quality educational options. They want their children to have a private school education comparable with the best ones on the open market and are willing to pay for this option. They too have a key role in the sustainability of the entire industry, as they are important investors and ambassadors for the industry as a whole. If the needs of this group are not met within the Jewish educational system, these

---

3   Excellence in secular education is not included, since it is likely to be a universal demand.

consumers will migrate to alternative general systems that are able to meet their demands for quality.

Educational entrepreneurs who target the high end of the market may thus be faced with the following dilemma: do they shoot for high-quality Jewish education within the context of private education, or do they shoot for high-quality private education within the context of Jewish education?

Given the above, it is possible to fully appreciate the contribution of Peter Geffen, whose leadership in the development of the Heschel School was highlighted in Chapter One. The Heschel School invested in sustaining innovation in both areas, offering an outstanding general education that competes with the best private schools and an outstanding Jewish education that competes with the best Jewish day schools.

Investment in Disruptive Innovation in order to Enhance Sustaining Innovation: Affordable Jewish Day Schools

The name of this section appears to be an oxymoron! We described sustaining innovation as that which invests in the high-end, demanding customers and disruptive innovation as aimed at attracting the overshot and noncustomers.

As has been pointed out, there are two types of customers at the high end of the Jewish day school market: those who are committed to quality comprehensive Jewish education and those who are committed to high-quality private education. While we discussed these as being two alternative markets, the high cost of Jewish day school education has de facto merged them into one. Parents who cannot afford the high tuition but do not want to apply for tuition relief are locked out of the system. Most Jewish day schools have become by default "Jewish private schools," affordable only to the affluent.

Gershon Distenfeld was deeply troubled by this predicament. He understood the anguish of committed families when they realized they could not afford quality comprehensive Jewish education for their children. Though they believed strongly in the ethos of Jewish education, the high cost of tuition "overshot" them, making day school education beyond their reach. Thus, Distenfeld spearheaded the establishment of a Jewish day school that would make "sustaining innovation" affordable. His research showed that through disruptive innovation, he could develop a school that offered the blended learning model.

Online learning

A remarkable outcome of Distenfeld's findings confirmed a finding in Christensen et al. [Christensen, Horn and Johnson, 2008]. Online digital learning had moved up the trajectory and was now in a position to offer a quality level of instruction.

Online courses offer four important educational advantages:

1. *They have access to expert faculty.* The producers of online courses have access to high-quality, expert faculty since they are not s limited by geography. The traditional classroom is limited to available faculty. If there are no expert faculty in a specific school in a specific subject area, the academic standards of the subject which is offered may be compromised.
2. *Learning is individualized.* In the traditional classroom, where there is a large group of students of varying levels and aptitudes, the same instruction is given to all students. In this situation the brightest students may be overlooked if the lesson is pitched below their level, while the weaker students may be overlooked if the lesson is geared to the level of the stronger students.
3. *Student progress is monitored in real time.* In the traditional classroom it is very difficult for the teacher to gauge if the student fully comprehends the material. Assignments and examinations will pick this up, but often this happens late in the course and as a result precious time is lost in which the situation might be remedied.

4. *Since the formal instruction is given by a third party, the faculty is able to give individualized attention to each student.* In the traditional classroom, the teacher has a dual role. He or she is responsible for group instruction and is a facilitator of the learning. Since these two activities cannot be performed simultaneously, as the first is given to the entire group and the second requires individualized attention, the teacher is faced with an either/or situation. In the digital classroom, there is a differentiation between the two roles. The formal instruction is provided online, while the facilitation of learning is provided by faculty who are present in the classroom. Faculty can give attention to each student without interrupting the instruction to the other members of the class.

While online instruction has the above advantages, still, a critical aspect of education is social and human interaction. It is of critical importance to interweave traditional, face-to-face instruction in the educational milieu. Hence the term "blended learning," the growing trend in which schools offer both frontal and online learning.

Blended learning is now growing at a rapid rate, and according to Christensen et al. [Christensen, Horn and Johnson, 2008], by the year 2019, 50 percent of all high school courses will be delivered online in some form or fashion.

The economic advantages of blended learning

The blended learning model requires professional faculty for face-to-face instruction. However, the learning facilitators need not be teaching professionals. There are many establishments which use university students for this role. Facilitators need to be fluent in the subject matter and have the empathy to work with children. This is a blue ocean of educational talent and is far more cost-effective to employ, and consequently the personnel expenditures, which are a high portion of formal education budgets, are far lower than traditional schools.

Targeting Overshot Customers through Disruptive Innovation.

In categorizing the market we distinguished between two types of overshot customers. The first is made up of those for whom Jewish day schools were an option yet were "overshot" because of the high price of private education. Affordable Jewish day schools would meet their needs.

The second type of overshot customers comprises those parents who would like a milieu with a Jewish flavor and a Jewish "cultural" education for their children. If this option does not exist they will not consider day school to be an option, as they feel that what is offered overshoots their needs. However, should there be a large enough group of parents of this type, a comprehensive cultural Jewish day school would certainly be an important disruptive innovation.

Targeting Noncustomers through Disruptive Innovation

As mentioned at the beginning of this chapter, the noncustomers comprise the largest segment of the Jewish education market. This group of parents will typically enroll their children in once- or twice-a-week Hebrew supplementary schools if they are members of a congregation; if they are unaffiliated their children might very well receive no Jewish education at all. This group is not ideologically opposed to comprehensive Jewish education (as opposed to the "never-will-be-customers"), and thus from a numerical perspective holds the largest potential for growth among all the segments.

It is with this group that Peter Deutsch, in establishing the Hebrew charter school concept, and Ana Robbins, in establishing the Jewish Kids Group, were highly successful. Their recruitment efforts reflected their understanding of the "jobs to be done" among the populations they served, and they skillfully ensured that the enterprises they established would enable these noncustomers to achieve their goals while receiving comprehensive Jewish schooling as well.

When the Ben Gamla schools opened in Florida, Deutsch discovered there was a large core of Jewish parents who were seeking a charter school as an alternative to the public schools in their area. Their prime motivation was excellent schooling for their children, and they believed the Ben Gamla schools would excel educationally and academically. These parents were not opposed to the Hebrew culture flavor of the school. Many parents believed it was important that their children learn a second language, and given their Jewish heritage felt comfortable with their children studying Hebrew.

When Ana Robbins consulted with her constituency in Atlanta, Georgia, regarding future directions for the Jewish Kids Group, it was they who articulated their need for a five-day-a-week after-school program. They were seeking an outstanding educational framework which would operate every weekday afternoon. Their "jobs to be done to done" were to hold a full-time job and to ensure their children were in a safe educational environment. Since these working parents trusted Robbins's skills as an educator they urged her to provide a solution within the context of her Jewish educational enterprise. Robbins realized that in order to succeed she needed to deliver a superior educational enterprise which would compete favorably with alternative after-school programs.

The opportunity for Jewish after-school programs to attract noncustomers to comprehensive Jewish education cannot be underestimated. Deutsch discovered this when he got to know Ben Gamla's parent body, whose needs were similar to those of Robbins's constituency.

With regard to after-school programs at Ben Gamla it is important to emphasize that there is a complete separation, both personal and legal, between the school, which delivers on its mission of Hebrew culture, and Peter Deutsch, who believes in the importance of Jewish education. In his private capacity Deutsch promoted the establishment of independent Jewish educational programs during after-school hours and realized very quickly that parents who enrolled their children in these programs were seeking comprehensive after-school programming for their children. Thus, if a sophisticated, educational after-school program were establishment adjacent to the school, or which rented the school facilities in the after-school hours for this purpose, many parents would be tempted to consider it as their primary after-school option.

Both Robbins and Deutsch pride themselves on their achievements in this area; students of their establishments who were previously noncustomers are now customers, and becoming consumers, of Jewish education.

The Promise of Investing in Sustaining Innovation and Disruptive Innovation

If a strategy of investing in both sustaining innovation and disruptive innovation were to be pursued, the "industry" of comprehensive formal Jewish education would be enriched as a whole.

Graduates of the sustaining innovative settings will become the engines that drive the system forward. These passionate and committed individuals will become the faculty of the disruptive systems, and through their demands the system as a whole will benefit.

Similarly, disruptive innovations will gradually move customers upmarket. Initially they will serve the low-end, non-demanding customers, but if successful they will be pursued by the higher end of the market as well. Programs developed for use in Hebrew afterschools will find their way into Jewish day schools. Finally, if the system is successful and the noncustomers not only become customers but consumers as well, Jewish day high school education will become an option for the new consumers of comprehensive formal Jewish education.

References

Anthony, S. D., M. W. Johnson, J. Sinfield and E. J. Altman (2008). *The Innovator's Guide to Growth: Putting Disruptive Innovation to Work*. Boston: Harvard Business Publishing.

Bowker (2012). "Self-Publishing Sees Triple-Digit Growth in Just Five Years." http://www.bowker.com/en-US/aboutus/press_room/2012/pr_10242012.shtml.

Christensen, C. M. (1997). *The Innovator's Dilemma*. Boston: Harvard Business Publishing.

Christensen, C. M., J. Grossman and J. Hwang (2008). *The Innovator's Prescription: A Disruptive Solution for Health Care*. New York: Mcgraw-Hill.

Christensen, C. M., M. B. Horn, and C. W. Johnson (2008). *Disrupting Class: How Disruptive Innovation Will Change the Way the World Learns*. New York: McGraw-Hill.

Christensen, C. M., and M.E. Raynor (2003). *The Innovator's Solution*. Boston: Harvard Business Publishing.

Distenfeld, G. (2012, September 14). "A New Model for Jewish Day Schools." *The Jewish Week*. Retrieved December 27, 2012. http://www.thejewishweek.com/editorial-opinion/opinion/new-model-jewish-day-schools.

ELItalks (2013). "About Us." Retrieved July 29, 2013. http://elitalks.org/.

Executive Jet Management (n.d.). "Charter Programs." Retrieved March 24, 2015. https://www.executivejetmanagement.com/private-jet-charter/charter-programs/.

Hebrew Charter School Center (2013). Home page. Retrieved July 28, 2013. http://www.hebrewcharters.org/.

The Hebrew Corner (2012). Home page. Retrieved December 21, 2012. http://thehebrewcorner.com/index.php.

JCoss (2013). Home page. Retrieved July 29, 2013. http://www.jcoss.org/welcome-to-jcoss.

JewishBoston.com (2012). "Sulam Brookline." Retrieved December 21, 2012. http://www.jewishboston.com/resources/23906-sulam-brookline.

Kesher. (2013). About page. Retrieved July 29, 2013. http://www.kesherweb.org/about/.

Lewin, T. (2012). "College Credit Eyed for Online Courses." *NYTimes* online ed. Retrieved November 13, 2012. http://www.nytimes.com/2012/11/14/education/moocs-to-be-evaluated-for-possible-college-credit.html?_r=0.

Mechon Hadar (2013). "Online Courses." Retrieved July 29, 2013. http://www.mechonhadar.org/online-learning.

National Charter School Resource Center (2013). "Understanding Charter Schools." Retrieved July 29, 2013. http://www.charterschoolcenter.org/priority-area/understanding-charter-schools.

Nitzan Network (n.d.). "Affiliated Programs." Retrieved September 20, 2015. http://www.nitzan.org/affiliated-programs.html.

Rosenbluth, S. (n.d.). "New Jewish High School Offering Customized Education for $5000 per Year." *Jewish Voice and Opinion*. Retrieved December 23, 2012. http://jewishvoiceandopinion.com/2010/11/pre-college-learning-center-nj%E2%80%99s-new-jewish-high-school-offering-customized-education-for-5000-per-year/.

Saxe, L., and B. Chazan, B. (2008). *Ten Days of Birthright Israel: A Journey in Young Adult Identity.* Boston: Brandeis University Press.

Scott, S. A. (2007). *Getting Our Groove Back: How to Energize American Jewry.* Jerusalem: Devora.

Sulam Brookline. (2012). Home page. Retrieved December 21, 2012. http://www.sulambrookline.org/.

TED-Ed (2013). Home page. Retrieved July 29, 2013. http://ed.ted.com/

TED Talks (2013). Home page. Retrieved July 29, 2013. http://www.ted.com/talks.

Virtual Beit Midrash (2013). Home page. Retrieved June 29, 2013. http://www.vbm-torah.org/.

WebYeshiva (2012). Home page. Retrieved December 23, 2012. http://www.webyeshiva.org/.

Wertheimer, J. (2010, March). "The High Cost of Jewish Living." *Commentary*.

Wertheimer, J., and S. Victor (2009). "Between Entrepreneurship and Jewish Mission: The Making of a Chabad Hebrew School." In J. Wertheimer (ed.), *Learning and Community: Jewish Supplementary Schools in the Twenty-First Century*. Waltham: Brandeis University Press, p. 82.

Wiener, J. (2012, March 27). "A Charter Network's Emerging Imprint." *The Jewish Week*.

Yeshivat He'Atid (n.d.). Home page. Retrieved September 16, 2016. http://www.yeshivatheatid.org/mission-statement/.

Chapter Eight

Attracting the Noncustomers

CENTRAL IDEA

IN ORDER TO ATTRACT NONCUSTOMERS WE NEED TO UNDERSTAND THE "JOBS TO BE DONE": THE JOBS THAT PROSPECTIVE PARTICIPANTS ASPIRE TO PERFORM.

Noncustomers are our largest market segment, and therefore inroads into this market hold great promise. How do we attract noncustomers to comprehensive Jewish education when it is not their priority?

This challenge is not only ours. It is faced by many commercial ventures which struggle to increase their market share and who continue to make major investments in developing growth strategies. To guide us in meeting our challenge in Jewish education, we will borrow an idea from the commercial world developed by Clayton Christensen in his research into disruptive innovation, which was discussed in the previous chapter: identifying "Jobs to be done."

The Motivation for Purchasing Milkshakes

A particular restaurant undertook market research in order to increase its sales of milkshakes [Christensen, Cook and Hall, 2006]. It segmented the milkshake market and assembled panels of focus groups which had the attributes of potential milkshake customers. Through these focus groups they explored which changes to the recipe or price would make the product more desirable. The groups gave the restaurant a clear indication of the customers' desires. However, when these improvements were implemented, sales did not increase.

A new set of researchers was sent to understand current customers' behavior patterns and motivations for purchasing milkshakes. A researcher sat in the milkshake parlor for eighteen hours and found that 40 percent of the milkshakes were purchased in the early morning. Most often these were the only items purchased, and the milkshakes were rarely consumed on the premises. The researchers interviewed these customers in order to understand their motivation for purchasing the milkshake.

They discovered that the customers had "hired" the milkshakes in order to achieve a common set of outcomes. "They faced a long, boring commute and needed something to make the commute more interesting" [Christensen and Raynor, 2003, p. 76].

These customers had other options for achieving this outcome. They could have purchased a bagel with cream cheese or a banana. However, the former potentially caused their hands to be sticky and the latter was consumed too quickly. The advantage of the milkshakes was clear; it could take as long as twenty minutes to drink since it came with a thin straw. In that way the boredom of the commute could be lessened. The milkshake was convenient because it could be consumed cleanly with one hand, and with a minimum risk of spillage.

This realization provided an important insight into understanding the customers' purchasing behavior. The restaurant thought it was competing against other milkshake vendors; in reality it was competing against other providers of solutions for boredom. These solutions included bagels and bananas, which could also be purchased as solutions for passing the time. Thus the "job to be done" was identified as overcoming boredom.

With this realization, the restaurant understood that if drinking a milkshake could become even more interesting they could beat the competition. Christensen and Raynor suggest that if the restaurant added tiny chunks of real fruit to the milkshake, thereby providing an element of surprise for the consumers, this might entice them to prefer the milkshake as a solution to the boredom challenge.

Citing the milkshake research as an example, Christensen and Raynor [Christensen and Raynor, 2003, p. 76] claim[1] that an effective way for growing the market is achieved by understanding what job the potential customers want to do when they purchase a product.

The Importance of Recognizing Jobs to be Done for Attracting Participants to Jewish Education

This paradigm is important, as it enables us to think differently about how we can attract potential students to Jewish learning endeavors. It is critical that we understand which jobs teens seek to be done, which jobs college students seek to be done, and which jobs young parents seek to be done. If Jewish learning frameworks were to provide quality solutions for these "jobs to be done," they would compete more successfully against the other alternatives. Similarly, once we understand which jobs our teen children are trying to do, we will be better able to offer alternative options that would both be acceptable to them and suit what we perceive as their best interests.

The jobs to be done is the "text"; Jewish education should be the "context"

The jobs to be done paradigm calls for making "text" the activity that enables the participant to accomplish his or her desired objective, while Jewish education provides the "context" within which it takes place. Jewish education should be offered as the "setting" as opposed to the prime activity, with the prime activity being potential participants' "jobs to be done."

The Chabad (Lubavitch) organization has succeeded in establishing educational endeavors based on this paradigm. Their choice of the term

---

1   This insight has its roots in the works of Richard Pedi, CEO of Gage Foods, and Anthony Ulwick, founder of Strategy. However, Christensen and Raynor are credited for its popularization.

"Chabad House," as opposed to the "Chabad Synagogue" or "Chabad Temple," indicates that their objective is for their home hospitality to be the text and for Judaism to be the context.

Chabad reaches out to many Jews who do not identify with its philosophy and who are not committed to Orthodox Judaism. They are invited to Chabad House to enjoy the hospitality a home offers. All are made welcome and their needs are taken care of in the spirit of home hospitality, in most cases without any request for fee for service. Within the intimacy of the house, the "jobs to be done" are ascertained and all efforts are made in order to develop activities that will enable their performance. Thus, on multiple campuses, the Chabad House is the home-away-from-home as described by Chazan and Bryfman [Chazan and Bryfman, 2006] in their study. College students, who spend long periods away from their families and neighborhoods, relish the warmth and caring that the Chabad House offers.

Chabad Houses: A "Home away from Home" for Israeli Backpackers

There is a widespread phenomenon of Israeli backpackers who travel to Southeast Asia, South America and Australasia following their stint of military service. For many this is a welcome break after their service and before they enter college or the workforce.

In all the major Israeli trekking areas Chabad has established Chabad Houses, which have become important addresses for many of the backpackers. In their quest to meet peers with whom to travel, as well as to enjoy home-cooked food, free internet and traditional meals on Shabbat and festivals, tens of thousands of backpackers frequent the Chabad Houses. In Bangkok, Chabad House hosts about 1,000 backpackers for the Passover seders, and for many of these backpackers the experience is a seminal Jewish educational experience. While there are Orthodox backpackers who frequent the Chabad Houses, the majority are secular. These participants, in addition to enjoying the social and gastronomic amenities that Chabad provides, all imbibe memorable Jewish experiences that often have long-term impact.

In order to succeed in their task, the Chabad "*shluchim*" (emissaries) need myriad skill sets that go far beyond educational expertise. They need to excel in running an information bureau, in organizing mega events and in establishing cordial relations with their neighbors to ensure that their activities will be looked upon favorably by the local population. This is all in addition to ensuring they have the finances to cover the costs of their activities.

Most important, however, they need to understand the psyches of the backpackers and their needs. They fully realize that the backpackers are seeking a "job to be done" for which Chabad House is a preferred option. In order to continue to draw these backpackers they have to excel in providing a worthwhile response.

Rabbi Nechemya Wilhelm

In 1995, twenty-two-year-old, Jerusalem-born Rabbi Nechemya Wilhelm, together with his young wife, arrived in Bangkok to become the first rabbi of Ohr Menachem Chabad House. The flagship establishment, founded by chief rabbi of Thailand Rabbi Yosef Chaim Kantor in 1994, was the first Chabad House to cater to the approximately 25,000 young Israeli backpackers who visited the country annually.

In an interview for this book, Rabbi Wilhelm notes that this figure has subsequently quadrupled, with most of the backpackers visiting at least one of the four Chabad Houses in Thailand. In high season, between four hundred and five hundred people pass through Chabad Bangkok's doors per day. During low season it could be 150 to two hundred. As for the Passover seders the numbers can reach eight hundred to one thousand, while for Rosh Hashanah Rabbi Wilhelm puts the figure at "over a thousand."

"They come because here they really have a home," he notes, referring to the reasonably priced restaurant ("so that people don't need to debate whether they should eat kosher or not"), the fifteen computers with email access and the free calls home – all of which are among the draw cards. "When you're traveling you want to have somebody to listen to you, somebody to help you with any problems," he added.

Regarding his own motivation he says, "I'm a shaliach of the Rebbe and I was educated this way: that we should be there for every Jew. I'm addicted to this work!

"You know what a feeling (it) is to treat five hundred people around your table on Friday night – people who in Israel would never walk into such a place, would never go to shul, people who I'm sure are seeing a nice Shabbat for the first time in their lives? In Israel, if you say, 'A chareidi, a dati leumi [Modern Orthodox] and a non-observant Jew are sitting at a table,' it sounds like the beginning of a joke – in Bangkok it's a reality."

While some may start making kiddush or putting on tefillin as a result of their experience, Rabbi Wilhelm's "100 percent success" derives from the fact that "everyone is moved," as Jewish people come together and get to know others who are different from them.

The most difficult part of the job, he says, is the parting involved, whether it be sending his children to school in Israel or taking leave of his visitors. "People are here with you for a week or two weeks and then they leave. Every day you are parting from people you really love, you get really close to."

From Context to Text; from Customers Motivated by Jobs to be Done to Consumers Motivated by the Social Vision

As discussed, the jobs to be done strategy is an important vehicle for attracting participants who do not highly value the learning enterprise itself. In a Jewish educational setting, the goal should be to encourage participants to be consumers of the social vision and to value Jewish education as an important vehicle for achieving this. The strategy, therefore, is to encourage the students to make the "context" their "text."

In order to achieve this, four steps need to be adopted: the jobs to be done experience needs to be of the highest quality, the provider must ensure that a bond of trust develops between the participants and the educators, the educational experience must be extremely positive and the participants should be encouraged to explore myriad educational opportunities in the wake of the jobs to be done encounter. We will now explore these steps one by one.

The jobs to be done experience needs to be of the highest quality

An important given in the jobs to be done paradigm is that noncustomers have multiple options for getting their jobs done. Their choice of the milkshake or of the Jewish educational offering is motivated by their perception that this product or service will be a successful vehicle for accomplishing their goal. If the restaurant wants the customers to return they need to ensure that the milkshake performs the jobs to be done in an optimal manner. Likewise, with the educational encounter it is critical that the experience be of the highest quality and the goals of the participant realized.

The provider must ensure that a bond of trust develops between the participants and the educators

We all become loyal customers of those we trust, be they medical practitioners, legal consultants or investment advisors. When we trust their expertise and feel they have our interests at heart, we will be prepared to consider options which without their advice would never have explored. In consulting with these experts, especially when we are ignorant of the subject matter, we feel the confidence to experiment and consider new options.

Likewise, if a Jewish educational endeavor is to succeed, there needs to be a deep sense of trust between the participant and the educator. Ideally the outstanding performance of the jobs to be done should become the building blocks of trust, and therefore they go hand in hand. This poignant point emerged when I interviewed Genia Janover, former principal of Bialik College in Melbourne, Australia.

Prior to focusing on Janover, let us take a brief glimpse at the Melbourne Jewish community.

There are approximately fifty thousand Jews in the greater Melbourne area. The community is vibrant, is committed to Israel and has a strong Jewish educational system. Approximately 70 percent of Jewish children in Melbourne attend a Jewish day school.

The Jewish day schools are diverse and cater to the diversity of Melbourne's Jewish population. Similar to communities in the United States, Melbourne has chareidi, Chabad and Modern Orthodox schools, but the majority of the day school population comprises students who are not observant of *halacha*, Jewish law. These students attend Mount Scopus College, a large community day school with Orthodox affiliation; King David, which was established by the Reform community; and Bialik College.

On its website, Bialik College describes its ethos as follows:

Bialik is unique as Australia's only cross-communal Jewish school embracing the entire Jewish community regardless of affiliation or practice.

Our students have a strong and positive relationship with Israel and they enjoy exploring the complexity of Jewish life. Their experience of Judaism is expansive and inclusive, embracing the reality that there are different paths for different people. [Bialik College]

Genia Janover

When Genia Janover took over as principal of Bialik College in 1989 there were around three hundred children at the school. Some three years previously, the school had been beset by a series of problems relating to its lay and educational leadership as well as to finances. Bialik was on the point of being absorbed into another school.

By the time Janover retired at the end of 2008, the numbers at the cross-communal, Jewish Zionist school had risen to 1,090. "I was the friend-raiser," she quipped in an interview for this book, referring to the expectation that not only would she lead the school educationally, she would also engender a sense of confidence and trust in it by building relationships.

Her appointment proved to be a popular one. Janover was a highly identified member of the Melbourne Jewish community and her reputation as deputy principal of the Leibler Yavneh College had preceded her.

"There was a feeling of confidence and of collegiality among the staff," she recalled, "and a very strong feeling that we were part of building something special, with a trusting, open and positive atmosphere. We employed good staff, and we developed strong relationships with students and with parents.

"I maintain that the primary role of the principal is to be the culture-builder," she stressed.

On Janover's impetus Bialik invested in teacher learning, demonstrating to the staff that the school valued them. This investment provided opportunities for their personal growth, while also improving outcomes for students. "I believe that the principal must be an enabler and supporter rather than a naysayer," she added. Given its target market, a large number of Bialik students could have chosen to attend a non-Jewish private school instead. How did Janover transform customers of Jewish education into consumers?

"Every enrollment came through me," she said. "I did the tours around the school with the parents, and the children where appropriate. I got to know the needs and what it was that parents were looking for.

"You got to know every child so that when you walked around the school you could address every child by name. You knew if there was a bar mitzvah, you knew if somebody was sick in the family.

"When parents feel that their child is known and understood, and they have a sense of belonging – that's what we all look for."

Many, including me personally, who visited Bialik during that period had the privilege to see Janover "in action." She knew every child by name and often inquired about their siblings who had graduated from the school. It was not uncommon to see her stop a student in the corridor with a "parental," caring embrace. Janover had made Bialik into a family.

In 2007, Janover's contribution was recognized by the Australian government with the Best National Achievement Award for Excellence by a Principal. "We took a school of 370 children that was really struggling hand to mouth and we created a beautiful, dynamic school where people came, literally, from all over the world to look at what was happening. Once you build that trust, with the teachers, the parents, the students, you can do most things – you build a powerhouse."

The educational experience must be extremely positive

The educational encounter between the participant and the educator presents a high-risk opportunity. The participant is willing to "put his or her toe in the water" in order to accomplish extraneous goals; the intention is usually to go only so far and no further.

In order to persuade the participant that it is worthwhile to immerse him- or herself further in educational endeavors, the "toe in the water" needs to be an extremely positive experience. Every effort should be made to ensure this. One positive experience provides the impetus for participation in the next. Conversely, if the experience is negative the participant may develop resistance and forgo any future encounters beyond those required.

Sensitivity to this potentially disastrous outcome was brought home to me by Professor Nechama Leibowitz (1905–1997), one of the outstanding Jewish scholars and educators of the last century. Nechama, as she was called by her devoted students, was a master not only of Bible but of the human spirit, and she had a profound impact on thousands of students, including me.

As part of my participation in the Jerusalem Fellows program, I had the privilege of studying with Nechama at her home in Jerusalem on a weekly basis for a period of two years. A highlight of the fellowship was a group Shabbat attended by the faculty, the fellows and their families. Nechama was a natural choice to be the scholar-in-residence for the Shabbat. In anticipation of her lesson on Shabbat morning, there was an air of excitement, particularly among the young children of the fellows, who were eager to sit in a lesson given by the legendary figure who had made such an impact on their parents. The lesson was limited to children ages seven and above, and they all waited together with their parents for Nechama to begin her lesson.

When Nechama entered the room and saw the children, she requested that they leave. We were a little taken aback and promised her that the children had been primed for the occasion and would be on their best behavior. However, Nechama stood her ground; she would not teach unless the children vacated the room. We protested that for our children this would be a memorable experience for which there had been widespread anticipation. Nechama remained firm, and all the children disappointedly vacated the room to enable the lesson to begin.

After an inspiring and insightful lecture, we questioned Nechama regarding her firm stance that the children should not participate.

She explained that if the contents of the class were geared to the parents, the class would be unintelligible to the children. As such, the children would have a negative experience and would perceive Bible study as boring and incomprehensible. A negative experience would be far worse than a non-experience!

The participants should be encouraged to explore myriad educational opportunities in the wake of the jobs to be done encounter

The jobs to be done encounter should be viewed as an investment which is similar to complimentary programs and applications offered on the web. These are offered as a first step toward purchase of the premium package. Numerous companies invest large amounts of resources in the development of basic programs that are offered gratis to the end user. This investment is of course a first step toward the building of a relationship with potential customers.

The logic behind this strategy is that potential customers need to be educated with regard to the opportunities and benefits a program offers. If the user were offered only the premium package with a request for payment, he or she would have no understanding of the program's value and would probably show no interest.

Similarly, our endgame should be to get buy in on a premium educational package, including additional intense educational experiences that will certainly be far more demanding in terms of time, and perhaps finances as well.

A highly creative and exceptional individual who has excelled in all of the above is Harold Grinspoon, one of *the* exceptional lay leaders of our time. Grinspoon skillfully combined his passion for and deep commitment to the Jewish people, his entrepreneurial ingenuity and his empathy for young parents and their children. In partnership with hundreds of Jewish communities, he has made the gift of Jewish books available to hundreds of thousands of families. These families have essentially signed up to become customers of Jewish educational materials.

Harold Grinspoon Creates the PJ Library

In 2003, Harold Grinspoon, a well-known philanthropist from Springfield, Massachusetts, heard a story on public radio about a literacy program started by country western singer Dolly Parton for children with minimal access to books. This program, the Imagination Library, sent complimentary books to families with children in the age range of birth to six.

Grinspoon, already a major donor to Jewish day schools, Jewish early childhood education and a host of general public causes, was intrigued and decided to fund the initiative in his home community of Springfield.

Later, Grinspoon attended a Passover seder at his son's home and noticed how the children engaged with the Jewish-themed books his daughter-in-law had given them as gifts. He began connecting the dots, thinking about the Imagination Library and his passion for the Jewish people, and how a project giving complementary Jewish-themed books to Jewish families could be implemented.

The name PJ Library was chosen, a reference to the pajamas children would be wearing when they snuggled up with their parents for a bedtime story. In a classic demonstration of "jobs to be done," the concept was to turn these special bedtime moments into Jewish moments.

Grinspoon has always been concerned about the impact of assimilation, and focuses his philanthropy on strengthening Jewish religious and cultural identity. He is particularly sensitive to the phenomenon of intermarried families drifting away from Judaism.

PJ Library launched in December 2005 in western Massachusetts with two hundred subscribers, comprising parents of young children who were recruited by various Jewish organizations. Jewish Community

Centers, preschools and synagogues were won over by the offer of the gift of books. The mailing lists of local Federations were also used to grow the program, with book samples offered to entice individuals to sign up.

In February 2006, a rabbi was so excited by the idea of the PJ Library that he used his discretionary fund as part of a matching grant from the Harold Grinspoon Foundation to start the program in Shreveport, the third largest city in Louisiana. This marked the first branch outside of western Massachusetts, with eighteen families joining the program. More were recruited over the next few months, largely as a result of grassroots efforts with friends and family of the foundation and of the participants

The PJ Library initiative has been highly successful in reaching those families who previously had no affiliation with the organized Jewish community. When its community partners – Federations, JCCs and synagogues – are asked how many individuals on the PJ list they had hitherto been unaware of, their responses range from 20 to 70 percent.

In May 2006, Grinspoon enlisted local community partners and Jewish Federations to cosign a letter to their constituents and include a free Jewish children's book in the envelope. PJ Library thus launched in Detroit in October with four hundred families, the first sizable community to sign on.

As of November 2015, PJ Library of North America sends out 140,000 books a month, with sixty thousand subscribers having aged out of the program to date.

PJ Library's market reach in communities ranges from 25 to 60 percent of Jewish families with children of eligible ages. According to recent research, 50 percent of recipients identify themselves as being Jewish in nontraditional ways, and they are reached mostly by networking. The PJ Library program officers work with local partners to create Jewish conversations in multifaceted ways. This serves to break down possible barriers for parents who are not necessarily comfortable coming through institutional doors. For a number of families, PJ Library provides their initial connection with the Jewish community.

An important impetus for the success of the program is that it is highly accessible. It reaches families where they are; they walk as far as their mailbox to retrieve the books, and their child is excited to tear open the book's envelope. If they feel a level of discomfort due to a perceived lack of Jewish knowledge or concepts, they can learn at the same rate as their child.

Additionally, provision of accessible information on the flaps of the books empowers parents to be their child's first Jewish educator. A strong contributing factor is that they are targeted at a critical time in their child's development – the first six years of a child's life – when parents are more open to thinking about their heritage and what they want to pass on to their children.

As mentioned, one remarkable success of PJ Library is in attracting a group that has been "invisible" to the organized Jewish community. Parents of young children often encounter two major challenges: financial pressure and time pressure. On the one hand, many young parents are working hard to pay back their student loans and mortgages while keeping up with the expenses of raising young children and paying for their education. On the other hand, they are under constant time pressure, often torn between the demands of the workplace and of home.

Faced with these pressures, membership in Jewish organizations is considered a luxury. As they carefully "count their pennies," many choose not to be members of the synagogue and have no links with any Jewish educational frameworks. Harold Grinspoon's brilliance is his ability to bring Jewish content into these homes by identifying young parents' jobs to be done. For many, those moments at the end of the workday when their children are about to go to sleep are "magic." Parents can focus on their children and devote quality time and attention. Reading a story to a young child creates an atmosphere of intimacy between parent and child, and these moments often provide children with lifelong memories.

In choosing a story to read to their children, parents will often have the following important criteria. The stories should be interesting, educational and not too long. Jewish content is not a priority, and consequently Jewish story books would not naturally make it to the child's bookshelf. In order to encourage parents to select a Jewish story, Grinspoon made an offer that was hard for Jewish parents to resist: the gift of high-quality books delivered to their home on a monthly basis.

The results have been remarkable. Jewish themes are now discussed by parents with their children on a daily basis, and perhaps more important, parents themselves are becoming interested in the content as well.

PJ Library has successfully mastered the dual challenges of providing a quality educational experience and encouraging customers to become consumers. As a result, Grinspoon has initiated two additional programs which call for increased commitment by both the children and their parents.

PJ Our Way was successfully piloted as a PJ Library follow-up program for children ages 9–11, in which children select their own books. In addition, the Harold Grinspoon Foundation is considering the complexities of establishing a wide-reaching and diverse adult learning program. With these two follow-up programs Grinspoon is aspiring to ensure that the sweet taste of Jewish values which hundreds of thousands of young parents and their children have now acquired will encourage both parents and their children to fill their lives with Jewish content.

References

Bialik College (n.d.). "Bialik's Ethos." Retrieved September 3, 2015. http://www.bialik.vic.edu.au/about-bialik/bialiks-ethos/.

Chazan, B., and D. Bryfman (2006, August). "Home Away from Home – a Research Study of the Shabbos Experience on Five University Campuses: An Informal Educational Model for Working with Young Jewish Adults." Chabad Campus International Foundation.

Christensen, C. M. (1997). *The Innovator's Dilemma.* Boston: Harvard Business Publishing.

Christensen, C. M., S. Cook and T. Hall (2006, January 15). "What Customers Want from Your Products." Harvard Business School Working Knowledge. Retrieved August 30, 2015. http://hbswk.hbs.edu/item/5170.html.

Christensen, C. M., and M.E. Raynor (2003). *The Innovator's Solution.* Boston: Harvard Business Publishing.

claytonchristensen.com (n.d.). "Biography." Retrieved August 31, 2015. http://www.claytonchristensen.com/biography/.

Chapter Nine

The Development of New Products and Processes

CENTRAL IDEA

BEFORE EMBARKING ON THE DEVELOPMENT OF NEW PRODUCTS OR PROCESSES, MULTIPLE OPTIONS SHOULD BE CONSIDERED.

In the previous three chapters we focused on growing the market for Jewish education. Growing the market and increasing the impact of Jewish education will depend, among other factors, on our ability to develop new products and processes. This chapter and the three that follow will present and illustrate a range of strategies available to the educational entrepreneur looking to create innovative educational experiences in his or her own community.

We are in a world which has been transformed by technological advances. These changes have led to modifications in our lifestyles, in our priorities, in our perception of time and in our perception of place. These changes, which continue to be in motion, require that we innovate and take full advantage of the new opportunities at hand. The need to invest in designing and developing new products and processes is a priority, and will be the focus of this chapter.

Florence Melton Establishes the Florence Melton Adult Mini-School

The Florence Melton Adult Mini-School (FMAMS) was the initiative of the late Florence Melton (1911–2007), an entrepreneur and inventor from Columbus, Ohio.[1] While her own Jewish education came via "osmosis" from her grandmother, she believed passionately in the importance of developing high-quality Jewish educational programs. Florence was one of the founding members of CAJE, the Coalition for the Advancement of Jewish Education. In addition, she initiated the Discovery Program, an experiential educational trip for Jewish teens to New York City.

Melton realized that there were generations of American Jewish adults who, like herself, had had no formal Jewish education. She frequented adult lectures and courses but found them unsatisfying, ultimately recognizing that she lacked context and systematic understanding of the subject matter. This led her to believe in the importance of developing a "school" for adults that would offer systematic, comprehensive courses in Jewish subject matter. She chose the concept "Mini-School" since she envisaged a framework that would have formal studies and be rigorous, similar to a school. However, since the studies would take place only once a week, she coined the phrase "mini-school."[2]

With this in mind, in 1980 Florence and her husband, Sam, gave a sizeable gift to the Melton Centre for Jewish Education at The Hebrew University of Jerusalem, for the purpose of developing a comprehensive sequential curriculum that would provide Jewish literacy for adults.

The rationale behind the initiative was Melton's vision that this program would be offered to Jewish adults far and wide, and would therefore require a large faculty. She felt it was important to provide the faculty with an in-depth curriculum that would equip them for the task of teaching high-quality courses.

---

1   Following the Second World War, Florence Melton discovered a glut of foam rubber and patented its use in the development of women's shoulder pads and slippers.

2   In 2012 the name was changed to the Florence Melton School of Adult Learning.

Her initiative led to the establishment of a global network of schools for adults – "mini-schools," which taught the courses that were developed at The Hebrew University. Students were required to make a sixty-week commitment for two years to ensure their systematic and comprehensive study of the material. The first mini-schools were piloted in the United States in 1986.

Under the leadership of Dr. Betsy Katz, who was appointed as the founding North American director in 1989, the mini-school grew rapidly in the United States and Canada. Following my appointment as international director, we expanded to Australia and the United Kingdom. By 2001, the entire network comprised over sixty schools.

Today the program continues to operate under the leadership of institute director Dr. Howard Deitcher and CEO Judy Kupchan, and thousands of adults continue to frequent the courses.

Melton's idea to establish schools for adults who would follow a set curriculum was considered radical, and consequently it was met with great skepticism. The skeptics challenged the assumption that adults would commit both their time and money to sixty weeks of study.

Invention

In 1991, I was offered the position of international director of the Florence Melton Adult Mini-School Institute. Upon entering the position, I was presented with a very well-thought-out set of courses. My predecessor's team had skillfully chosen the areas and concepts that should be the basis of a curriculum in adult Jewish literacy. On this basis they drafted comprehensive lesson plans. These were tested in the field and following feedback the curriculum was launched.

While the curriculum was well conceived, it did not succeed in the field. The faculty enjoyed the course outlines and breadth of concepts to be covered. Yet very few teachers taught the prescribed material. My brief was to develop a set of new course materials that would work for both the faculty and the students.

Redesigning the curriculum felt like an insurmountable challenge. At the time, in the area of adult learning, the concept of a prescribed curriculum of study was nonexistent outside of accredited programs. Credit-granting educational programs require a curriculum to ensure that students master a prescribed body of material, upon which they are tested. What would be the rationale for a prescribed, mandatory curriculum in voluntary study taking place during one's leisure time?

Furthermore, there is an assumption in the field of adult learning that faculty who teach adults are averse to teaching course materials that they do not design themselves. They love the creativity of teaching and the challenge of preparing their own lesson contents and lesson plans. This was borne out in my predecessor's product. Thus while my charge was the development of a curriculum, there was a strong chance that the faculty would never use it!

My first four years as director were invested in developing a new conceptual framework comprising the following cardinal principles:

- The curriculum would adopt the liberal arts approach with a focus on Jewish cultural literacy.
- The curriculum would provide multiple sources that would require the faculty to embark on self-study in preparation for lessons.
- The courses would be based on primary texts where possible.
- The texts would be chosen on the basis of the ideas they portrayed and the interest they would evoke in the classroom.
- The texts would always include myriad diverse positions.
- The curriculum would include positions across the denominational spectrum, with a focus on understanding their assumptions and implications.
- The curriculum would be non-prescriptive and nonjudgmental.

This framework was developed in conjunction with a number of curriculum writers who came and went, with the real breakthrough being achieved with the recruitment of an excellent team. The team comprised Dr. David Harbater, Gary Shapiro, Dr. Marc Rosenstein and Dafna Siegman. These talented individuals identified with the new core values of the curriculum, had subject matter expertise and were deeply sensitive to the faculty and the students. They developed materials that became the building blocks for success, as they evoked interest among the diverse faculty and their diverse student bodies.

The hundreds of faculty who taught the materials my team had developed, together with the tens of thousands of students who studied them, are testimony that the curriculum was indeed successful, albeit following a decade of intense development activity.

Since the year 2002, Rabbi Morey Schwartz took over the position of director of curriculum, taking the curriculum in new directions. In addition, he creatively designed a new set of courses for graduates of the mini-school.

This account highlights the arduous path followed by those who embark on developing a new product. An important first principle is that invention rarely commences from scratch. All inventors build on knowledge generated by others. In our situation we were extremely fortunate to be able to build on the pioneering work of the first curriculum team. Their design of the course outlines was a crucial and brilliant first step, and they certainly have a share in the final product as well.

In this discussion we have highlighted a top-down approach, i.e., the ideas and innovations which were generated by experts at a university. Those who use this approach often encounter the challenge of marketing their initiative to the target population, with major effort required to demonstrate that their product or service can yield important value for the customer and address his or her needs.

An alternative approach to development works from the bottom-up, beginning with an understanding of the customer and his or her milieu and then seeking to develop a product or process that meets the customer's needs. This is known as the "design thinking" approach.

The Design Thinking Approach

The design thinking approach, which originated in the commercial sector, is a methodology for the development of products and processes. While in many areas designers are brought into the development process in its closing stages in order to improve the aesthetics and/or functionalities of products and processes, design thinking dictates a focus on design in the initial stages of conceptualization of the new product or process.

The design thinking approach comprises the following three important components:

- *A research process that focuses on the potential customer.* Researchers develop empathy for potential users and a deep understanding of their needs and lifestyles. As opposed to the top-down approach which commences with the expertise of the inventor and in the marketing stage grapples with the needs of the customer, in the design thinking approach the very first stage requires an understanding of the potential customer.

Design thinking begins with observing and understanding the potential user and the challenges he or she faces in daily life. The approach should be empathic, with the goal of completely identifying with the potential customer. Potential customers are studied, and stories about their lifestyles are woven together by the observers in order for designers to obtain a rich understanding of the cultural context of the end user.

- *A collaborative approach for development of the products and processes, comprised of teams of individuals from multiple disciplines.* This approach ensures that the end product or process not only meets the needs of the customer but is deliverable and economically viable for the potential distributors as well.

This approach is in stark contrast with a "solo development" approach which relies on the expertise and genius of a single gifted individual for the development of products and processes.

- *3. The building of prototypes that enable the team to test the product or process in a beta stage before it is rolled out.* The development of prototypes enables the development team to test the product and/or process under "real conditions." Ultimately, reality is the optimal testing ground. Prior to the development of an expensive product line, prototypes are modified or discarded depending on the success, or alternatively, lack of success, in the early development stage.

Design thinking in action

According to Tim Brown [Brown, 2008], the roots of design thinking can be traced to Thomas Edison. Edison, who was a prolific inventor with over 1,000 US patents, invented the light bulb in 1879. Edison astutely understood the importance of electricity as a means of serving the end user in multiple ways and the impact it could have on the end user's lifestyle. In addition to his empathy for the end user, Edison utilized the other principles of design theory: teams of collaborators worked in his laboratory, and he developed prototypes for all his inventions.

IDEO: a company that specializes in design thinking

A company that both champions design thinking and uses this approach in the development of new products and services is IDEO.

IDEO was established in 1991 as a result of a merger between David Kelley's company, Design, which designed Apple's mouse in 1982, and ID Two, a company that designed the first laptop in the same year [Brown and Wyatt, 2010]. Initially IDEO focused on the traditional design of digital products such as the Palm V. They were famous for their product designs, which excelled in both aesthetics and functionality.

By 2001, increasingly urged to tackle problems that were beyond their traditional design activities, IDEO began investing in the design of systems and services that created social value. These included a health care foundation that asked IDEO to reform the organization with a focus on meeting the patients' needs, and a university that strove to develop alternative learning environments to supplement its traditional classrooms. According to Brown and Wyatt [Brown and Wyatt, 2010], this led IDEO to move from the design of consumer products to the design of consumer experiences, adding another important dimension to the utilization of the design thinking approach.

Design thinking in the Jewish sphere

Within the broader sphere of Jewish life one can find many examples of design thinking. The Orthodox Tzohar Rabbinical Association in Israel has, for example, embraced design thinking in its design of Orthodox marriage ceremonies [Tzohar].

Tzohar rabbis design creative marriage ceremonies

In Israel, the Orthodox rabbinate has the monopoly on marriage in the Jewish sector. In the early 1990s couples flew at increasing rates to other countries to obtain a civil marriage, a clear indication of their rejection of the marriage ceremony performed by the rabbinate. In 1995 the Tzohar Rabbinical Association was founded by a group of Modern Orthodox rabbis committed to designing a marriage ceremony that would meet both the lifestyle and cultural preferences of secular Israeli couples and the requirements of Jewish law.

Tzohar rabbis design each marriage ceremony in partnership with the couple, resulting in highly creative ceremonies. They include contemporary music and poetry, ensuring that the experience will be meaningful for the bride and bridegroom, their families and their friends. Tzohar marriage ceremonies are becoming increasingly popular. Many couples who would have explored other alternatives are now willing to choose the Tzohar option.

Design thinking in Jewish education

In reviewing the field of Jewish education and particularly that of informal education, one certainly encounters gifted educators who are intuitive experts in design theory. They design programs grounded in the participants' weltanschauung, which hold the attention of their students. They know how to "set the scene" for educational experiences that are long remembered. Memorable camp moments are the result of these well-planned and -designed educational programs that are highly attentive to the lifestyles and the values of the participants.

In the area of formal Jewish education, design thinking is still in its early stages. Major pioneering work in this field has been done, with a strong focus on the importance of empathy within formal educational settings. Empathy is an underpinning of design thinking, and *the* outstanding educator who made this a focus of her work in faculty development is Dr. Ora Zohar. She established the National Center for Staff Development at The Hebrew University of Jerusalem, which has had a profound impact on thousands of faculty and their students both in Israel and abroad.

At the center, Zohar focused on the teacher as a human being, on the practice of teaching and on the cultivation of significance, i.e., how to be a significant figure in the lives of one's students. For Zohar, the design of successful educational programming requires first and foremost the establishment of a significant relationship between teacher and student.

Ora Zohar establishes the National Center for Staff Development

In 1958, Ora Zohar came on aliyah from New York and spent a decade teaching English to Israeli high school students. In addition to her teaching she assumed the role of mechanechet, "class educator" or homeroom teacher. In Israeli high schools, in addition to the students having subject matter teachers, one teacher assumes the role of class educator and is assigned teaching hours in order to deal with educational issues [Zohar, 2015].

Zohar excelled in these roles, applying unique approaches to her interaction with the students. She placed student-teacher interaction as the centerpiece of her teaching and viewed the school as primarily an interactive human environment. This approach was in sharp contrast to the prevailing approach in Israeli high schools, according to which the teachers were trained as subject matter experts with the primary role of transmitting knowledge to the students.

Given her success, Zohar became a trainer of English teachers at a university, applying her unique approach to teaching. In the summer of 1973 she was offered the opportunity to do a PhD at the University of Massachusetts at Amherst under the supervision of Professor Dwight Allen. On a visit to Israel as a guest of the Ministry of Education, Dwight had met Zohar and observed her in action. He was highly impressed by her abilities and aptitude, and on that basis offered her the opportunity to enroll in a doctoral program at Amherst.

At Amherst, in addition to her research Zohar worked in the in-service training clinic as a teacher improvement specialist. Specialists were assigned to work with the university faculty on a one-on-one basis in order to improve their teaching skills. Zohar was highly impressed by the clinic approach and its impact on the teachers. However, she felt that while the one-on-one work was effective, it would not be economically feasible were it to be implemented on a large scale. She thus toyed with the idea of a teachers' clinic that would adopt a group approach combining Allen's techniques with the facilitation techniques of the humanist Carl Rogers. Zohar was given the opportunity to test this idea at a Jewish high school in New York, where she gave a four-day, in-service seminar to the teaching staff. Her approach proved to be highly successful.

Zohar envisioned the creation of a national center in Israel that would provide "a structured professional growth program for teachers of kindergarten through twelfth grades regardless of subject specialty," and it took two years following her return to Israel for the idea to take root.

In 1976 Professor Seymour Fox, dean of the School of Education at The Hebrew University of Jerusalem, offered Zohar the opportunity to implement her vision at the School of Education. She established the National Center for Staff Development in 1977, and it operated until 2005. During that period Zohar, together with her dedicated staff whom she had trained, provided in-service training workshops to thousands of teachers, and at a second stage to hundreds of principals as well. At these workshops teachers focus on listening to their students and developing empathy for them. They also focus on their own growth as educators and facilitators of their students' growth. The impact of Zohar's unique approach was not only felt by the faculty that studied with her and her staff but by the multitudes of students whose classroom experiences were impacted by her approach.

In addition to her workshops in Israel, in 1982 Zohar was invited to give workshops at Mount Scopus College in Melbourne, Australia, one of the largest Jewish day schools in the world. Thereafter she impacted teachers in other cities in Australia, as well as in South Africa, the United States, Canada, Mexico and Hungary.

Alternatives to Developing from Scratch

As illustrated in the development of curriculum at the Florence Melton Adult Mini-Schools, the development of new products (or processes) may turn out to be a lengthy and arduous process. From the start there is a risk that the product or process will not be successful, despite major investments of time and resources. A second risk is that the product or process may be obsolete by the time it reaches fruition, which is prevalent in the area of curriculum development within the formal education system.

Curriculum development assumes a level of prevailing technologies. With the rapid advances in technology today, if a curriculum development project were to stretch over a four-year period, the technological realities at the time of implementation may be radically different from those that existed four years previously. Curricula developed before the advent of YouTube, for instance, could be considered obsolete in the post-YouTube area. Similarly, a curriculum developed before the advent of tablets would need to be modified for the post-tablet era.

Different options

What, then, are the alternatives to developing Jewish educational programs from scratch?

It is possible to take existing products and processes and modify them for current need. In doing so there are four distinct options: replication, copy and modification, borrowing and importation. Let us start with the options closest to the source and thereafter explore those farther afield.

Replication of successful Jewish educational models

This strategy is highly cost-efficient and low risk. When successful Jewish educational models are developed the field as a whole can benefit from their replication. In a field in which resources are limited, replication should be the preferred strategy. With this in mind, we chose to focus in Chapter One on four entrepreneurs who have developed replicable models.

Replication, however, is not easy. Education is a human endeavor, highly influenced by unique and charismatic personalities. Many outstanding educators have developed new models, but to be suitable for replication they need to be designed in a way that can be implemented with success by other very good personnel.

Identifying the theory of change

In Chapter Five we discussed in detail the concept, "theory of change." Replication is possible only if we are able to identify the micro theory of change. What are the essential elements of the project we are attempting to replicate?

Organizations that are cognizant of their theories of change are able to replicate using the branch and/or franchise format. In the commercial world this is highly prevalent among fashion stores, supermarkets and coffee shops. Those of us who love sipping a Grande black coffee at Starbucks will feel at home in any Starbucks coffee shop. What makes each store successful even though they are situated in different geographical areas, have different staff and serve different populations? It is their theory of change, which they replicate. It is not only the format and layout of the store, it is the DNA of the culture as well.

While replication of successful models is desirable, it is not always possible. What are our options if we cannot replicate the model?

Copy and modification of successful educational models
If an established endeavor has a plausible macro theory of change,[3] it is possible to copy and modify it without the need to replicate the micro theory of change.

---

3   See Chapter Five for a discussion of the macro theory of change.

As an example we have the proliferation of Jewish camps that share the plausible macro theory according to which high-impact Jewish education is possible if it takes place in a residential social milieu. The camps differ from each other in terms of their culture and emphases, but as Jewish sleepover camps they are similar. In planning their activities, other camps can copy and modify successful programs and assume a reasonable chance of success.

Borrowing models from general education

There are multiple successful models within the realm of general education from which we can "borrow." This was the strategy used by Peter Deutsch when he founded the Hebrew charter schools, as described in Chapter One. He did not invent the charter school concept; he merely borrowed the model and "tweaked" it for Hebrew education purposes.

Deutsch continued to use this strategy when designing the supplementary Jewish studies program offered to the students outside of school hours. He studied the Mormon approach to religious education and imported it into the Jewish educational setting.

The Mormons face a similar challenge in their aspiration to ensure that their children receive a religious education. Their children attend public schools which are adjacent to a Mormon religious school building. They are given "release-time" at the public school, wherein they move across to the Mormon Supplementary School building for their religious education classes. When release-time is over they return to the public school. This approach was used for supplementary Jewish high school education which paralleled the studies at one of the Hebrew charter schools. [Shulzke, 2012].

Similarly, the PJ Library founded by Harold Grinspoon adapted the idea developed by Dolly Parton in her Imagination Library.

The potential for enriching Jewish education through borrowing from general education is growing with the growth in learning opportunities being developed in the digital era. Gatherings on Jewish subjects a la TED Talks would probably attract large audiences; the free MOOC (Massive Open Online Courses) courses offered by the top universities in the world could be a great idea for adult Jewish education, as well as the multiple online learning platforms available today.

Importation from seemingly unrelated fields
Since education is primarily an arena of human interaction, we should not limit ourselves to building on ideas and models grounded in the educational milieu. Creative ideas exist in other areas as well, and when relevant it is important to "import" them if they are in sync with the target population.

An Israeli organization that used creative importation with great success was the *Tav Hachevrati*.

The Tav Hachevrati: social certification
In 2004, a group of Israeli young adults, Chili Tropper, Shmuli Bing, Efrat Degani and Assaf Banner, formed an organization called B'ma'agalei Tzedek for the promotion of social justice. The initial venture was a publication that highlighted the importance of social justice, soon after which they launched the *tav hachevrati* (social certification) project.

In Jerusalem where they lived, coffee shops and restaurants turned a blind eye to the labor laws regulating the payment of a minimum wage to their workers. Thus the kitchen workers were often exploited, as were the waiters and waitresses. In addition, many of these establishments were inaccessible to customers with disabilities, who consequently were prevented from visiting them.

Based on the practice of many Jerusalemites who patronized only food establishments that displayed kosher certification, the group decided to introduce an alternate system of *social* certification, to be given to establishments that paid fair wages and provided accessibility to people with disabilities. They asserted pressure on places that refused to meet the requirements for social certification, and embarked on a public campaign to urge consumers to visit only those establishments that displayed the social certification.

The campaign was very successful, with over 50 percent of Jerusalem establishments applying for social certification. The campaign was launched in other cities as well. Regretfully, however, the full potential of the certification is yet to be realized.

Importation of ideas for Jewish education

With regard to Jewish education, I often import ideas from other areas. For example, an important pedagogic lesson I teach is drawn and adapted from the mega store IKEA.

IKEA is a global chain that is highly successful in attracting customers and convincing them to make purchases, often far beyond their original intentions. Their stores are skillfully designed. On the upper level, customers move through a maze of showrooms. They note which items they wish to purchase, and on the bottom floor gather these items and move across to the checkout stands.

While moving through the store on one occasion, I tried to work out the secret behind IKEA's success. Their ability to attract customers was not difficult to fathom. They offered easy parking facilities, a cheap restaurant and free childcare. Furthermore, their furniture designs were often creative. In making the sale, however, it was the showroom layout that gave them the competitive edge.

When one makes a purchase of a kitchen faucet at a regular store he or she will often be faced with a wide range of products, and in making a purchase will need to imagine his or her kitchen and try to figure out which faucet will look best. At IKEA everything is sold in context, and thus one sees the faucet within a kitchen. The customer is able to view the faucet in a natural setting as it blends in with the kitchen sink and other appliances. Furthermore, the customer may be tempted to purchase other kitchen amenities that match the style of the faucet, consequently buying and spending more than he or she originally intended.

This idea of marketing an item in its natural context is a major pedagogic idea as well. When conveying to students the concept of Shabbat and the rationale behind the different rituals, they can understand and make a "purchase" only if the concepts and rationales are taught in their natural context, i.e., in the context of a Shabbat experience. Therefore, in teaching Jewish lifestyle concepts, experiential education that creates the social and natural context, as opposed to frontal classroom teaching, is the obvious format.

References

Brown, T. (2008). "Design Thinking." *Harvard Business Review*: 84–95.

Brown, T., and J. Wyatt (2010). "Design Thinking for Social Innovation." *Stanford Social Innovation Review* (25).

Chesbrough, H. W. (2003). *Open Innovation: The New Imperative for Creating and Profiting from Technology.* Cambridge: Harvard University Press.

Christensen, C. M., and M.E. Raynor (2003). *The Innovator's Solution.* Boston: Harvard Business Publishing.

Schwab, J. J. (1969, November). "The Practical: A Language for Curriculum." *The School Review*: 1–23.

Shulzke, E. (2012, September 10). "Hebrew Charter School Founder Looks to 'Mormon School.'" Deseret News. Retrieved March 26, 2015. http://www.deseretnews.com/article/765603214/Hebrew-charter-school-founder-looks-to-Mormon-model.html?pg=all.

Tzohar (n.d.). "What We Do." Retrieved November 16, 2015. http://www.tzohar.org.il/English/what-we-do/.

Zohar, O. (2015). *For Teachers with Love: Helping Educators Become Significant.* Crows Nest, NSW: EA Books.

Chapter Ten

Bridging

CENTRAL IDEA

THE BRIDGING STRATEGY LINKS TWO SIDES WHOSE INTERACTION CREATES SOCIAL VALUE. THE BRIDGE IS DESIGNED TO MAXIMIZE THE IMPACT OF THE INTERACTION

A few years ago my wife was treated for an ailment by a certain medical practitioner. During the treatment she discovered that the practitioner was a relative she had never met and that he was an eligible bachelor. When she completed the treatment, she thought about a good friend of our daughter whom we had often hosted in our home. On the spur of the moment it occurred to her that they might be suited to each other. She decided to test the waters. She asked him if he was prepared to meet someone who she thought was suitable. He responded that he was weary of blind dates. However, given the newly discovered family connection with my wife, he consented.

The match turned out to be successful and today the couple are the proud and happy parents of two young children!

This episode highlights the power of "bridging." My wife's efforts in bringing the couple together were modest. The impact, however, was enormous, bringing lifelong happiness to these two individuals.

Bridging is an innovation strategy predominant in the commercial[1] and social sectors alike, and given our focus we will primarily explore it within the context of Jewish education.

---

1   Google is an outstanding example of bridging; it links the web surfer to a website.

Bridging acts as a catalyst for the interaction of two forces that had previously operated independently of each other. The resulting interaction generates widespread educational value that could not have been achieved otherwise. Bridging requires that the innovator have a sharp, discerning eye and an innovative edge. He or she must think laterally and creatively, and contemplate the value that could be attained if two sides that exist or operate independently could be brought into interaction. Once this is assessed, the innovator needs to design a bridge between them so they will be able to interact freely.

Within the realm of general social entrepreneurship, the power of bridging is illustrated by Childline.

Childline UK

Childline is an organization that offers a helpline for abused children. It was founded in the United Kingdom in 1986 and now operates internationally as well.

The impetus for the birth of Childline came from the BBC TV consumer series called *That's Life!* hosted by Esther Rantzen. In the spring of 1986, the BBC ran a program on child abuse. After the program they ran a helpline for twenty-four hours, inviting adults and children alike to call in. The response was beyond all expectations, with the lines jammed by adults who were abused as children and children who were presently being abused. Most of the young callers insisted on remaining anonymous while confiding details of terrible cruelty they had encountered [Harrison, 2000].

This event led to a realization that child abuse was a widespread phenomenon and that children were seeking an avenue to solicit support. In response, the BBC established a 24/7 helpline in coordination with a number of welfare organizations. The helpline was launched in October 1986, six months following the broadcast of the *That's Life!* program on child violence. On the opening day, 55,000 callers attempted to call in. The helpline continues to this day, and as many as 4,500 people, most of whom are children, call in per day.

Childline has an easy-to-remember number, and the lines are staffed with thousands of volunteers supported by professionals. The calls are completely free in order to ensure easy access. To guarantee the anonymous identity of the caller, calls do not appear on any of the telephone accounts. Thus a call can be made from literally any private or public telephone without leaving "footprints."

Childline demonstrates the effectiveness of the bridging innovation. Prior to the founding of the organization, welfare authorities did what they could to help abused children. However, they had no insight into the scope of the problem, nor did they have a mechanism for reaching out to the victims. Similarly, the victims, who may have been desperate for support, were helpless, despite the willingness of the authorities to come to their aid. The free, anonymous telephone link provides the bridge between those who need help and those who are willing to provide it. The cost of the bridge is insignificant relative to the social value attained. The Childline "bridge" enabled welfare organizations to unleash forces and resources that were hitherto completely dormant.

Bridging in Jewish Education

Within the realm of Jewish education, entrepreneurs have used the bridging strategy in the following two areas:

1. *Providing a link to a missing "P."* In Chapter Six we mentioned the "three Ps," participants, personnel and pennies, all of which are crucial for the development and delivery of an educational experience. In the event that one of the Ps is elusive, it may be accessed with the use of bridging.

2. *Providing a link between different populations in order to create social value.* In this situation the bridge architect senses the important social value which could be attained by the interaction of diverse populations in an educational setting.

1. Providing a link to a missing "P"

In Jewish education, we face a major challenge of accessing the three foundational components, i.e., the participants, the personnel and the pennies. A resourceful entrepreneur might be able to access funding and recruit personnel yet be unable to recruit students. A second may be able to recruit students and personnel but is unable to attract funding, and a third may be able to attract funding and recruit students while being unable to recruit personnel. A frustrating aspect of this predicament is that the entrepreneur might be aware of the existence of the missing component but can't connect with it.

The innovative bridge entrepreneur is able to design a creative bridge to the missing component, thus ensuring the success of the enterprise.

Types and examples of bridges to each of the three components are as follows:

Building a bridge to participants

The most important component is of course the participants. Success is measured in terms of the educational impact experienced by the participants. Their recruitment is a critical first step.

Designing a bridge between organizations and potential participants

One of the challenges educational organizations face is connecting with potential students who are currently noncustomers. Many educational organizations are proud of their educational offerings. Their graduates are generally happy and their programs are considered to be of a high quality. Nevertheless, these organizations are frustrated. They have the capacity to enroll many more students yet the "seats remain empty."

Innovative entrepreneurial endeavors have identified this as both a major challenge and a major opportunity. Designing a bridge between the potential students and the organizations could lead to major educational impact.

BunkConnect

An innovative bridge of this type is BunkConnect, designed by
Foundation for Jewish Camp [Foundation for Jewish Camp]. This
initiative aims to attract new participants to Jewish overnight camps
by offering them a highly subsidized rate. BunkConnect defines a
first-time camper as a child who has not attended a nonprofit Jewish
overnight camp for twelve or more consecutive days. First-time
camper status is determined separately for each child in a family.

A second major bridge of this type is Masa, which functions
as a dual-purpose bridge. Its mission to provide a meeting ground
between young Jewish adults, ages 18–30, and Israel. In addition,
it operates as a bridge between Israel educational organizations and
potential participants. Masa was the brainchild of Alan Hoffmann,
the current CEO and director general of the Jewish Agency; Sallai
Meridor, past chairman of the Jewish Agency Executive and the late
prime minister Ariel Sharon.

Alan Hoffmann

*In the realm of social entrepreneurship, Hoffman is a gifted
entrepreneur in his own right and an outstanding mentor of others.*

*Hoffman was born in South Africa and came on aliyah in
1967. His professional career includes serving as director of the
Melton Centre for Jewish Education at the Hebrew University,
head of the Mandel Center for Jewish Continuity at The Hebrew
University and director general of the education department of
the Jewish Agency.*

*In these three positions Hoffman created high-impact programs
with exceptional out-of-the-box thinking. As director of the Melton
Centre he founded the Florence Melton Adult Mini-School. During his
tenure at Mandel he founded Revivim, a high-profile, elite academic
program that trains Bible and Jewish Thought faculty for secular
Israeli high schools, and in his first years at the Jewish Agency he
established Masa.*

I had the privilege of working with Hoffman from 1991 to 1995, when I was international director of the Florence Melton Adult Mini-School, and while my academic career in the field of social entrepreneurship commenced in 2003, my professional internship in this area began at the Melton Centre. Working with Hoffman proved to be an ongoing seminar of the highest level in professional development. He always believed in thinking big and aspiring for high-level impact. His creative thinking was infectious and his support was a crucial pillar when creativity ran the risk of failure.

Throughout his career, Hoffman was and continues to be a mentor par excellence. Those he mentored two decades ago (including me) continue to solicit his advice on a periodic basis.

Masa

Masa Israel was established in 2004 by the Jewish Agency in partnership with the Israeli government. At a joint meeting between Prime Minister Sharon; Sallai Meridor, chairman of the Jewish Agency Executive; and Alan Hoffmann, director general of the Agency's Education Department, which took place a year after Sharon took office as prime minister, the fundamentals of the program were agreed upon.

Sharon, who until then believed that all available funds should be earmarked for *aliyah*, came to the realization that if Diaspora Jews did not have a strong Jewish identity they would not contemplate *aliyah*, and those that remained in their home communities would become more and more disconnected from Israel. He became convinced of the importance of the Masa vision for strengthening the Jewish identity of young adults by enabling them to spend a few months to a year in Israel on an educational program. Subsequently, Sharon made a commitment to the project on behalf of the Israeli government, while the Jewish Agency, supported by North American Federations and Keren Hayesod, which represents communities outside of North America, made a matching commitment.

Until the advent of Masa, the overwhelming proportion of young adults studying in Israel for a few months or more came from Orthodox backgrounds. Masa, primarily focusing on the non-Orthodox sector, set itself a goal of bringing cohorts of as many as twenty thousand young adults per year to Israel, a large segment of the potential market. In the 2009–2010 academic year, a mere five years following its inception, had reached almost 50 percent of its target growth, and with a steady growth of 10 percent participation per year, is on the way to achieving its goal.

When Masa was conceptualized the Jewish Agency made a very important decision: rather than being an operating organization, it would serve as a catalyst that would bridge potential participants with Israeli educational organizations. In order to achieve its bridging mission it created a "bridge organization" that operates as follows:

- It offers a financial grant for all Jewish young adults ages 18–30 who participate in a five- to twelve-month, organized experience in Israel under the Masa umbrella.
- It validates the core educational components of Israeli programs and grants their participants eligibility to receive Masa funding.
- It helps multiple organizations develop long-term Israel programs, thereby expanding the choice of offerings available to Masa participants.
- It offers a marketing platform for these organizations, thereby increasing their numbers of participants.

In terms of ROI (return on investment), Masa is very "profitable." The grants given cover only a small portion of the tuition costs per participant, yet they are sufficient to provide the "tipping point." These grants encourage the field at large to make their own investments, resulting in an expanding of the field.

Designing a bridge to noncustomers

Financial incentives for the attraction of participants are effective if there is a potential customer market. Potential customers may consider the option at hand if it is economically attractive. Noncustomers, however, will probably be oblivious to any option, given their lack of interest in the educational initiatives.

How does one then build a bridge to the noncustomers? Chabad is an organization that has creatively succeeded in this feat.

Chabad builds a bridge to students on campus

Chabad (Lubavitch) has achieved notable success in connecting with Jewish students in colleges and universities through their campus Chabad Houses. This is a remarkable achievement since many of those who frequent Chabad activities do not identify with the core Chabad Orthodox ideology. Many come from liberal, non-Orthodox backgrounds, and would feel far more comfortable in egalitarian synagogue settings or in other cultural settings that resemble their family's lifestyle.

A comprehensive analysis of the Chabad method is beyond the scope of this book, and therefore a limited discussion of one aspect will follow.

Rabbi Menachem Mendel Schneerson, who became the head of the Chabad movement in 1951, made outreach a focus of his incumbency. He skillfully built his outreach strategy on the dedication and commitment of his *shluchim* (emissaries). These emissaries, who were personally appointed by "the Rebbe," traveled far and wide, and their presence was felt in many communities. Rabbi Schneerson did not initiate the *shluchim* model; he changed the function and focus of the emissaries. Whereas the Rebbe's predecessors had used the *shluchim* to keep in contact with their loyal Chassidim, Rabbi Schneerson used them as a vehicle for reaching out to Jews who did not observe *halacha* (Jewish law). The *shluchim* targeted the noncommitted with the explicit goal of strengthening their Jewish identity.

This change of mission precipitated a major innovation, the establishment of the Chabad Houses on university campuses. The first Chabad House on campus was established by Rabbi Shlomo Cunin at UCLA in 1969, and this model has been replicated on multiple campuses in North America and beyond [Fishkoff, 2001, p. 94].

The establishment of a campus Jewish "house" is not unique to Chabad. On many campuses in Canada, The United Kingdom and Australia there were Hillel Houses. The Chabad innovation was in transforming the "house" concept into one of "home." For Chabad the establishment of a Chabad House with a home connotation on campus reflected a strategic goal. Chabad Houses would provide the bridge for attracting the target population.

For many Jewish students, the campus experience presents a personal challenge. If the campuses are geographically distant from the students' home cities and they cannot go home regularly, being away from their families might not be easy. Thus many of these students are attracted to a place with home cooking and a home ambience.

In their important research on Chabad on campus, and particularly the hosting of Shabbat meals, Chazan and Bryfman [Chazan and Bryfman, 2006] focus on the Chabad House as being a "home away from home." As Joe Reimer noted in his introduction to this research, "The importance of home and the personal touch" are the critical underpinnings of this experience. "To attend Shabbat at Chabad, students enter the home of the rabbi and his family and meet that family as they are celebrating Shabbat. Students are greeted warmly and personally, and the rabbi makes a special effort to learn each student's name."

The Chabad House has succeeded globally in attracting potential students; it is an outstanding bridge to those who would have probably never engaged in Chabad's educational programs.

Building a bridge to personnel

In their quest to develop an educational enterprise, educational entrepreneurs are often confounded by a lack of quality personnel. This limits the ability of the enterprise to achieve high impact. The optimal long-term strategy for an educational endeavor is to recruit, develop and train local personnel. The problem is that it can prove to be costly. Furthermore, this strategy requires a considerable time lag before the community is able to enjoy the fruits of its investment. Faced with this challenge, the bridge innovator takes a "shortcut," contemplating whether it is possible to build a bridge to competent personnel who can make the educational endeavor successful.

Three different bridge models have been designed for this purpose:

1. *The shlichut (emissary) bridge.* According to this model, organizations send personnel to communities for a limited period of time after which they return home.
2. *The virtual bridge.* In this model, the faculty reside in their home region and are linked virtually to the students.
3. *The local personnel bridge.* In this model, a bridge is developed that enables quality personnel not engaged in Jewish education to assume educational roles for the purpose of the endeavor.

The *shlichut* bridge

The *shlichut* bridge imports quality personnel for limited periods of time. In most circumstances, this bridge facilitates the travel of personnel who live in Israel to work in communities across the globe. The *shlichim*[2] may travel for a short-term period, for example

---

2   There is a major difference between the Chabad *shluchim* model and the Israeli *shlichut* model. In the former there is a long-term (and often lifelong) commitment to the community they serve. In the latter the service is deemed temporary and the emissaries are bound to return to Israel after a given period.

as counselors in a summer camp, or for as long as a four-year term as *shlichim* in Jewish day schools, in youth movements or to the community at large.

The *shlichut* bridge was inaugurated by the Jewish Agency as a vehicle for strengthening ties between Israel and local communities in the Diaspora, and to this today the Agency continues to be the primary facilitator of long-term missions.

A number of additional organizations, independent of the Jewish Agency, also facilitate yearlong missions. Many of these organizations send volunteers. They include Torah MiTzion, Bat Ami National Service volunteers, and *"Shin Shinim"* – a pre-military, yearlong voluntary service corps.

An advantage of the *shlichut* bridge is that outstanding personnel can be brought to Jewish communities, giving local students opportunities to interact with educators they would otherwise never meet. This has the potential for high educational impact.

A second advantage is the financial one, particularly when *shlichim* serve in a volunteer capacity. While living and transportation costs are covered by the organization, primary compensation costs are saved. On the other hand, when *shlichim* are hired as professionals, the costs of relocating the *shaliach* and his or her family, in addition to the compensation package, may be prohibitive.

The main disadvantage of the *shlichut* system is the limited timeframe of a *shaliach*'s service. In order to make an impact in a community, the *shaliach* needs to undergo an often lengthy period of acculturation. Thus, by the time the *shaliach* reaches his or her full potential it may be time to return home.

The virtual bridge

With the development of broadband and web conferencing, it is now possible to conduct classes with teacher and students in different geographical locales. WebYeshiva has developed a virtual bridge for teaching students all over the world. Founded in 2007 by Rabbi Jeff

Sacks under the supervision of Rabbi Chaim Brovender, WebYeshiva continues to be the leading organization providing synchronic lessons in distant geographical locations [WebYeshiva]

Among the for-profit educational providers, eTeacher offers biblical and modern Hebrew instruction to small groups of students. The teachers reside in Israel and instruction is given to different groups all over the globe [eTeacher].

A major advantage of the virtual bridge is that it provides access to high-quality personnel wherever they reside, while participants pay only for the instruction itself since there is no need to physically transport the faculty and pay transportation costs and travel time.

A disadvantage of the virtual bridge is the lack of face-to-face interaction between teacher and student, often an important element of the classroom experience. Thus, despite its considerable virtues, on its own the virtual bridge will lack the capacity for achieving some of the educational entrepreneur's desired outcomes.

The local personnel bridge

A potential resource for personnel is professionals who have had a rich Jewish education and youth movement experience but who have not followed a career path in Jewish education. Particularly in cities with small Jewish populations and a dearth of professional Jewish educators, these individuals may be a rich potential resource.

In many situations the entrepreneur is faced with a formidable challenge when attempting to build a bridge to these individuals, as they are often extremely busy and are not able or willing to allocate sufficient time for adequate course preparation and professional development.

An organization that successfully met this challenge is the Florence Melton Adult Mini-School, which was discussed in the previous chapter. This organization, which I had the privilege of heading for two decades, was able to attract a small group of outstanding nonprofessional educators to teach its courses. Among them was Simon Myerson from Leeds, United Kingdom, and the "bridge" that enabled him to assume a faculty position was the Mini-School curriculum.

Simon Myerson QC

In the year 1999, the Florence Melton Adult Mini-School advertised in Leeds, United Kingdom, that it would be opening in the fall. This community of about six thousand Jews who live about forty miles from Manchester is comprised of many people who belong to Orthodox synagogues but do not follow an Orthodox lifestyle.

Simon Myerson, a local forty-year-old lawyer, saw the advertisement and decided to enroll in the Mini-School. However, a former colleague of his called him later in the week to convince him that instead of enrolling as a student he should apply to be a teacher. Myerson was a little taken aback by this suggestion, but he was assured that there was a written curriculum and that with the use of the faculty guide, he would be able to master the material.

Myerson was an observant Jew from a Leeds home in which his mother was observant and his father not. He remembers that Shabbat at home was a mixed experience: a traditional Friday night dinner, with his father going to work on Shabbat morning. Following the traditional lunch, the afternoon was spent watching sports on television.

At the age of twelve Myerson was sent to Carmel College, a private Jewish boarding school with an open Orthodox atmosphere. He loved the education at Carmel and felt a strong affiliation with Orthodox Judaism, yet he did not define himself as strictly Orthodox.

Myerson went on to study law at Cambridge University, and there became head of the Union of Jewish Students. In this position, he decided to become more observant and donned a kippah on a daily basis. At Cambridge he met Nicole, and they decided to marry and set up an Orthodox home in Leeds. This was a conscious decision on the part of both Simon and Nicole, who both highly valued the importance of choice.

The advertisement for the mini-school emphasized intellectual learning in an open environment, and this is what grabbed Myerson's attention. He was now fifteen years into his profession as a lawyer and was intrigued by the opportunity to teach. He decided to apply for the position of instructor. He was required to give a model lesson and was handed the Purim story to prepare. Myerson recalls reading the curriculum and feeling challenged by the questions it posed. He mulled over this lesson for hours, and delivered what proved to be an outstanding lesson.

Initially Myerson was very apprehensive about teaching in the mini-school. He felt he was in essence only a lesson ahead of his students, and thus preparing the material needed to be a high priority. It took him a minimum of five hours a week to prepare, and he recalls that he went from being an avid reader of fiction to being an avid student of Jewish text and Jewish thought.

Myerson's teaching improved from week to week, and his influence on the students was profound. The intellectual engagement and social dynamic in the classroom were instrumental in developing the Leeds mini-school learning community, and Myerson sensed this opportunity for community impact.

On a personal level, Myerson felt privileged to be an educator. He understood the financial constraints of the Leeds community and donated his time for the course. In order to improve his professional skills as an educator, he personally financed his participation in a 2002 Hebrew University seminar for faculty, and this seminar produced lasting results for him.

As the mini-school progressed and the pool of eager students graduated, Myerson turned his attention to recruiting the new cohorts. Every Yom Kippur he would give model lessons in two different synagogues, using the lessons as a draw card for the course. In this manner he was able to attract students who had never intended to make a two-year commitment to study in a Jewish literacy program, thereby also ensuring the ongoing vitality of the school.

After eleven years the mini-school in Leeds had run its course. Eight to 10 percent of all Jewish adults in the city had taken the courses, and the impact on the community was felt across the board.

On personal reflection Myerson never saw his future in education, and if it were not for the persuasive call from his colleague he might not have embarked on his teaching journey. The curriculum was the bridge that convinced him to make the move. However, eventually it was the sense of intellectual challenge and the fulfillment derived from impacting the community that captured his soul. These dimensions of the bridge should not be underestimated.

Myerson's experience emphasizes the importance of support and satisfaction, always critical factors when accessing nonprofessional Jewish educators. When financial incentives are not a factor, it is crucial that personnel have the support that enables them to teach without excess preparation, and satisfaction which enhances their motivation.

Building a bridge to pennies

This bridge has great strategic importance in the area of entrepreneurship in Jewish education. Creative innovators who have developed programs require access to funders, and similarly funders need to be able to identify programs that have great potential for high impact.

It was with this group in mind that Slingshot, an organization that bridges between next-gen contributors and innovative organizations, was established.

Slingshot

The idea for Slingshot developed organically in 2004 following a weekend retreat for a dozen young Jews who were preparing to become involved in their family foundations. Participants were hoping to learn how to navigate the alphabet soup of the Jewish community and to sort out which organizations resonated for them and their peers. They came up with the idea of producing a Zagat-style guidebook, and with the help of staff from the Andrea and Charles Bronfman Philanthropies they worked to produce Slingshot: A Resource Guide to Jewish Innovation. In the guide they identified, for themselves and their peers, the fifty most innovative nonprofits in the North American Jewish community.

In 2007, the next-generation funders responsible for Slingshot took their concept a step further and created the Slingshot Fund, a network where young philanthropists recruit each other to support Jewish organizations that resonate with their generation. The Slingshot Fund exposes next-generation funders to a professional grant-making process. While many come from families involved in philanthropy, most have yet to review grant proposals, conduct site visits and make allocation decisions. In conjunction with a group of their peers, Slingshot offers them the opportunity to develop these skills and learn from experts in the field, while leveraging their small gifts into a significant grant pool.

Slingshot's mission is to inspire the Jewish community – as well as grow its capacity – to be innovative, focusing on the role of philanthropy in supporting that innovation.

Slingshot builds a bridge between innovative organizations and funders in the following three ways:

- It publishes an annual list of innovative organizations that have received Slingshot approval as worthy of investing in. These organizations are selected on the basis of an application process and an in-depth evaluation by Slingshot. Organizations listed in the guide have a high chance of receiving support from funders who desire to support organizations that carry the Slingshot seal of approval.
- It invites the organizations that appear in the guide to apply for funding from Slingshot funders, and a small number are awarded grants ranging from $10,000 to $30,000 per annum.

- It organizes an annual Slingshot Day when funders and innovative organizations are brought together to network and explore funding support.

Slingshot thus operates two bridges: the Slingshot Guide, which highlights innovative organizations worthy of support, and a Slingshot Day, which brings innovative organizations and funders together.[3]

Hopefully the lead taken by Slingshot will be emulated by other funding bodies, with a view to building bridges between entrepreneurs and funders.

2. Providing a link between different populations in order to create social value

While we speak about the "Jewish people," we are a very diverse population group. We live in different areas across the globe and have different lifestyles.

It is our propensity to establish local Jewish communities in those places to which we migrate. In the societies where we have taken root, we have adopted many of the facets of the larger society. In addition, we follow diverse lifestyles with different levels of commitment to Judaism, to the Jewish people and to Israel. Among those of us who have a strong commitment to these three "pillars," the commitment is expressed in various ways.

Diversity has the potential to be both a strength and a weakness. If each segment of the Jewish people is able to enrich one another, diversity is a source of strength for both the individual community and the Jewish people at large. Alternatively, if diversity leads to inner tensions or isolation it might be seen as a point of weakness, having a detrimental effect on the broader community.

---

3   In 2015, Slingshot rethought the concept of Slingshot Day and decided to discontinue it.

It is with this in mind that a number of educational entrepreneurs have made it their mission to build a bridge between culturally and ideologically diverse populations and/or between geographically diverse populations. The premise of these entrepreneurs is that if we establish a bridge between the diverse populations within an educational setting, we can harness the diversity to strengthen each group as well as the Jewish people at large.

Two examples of this phenomenon are Vivienne Anstey's endeavors in South Africa and Gesher's programs in Israel

Vivienne Anstey champions cross-community bridges in South Africa

In South Africa the local Jewish community has been seriously challenged with the political changes which have taken place over the past twenty-five years.

In the previous era population groups were encouraged to maintain their separate identity. Within this climate, the Jewish community succeeded in fostering a strong sense of Jewish identity in its members, and to this day South African Jews, wherever they reside, are known for their strong Jewish identity.

With the dismantling of apartheid in the early 1990s, however, social integration has now become an important virtue. In the wake of these new realities the Jewish community is at a crossroads, with many choosing to emigrate.

Within this complexity, Vivienne Anstey, a Cape Town social activist, has dedicated herself to building bridges across the community, and by doing so build a bridge from the past to the future.

Vivienne, who was born and raised in Cape Town and studied at the Brandeis University Hornstein Professional Jewish Leadership Program, has championed the development of new community paradigms, which she believes will enable the community to master its challenges. Part of this strategy is the sponsoring of cross-community Jewish educational initiatives. In a professional capacity she brought the Melton Adult Mini-School to Cape Town in 2005, while in a lay capacity she initiated the establishment of Limmud4 in South Africa in 2007. Both initiatives reflect her aspiration to build cross-community bridges and to include members of the Jewish community across the spectrum.

.*Gesher designs a cross-community bride in Israel*

Gesher, the Hebrew word for bridge, was established over forty years ago by Rabbi Dr. Danny Tropper, an Orthodox rabbi who came on *aliyah* from the United States.

Rabbi Tropper was deeply troubled by the rifts in Israeli society and he established Gesher in order to heal these rifts. He was particularly troubled by the rift between the secular and religious populations, which in many instances lived in their own enclaves and which studied in separate school systems from kindergarten through twelfth grade.

As Rabbi Tropper expressed it:

Our Jewish identity, which should serve to unite the diverse Jewish people in Israel, has instead been the cause of a deep rift between communities. This split has resulted in anger and alienation and is tearing the nation apart. Healing the rift can only come by way of enlightened Jewish education that can become the common denominator for genuine dialogue between different sectors of the nation. [Gesher]

Gesher's original educational model comprised overnight seminars that brought together schools from the secular and Orthodox sectors. At these seminars an attempt was made to focus on dialogue and mutual understanding. Lifelong friendships were forged between the participants and thus the impact was long term.

---

4   Limmud is discussed in detail in the following chapter.

Over the years Gesher has continued to introduce innovative educational endeavors, including programs run for soldiers in the Israel Defense Forces. Today a Gesher seminar is part and parcel of the IDF's officer training course, reflecting its strategic importance for the leaders of tomorrow.

As illustrated in the above examples, bridging is a powerful innovative strategy, given its ability to harness the power of existing elements.

References

Chazan, B., and D. Bryfman (2006, August). "Home Away from Home – a Research Study of the Shabbos Experience on Five University Campuses: An Informal Educational Model for Working with Young Jewish Adults." Chabad Campus International Foundation.

Dress for Success (n.d.). "What We Do." Retrieved January 26, 2013. http://www.dressforsuccess.org/whatwedo.aspx.

eTeacher (n.d.). "eLearn Together Grow Together." Retrieved December 1, 2015. eteacherHebrew: http://lp.eteacherhebrew.com/lp_biblical_and_hebrew_together_vid-en.html?cid=17&adgroup=e-teacher&creative=60465197346&keyword=e%20teacher&placement=&matchtype=e&adposition=1t1&gclid=CP_63aLauckCFVWdG-wodpo8O2Q.

Fishkoff, S. (2001). *The Rebbe's Army.* New York: Schocken.

Foundation for Jewish Camp (n.d.). "BunkConnect." Retrieved December 8, 2015. http://www.jewishcamp.org/bunk-connect/faq.

Gesher (n.d.). "Bridging Rifts in Israeli Society." Retrieved December 3, 2015. http://www.gesherusa.org/what-is-gesher.

Harrison, H. (2000). "Childline: The First Twelve Years." *Arch Dis Child (Archives of Disease in Childhood)*: 283–285.

National Public Radio (n.d.). "Nancy Lublin, Founder of Dress for Success." Retrieved January 26, 2013. http://www.npr.org/2010/10/21/130727578/ nancy-lublin-founder-of-dress-for-success.

Unity Prize (n.d.). "The Prize." Retrieved December 3, 2015. http://www. unityprize.org/en.

WebYeshiva (n.d.). Home page. Retrieved December 1, 2015. http://www. webyeshiva.org/.

Chapter Eleven

Design of Platforms

CENTRAL IDEA

PLATFORMS ARE POWERFUL MECHANISMS THAT CREATE EDUCATIONAL
VALUE BY PROVIDING VIRTUAL, PHYSICAL AND ORGANIZATIONAL
INFRASTRUCTURES THAT ENABLE OTHERS TO PERFORM.

Imagine a "compendium" of Jewish educational resources designed
by thousands of knowledgeable individuals and utilized by hundreds
of thousands. This compendium could be comprised of classic and
contemporary sources drawn from the Jewish people's diverse
populations. Everyone who is knowledgeable would be invited to
contribute. Contributions would be made by young and old, those
who live in Israel and those who live in the Diaspora, secular and
traditional, and from across the denominational spectrum including
the ultra-Orthodox.

This compendium could be made both accessible and appealing to
the multiple segments of the Jewish people. An individual interested
in learning how to build a *sukkah* for the first time, for example,
could find a five-minute YouTube video on the subject. Another,
searching for the existential meaning of dwelling in a *sukkah*, could
read personal insights from those who dwell in their *sukkah* every
year on the festival of Sukkot. Still others dedicated to studying the
traditional sources for the *sukkah* could do so with a rich collection
of commentaries.

A compendium of educational materials may sound like a very
expensive and futuristic project. In reality, taking into account
its social and educational value, it is comparatively cheap and
technologically possible to construct.

The idea of a compendium is not radically different from a number of recent innovations that have attracted major traffic and brought great wealth to their founders and investors, including Facebook, eBay, Uber and Airbnb. They are all innovative platforms developed to enable others to be active. The platforms provide a "structure" and a second party provides the content. This content serves a third party, who is the ultimate beneficiary. Platforms are thus structures designed to enable others to interact.

The major advantage of the platform design strategy is that the innovator invests in neither the activity nor the content. He or she provides a locus in which others can establish a presence by providing the content and activities that attract the end users.

Types of Platforms

In analyzing platforms it is possible to differentiate between four major types: virtual platforms, bricks and mortar platforms, organizational platforms and organizational support platforms.

Virtual platforms

Virtual platforms are web-based "constructions" and require that both the active contributor and the beneficiary be linked to the web. Given the proliferation of smartphones and tablets, it fair to assume that virtual platforms are highly accessible to our target population.

As mentioned, a key feature of the platform is its dependence on others to provide the content. How is this content solicited? Through crowdsourcing, which has become an extremely popular strategy in recent years.

Crowdsourcing

The concept "crowdsourcing" was popularized by Jeff Howe in his landmark article, "The Rise of Crowdsourcing," which was published in *Wireless* magazine in June 2006 [Howe, 2006].

Howe noticed a growing trend of outsourcing that differed from the traditional model. Traditional outsourcing is giving a job to an outside party who has expertise in the area, with a contractual commitment for payment. By contrast, the new trend involved outsourcing to the general public – an unidentified "crowd" of people – and not to a designated party. Multiple providers could work on the project, with compensation paid only to the provider who delivers the desired product or process.

The growth of this phenomenon was a by-product of newly developed Internet platforms that facilitated the process.

Salient features of crowdsourcing

- A call is made to the general public and is thus open to all: young and old, amateurs and professionals alike.
- It encourages new approaches and out-of-the-box thinking, since "the crowd" is not locked into traditional paradigms.
- The innovation process becomes democratized. Novices and veterans compete on the same playing field, with no advantage given to experts.
- It enables companies and organizations to utilize multiple untapped resources.
- The company or organization that issues the call does not expose itself to risk; it pays compensation only if its requirements are met.

Historical precedents for crowdsourcing

The solicitation of ideas and innovative models is not novel. There are many occurrences in history when the government or companies turned to the public for ideas and/or development of a new product. These include the following:

- In 1714, the British government offered the Longitude Prize of £20,000 to any individual who could solve a serious navigation problem. Ultimately this prize was won by the son of a carpenter, who submitted a highly creative and reliable solution [DesignCrowd, 2010].

- In the late nineteenth century, Professor James Murray led a team of volunteers who compiled the *Oxford Dictionary*. Hundreds of volunteers submitted slips of paper with definitions, which Murray and his team collated and filed [Lanxon, 2011].

- In 1936, Toyota staged a contest for the design of its new logo. The company received 27,000 responses and the logo used by Toyota today can be traced to the winner of that contest [DesignCrowd, 2010].

- In 1955, The premier of the New South Wales State initiated a contest with a £5,000 prize for design of a building in the Sydney Harbor, which became the Sydney Opera House. Over two hundred individuals from thirty countries sent in entries. The winning design became one of Sydney's most famous landmarks [Sydney Opera House].

Roots of crowdsourcing in the Jewish tradition

Crowdsourcing in the Jewish tradition dates back to the fall of the second Temple and the establishment of Yavneh in 70 CE.

As explained in Chapter One, the fall of the Temple became a catalyst for the development of rabbinic Judaism, which focused on the study of Torah as an important aspect of religious practice. This change of focus led to the democratization of Judaism. In Temple times, only the Kohanim (priests), the descendants of Moses' brother Aaron, could head the religious hierarchy. Sacrificial ritual was the exclusive right of the Kohanim and thus the Jewish religion functioned as a meritocracy.

Following the destruction of the Temple, the religious hierarchy was comprised of the Sages. The Sages were individuals who earned their authority through proven wisdom following years of dedicated Torah study. Since Torah study was open to all, anyone could rise to a position of religious leadership, irrespective of lineage.

This change is reflected in the *Mishneh Torah*, written by Moses Maimonides (1135–1204):

> The Jewish people were privileged to receive three crowns: the crown of Torah, the crown of priesthood and the crown of royalty. Aaron (and his descendants) received the crown of priesthood...David (and his descendants) received the crown of royalty...while the crown of Torah is placed in abeyance, waiting to be claimed (*Sefer Hamada*, Laws of Torah Study 3:1).

The last sentence of the paragraph is an open call to the public to come forward, study and claim the crown of Torah, i.e., to assume the mantle of religious leadership. In other words, following the destruction of the Temple Judaism became dependent on crowdsourcing for its religious leadership!

Maimonides did not limit himself to an open call to the public to study. He implored the Sages to take responsibility for tutoring the children of the entire community. Ideally, he wrote, this tutoring should be without payment to ensure maximum participation. Such an educated public would thereby ensure that crowdsourcing would meet with success.

Virtual platforms and crowdsourcing

Virtual platforms reliant on crowdsourcing for their activity have a major potential impact for education, as they have two very important virtues:

1. They are able to draw upon multiple untapped resources across the religious and geographical spectra.
2. If participants volunteer their services, the costs of the educational endeavor are limited to the upkeep of the platform only.

An example of a crowdsourcing platform that has made a major impact is Wikipedia, founded as a nonprofit enterprise by Jimmy Wales and Larry Sanger in 2001 [Wikipedia]. This online encyclopedia is totally dependent on the "crowd" for its content and for its being updated.

While Wikipedia has been exploited by companies as a type of advertising, and its authority may be in question, it nonetheless plays a major disruptive role by providing accessible information to millions of web users who otherwise would lack immediate access to information.

In the area of Jewish education, we have yet to utilize the full potential of crowdsourcing platforms. A recent educational platform partially based on crowdsourcing that is making a major impact is 929 Tanach Beyachad ("Bible Together"), a platform for the in-depth study of the Bible.

929 Tanach Beyachad

In 2010, Avi Wortzman, at the time of this writing the Israeli deputy minister of education, initiated the daily study of Bible, one chapter a day. While daily study of a chapter is itself not a new idea, Wortzman made it popular, even among segments of the population previously unengaged in Bible study. To do so he galvanized interest among public and cultural figures, as well as educators and philanthropists. In 2013, the Center for Educational Technology commenced work on a learning platform, and in December 2014, spearheaded by Rabbi Dr. Benny Lau, the platform was launched. The platform was coined "929," reflecting the 929 chapters of the Bible.

Study takes place daily from Sunday through Thursday, a chapter a day, and the weekend is utilized for review. The platform provides the text, in both written and audio form, and access to traditional sources. The public is invited to contribute their comments, thereby enhancing study through this crowdsourcing.

Thousands of people have joined this daily study since its inception. National radio now runs a weekly program to discuss the chapters, and study groups continue to grow and flourish.

The goal is to complete the first cycle in the summer of 2018, coinciding with the seventieth anniversary of the establishment of the State of Israel [929.org.il].

Bricks and mortar platforms

The bricks and mortar Jewish educational platform is a physical construction designed to house multiple educational activities.

In the commercial world, a familiar example of a bricks and mortar platform is the shopping mall. Those who design the "mall platform" understand the need to attract potential customers and to offer them an experience that will be an impetus for them to return. Thus the malls will try to attract anchor stores that organically attract customers on a regular basis, and a wide range of other stores that focus on the target market.

In order to ensure that going to the mall is more than a mere shopping expedition, malls will usually house an array of coffee shops and restaurants and often provide various forms of entertainment as well.

The importance of choice: the mall theory

A key strategy adopted by malls to attract many customers is to host multiple stores that offer similar merchandise. For example, in the larger malls there will be a number of department stores, a number of clothing stores and a number of stores that stock digital and electrical appliances. This strategy is based on the theory that choice is crucial for the attraction of potential customers. While consumers who always purchase at a specific store will seek it out wherever it is located, occasional customers and noncustomers will be attracted by the choices offered by the multiple vendors.

The "mall theory" might seem counterintuitive; surely a store should be far more successful if the competition is geographically distant! In reality, stores seek to operate near their competitors. While they may lose customers to their neighboring competitors, ultimately there will be a net gain of customers. The proximity of multiple stores that stock similar items is a strong draw for potential customers, such that all the stores in the vicinity stand to gain.

Bricks and mortar Jewish educational platforms

Within the realm of Jewish education, we too have purposely built bricks and mortar platforms that provide multiple options for potential customers. An example of this platform in North America is the Jewish Community Centers, which provide a rich array of options for the family and for different age groups. They pride themselves on their ability to attract large segments of the Jewish community to their programs.[1] Their salient features include the following:

- *They offer multiple Jewish educational activities and experiences.* Similar to shopping malls, bricks and mortar educational platforms need to be highly creative in order to attract potential participants. A wide range of parallel activities appealing to different ages is necessary to ensure that the participants have multiple and attractive choices. In addition, there needs to be

---

1   It must be noted that in the strict sense Jewish Community Centers do not fit the definition of "platforms" because they operate many of their programs themselves. However, we have included them in this category since many of their programs, like PJ Library, are offered in partnership with other organizations.

culinary choices as well as other events that will attract the potential customer.

- *They create a "Jewish space."* In the past, Jews grew up in homes with a rich Jewish atmosphere. There were Jewish foods on the table, the festivals were celebrated and there was Jewish music in the home. Today, with the high rate of intermarriage, the number of Jews who have "Jewish homes" is dwindling. Similarly, many Jews lived in Jewish neighborhoods with a Jewish ambience, or frequented synagogues, while today many no longer do. These changes have created a deep educational need for a "Jewish space" with Jewish ambience, where a maximal effort is made to ensure that individuals who frequent the facility will be emersed in Jewish culture. The cultural ambience is created through artifacts, pictures, signs, music and traditional Jewish cuisine.

- *They nurture Jewish social networks.* A major and important feature of the bricks and mortar platforms is the social interaction and networking they make possible. It is this networking that develops Jewish community and strengthens Jewish identity.

A Jewish Community Center that has taken full advantage of the educational possibilities afforded by a bricks and mortar platform is the Harry and Rose Samson Family Jewish Community Center in Milwaukee, Wisconsin.

The Harry and Rose Samson Family Jewish Community Center

The Harry and Rose Samson Family Jewish Community Center in Milwaukee is a central platform in the Milwaukee Jewish community for Jewish educational activities. The overwhelming majority of the thirty thousand-strong Milwaukee Jewish community participates at least once a year in a JCC activity, a figure that highlights its central role in the community.

On entering the JCC one is struck by its Jewish character and immediately feels him- or herself to be entering a Jewish space. Posters that emphasize Jewish values adorn the walls. The single kosher facility in the city is housed here and is a focal meeting place, and the renowned media center, which stocks over one thousand Jewish movies, is a large-scale lending facility for the community.

Jewish programming at the JCC is intense. The early childhood centers are enriched by a rabbi educator. PJ Library is highly popular among the young families, and PJ events are well attended. Sports activities for kids are pursued with a focus on Jewish values, and the JCC overnight camps are renowned for their high-impact Jewish experiences.

While the JCC is frequented by members on a daily basis, on at least four occasions during the year it is filled with many non-members. On Purim, Hanukah, Yom Ha'atzma'ut (Israel Independence Day) and Yom Hashoah (Holocaust Memorial Day), community-wide events are held at the JCC, thereby reminding the larger Jewish community of their Jewishness and their link with Israel.

The JCC's commitment to being a platform for Jewish education should not be taken for granted. At least 30 percent of the membership is not Jewish, a situation that could lead the center to minimize Jewish educational elements. Nevertheless, through the strong leadership of Mark Shapiro, executive drector since 2007, Jewish education remains a high priority.

In addition to Mark Shapiro, the JCC is blessed with the services of Jewish educator Jody Hirsh, who was awarded the Morton L. Mandel Jewish Educational Leadership Award in 2014 by the JCCA [JCC Association of North America, 2014].

Jody Hirsh

Hirsh is a veteran JCC educator. In 1992 he was appointed as the first Jewish educator at the Houston JCC, and three years later he became the Jewish educator at the JCC in Hong Kong. In 1997 he returned to the United States to take the position of Jewish educator at the Milwaukee JCC, a position he continues to hold at the time of this writing.

I had the privilege of studying with Hirsh from 1989 to 1991, when we both participated in the Jerusalem Fellows Program. I was struck by his mastery of Torah text, of the arts, of music and of Jewish culture in general. In addition, he has a passionate love of Israel and the Jewish people.

On bringing these traits to Milwaukee, Hirsh leveraged the power of the JCC platform to ensure that Jewish education would permeate in both formal and informal settings. Small wonder the Morton Mandel award noted that "Jody's breadth and depth of knowledge, his creative imagination, and his interest in the learning process make him the 'Gold Standard' for JCC Jewish educators."

Hirsh's influence on Jewish programming is not limited to the Milwaukee JCC. His mystery game continues to be played at the Citadel Museum in Jerusalem, and his Jewish Artists' Laboratory operates not only in Milwaukee but in Madison and Minneapolis as well.

Transforming an existing organization into a platform

While purpose-built bricks and mortar platforms are the ideal, it is possible to develop a bricks and mortar platform from an existing infrastructure. This is particularly important today when demographic shifts lead to the underutilization of extensive facilities, either partially or fully. In this situation it may be possible to transform an organization with bricks and mortar facilities into a platform, enabling it to make a major educational contribution to the community.

This was the challenge that Dr. Hilton Immerman faced when he took on the joint positions of Hillel director and master of Shalom College, both of which were at the University of New South Wales in Sydney, Australia, and transformed them into the Shalom Institute.

From Shalom College to the Shalom Institute

When Hilton Immerman, a South African native then in his mid-thirties, took up the position of master of Shalom College and director of Hillel at the University of New South Wales in 1989, little did he dream that he would be the game changer who was to have an impact on the entire Jewish community of Sydney and beyond.

Shalom College was a dormitory for university students, offering a kosher facility and accommodation to Jewish students who were non-Sydney residents. The building's space far exceeded the needs of the Jewish students. With quality accommodation on campus being a general need, Immerman identified a potential income stream for his future plans to make Shalom a nexus of community educational programs. He essentially made a paradigm shift and, marshalling his entrepreneurial and innovative abilities, set about transforming a facility for Jewish college students into an educational platform for the wider Jewish community.

Immerman is the first to admit that he didn't have a grand vision when he started, but as he looked around the community it gradually dawned on him that it lacked the wonderful programs available overseas. The dearth of activities for young adults in particular was akin to a black hole, and the campus was essentially the last stop. Gathering all the role-players, Hilton persuaded them that it would be a good thing for the community if young adult events could be coordinated and put on a more professional footing.

Immerman skilfully managed to get his board's buy in to deviate from Shalom's core business, as each of his ideas was backed up by a solid rationale, a proposal and a business plan.

In 1993 Immerman advocated for bringing in the Florence Melton Mini-School to address the lack of adult Jewish education, convincing his board that a strong community was a Jewishly literate one. In addition to benefiting the community, the program would bring credit to Shalom. In 1999, Shalom College inaugurated Limmud-Oz, the first Limmud outside the United Kingdom. The following year it convened the Sydney Jewish Writers' Festival.

A community capital appeal in 2001 for Shalom College resulted in significant growth. Immerman had seen that Shalom was always in demand for other organizations to rent out, and realized that if its size were to be increased by 50 percent, the income that could be generated would be substantial. The appeal, together with the support of a major donor, enabled Shalom to add major facilities, including a mini-conference center for running the programs he envisaged.

To this day the Shalom Institute continues to be Sydney's premier educational platform, spearheading new partnerships and new initiatives. Shalom Baby was launched in 2008 and Shalom Tots in 2010. PJ Library was added to the platform in 2011 and Moishe House was launched by the institute in 2013.

In 2005, Shalom College inaugurated a significant tikkun olam (social justice) program to help close the professional gap between indigenous and non-indigenous Australians. The program aimed to increase the number of indigenous professionals by providing residential scholarships for aboriginal Australians. It is called the Shalom Gamarada Ngiyani Yana program – translated as "we walk together as friends." To date a total of eighty students have been assisted, with twenty graduates – fifteen of whom are qualified doctors. This initiative drew many less affiliated Jews to support Shalom's work, and has promoted very strong and positive relations between the Jewish and aboriginal communities across Australia.

It must be noted that Immerman ensured that the original core mission of the organization would continue to be fulfilled. Although the Shalom Institute has incorporated Shalom College, the latter continues to provide support, food and lodging to the students on campus. The creativity was in developing a platform that would address the needs of other populations, thereby enhancing its community impact.

Organizational platforms

Organizational platforms are those that are designed for live events but which lack a physical infrastructure. They operate events over a limited period of time and focus on a specific target market, renting facilities for these events.

A prime example of organizational platforms in the commercial e-world is an itinerant fair. Fair organizers find a suitable facility that can house the fair for a limited time and invite merchants to display their wares. In operating this platform, the organizers expose new merchants to potential customers and provide local customers with access to reconvened merchants from other areas.

In the educational realm, an organizational platform is one that arranges conferences that provide a wide range of educational options and experiences. In order to facilitate this, it rents suitable facilities on an ad hoc basis that will meet the needs of the organizers and the program.

Similar to the itinerant fair, educational organizational platforms deliver a brief yet rich experience that is highly attractive because of the choices it offers. In addition, the social milieu creates a major opportunity for networking and for social interaction.

How organizational platforms differ from bricks and mortar platforms

Organizational platforms resemble bricks and mortar platforms in that they operate in a physical space and offer a wide range of educational options and experiences to participants. However, they differ in the following ways:

- They operate for a limited time period.
- They need to rent a facility and thus are dependent on outside availability.
- They bring the platform to target populations by choosing venues in close proximity.
- They do not have the expense of maintaining a permanent physical structure.
- They do not have the expense of maintaining an ongoing, comprehensive organizational structure.

An organization that has excelled in designing and replicating a Jewish educational platform is the Limmud Conference.

The Limmud Conference

The Limmud Conference is an example of an organizational platform. Over a brief period of time, ranging from one day to five, Limmud brings together scores of presenters from different religious and political perspectives and offers participants an intense, varied and rich learning and cultural experience. Participants range from college age to seniors. They come from diverse backgrounds and are attracted by the intense intellectual, cultural and social activity offered by this platform. Generally, Limmud conferences are very well attended, attracting over 2,500 participants in the larger community conferences and hundreds in the smaller.

A powerful aspect of the Limmud learning experience is its deep commitment to operating as an open platform without limiting the views being offered. With an ethos of egalitarianism, participants don name tags that indicate only their first and last names. The program is designed to encourage debate and ensure that the intellectual activity reflects the myriad opinions in the Jewish community.

Having attended the Limmud UK Conference over a decade ago, I was struck by the vibrant, open-air market atmosphere. Those who frequent open-air markets, such as Pike Place Market in Seattle,

Washington, and Machaneh Yehudah in Jerusalem, know that the abundance of stalls selling fresh produce and other wares, along with the vitality, fragrances and "hum" of the open-air market, make visiting a worthwhile experience. Likewise, Limmud participants are struck by its powerful, "open-air market" feel. The richness and freshness of the program, the vitality and constant hum, are all vital aspects of the Limmud experience.

Limmud's beginnings

The Limmud Conference was founded in the United Kingdom. It was developed on the Coalition of Alternatives in Jewish Education (CAJE) model. This North American-based conference brought together hundreds of Jewish education professionals annually and offered a multiple array of workshops for professional development. In the late 1970s, Clive Lawton, Alistair Falk, Michael May and Rabbi Michael Rosen attended the CAJE conference. They were excited by their experience and founded Limmud in the United Kingdom in 1980.

From a small conference for educators to a large education convention

The Limmud UK conference in its current form differs from its initial setup, which was an in-service professional conference for Jewish educators. Today the conference attracts the wider community. Furthermore, whereas during the first decade Limmud conferences attracted up to 250 participants, today it attracts up to ten times that amount. While it still perceives itself to be a conference, Limmud far more resembles a convention.

This growth trajectory should not be taken for granted. Most large conferences rely on affiliate organizations to support them and are consequently "guaranteed" a large number of participants. In North America, Jewish conferences of this magnitude are run by the national organizations. The Jewish Federation of North America runs the annual General Assembly and the Jewish Community Centers Association (JCCA) runs the JCC biennial conference. Other large conferences are run by specific organizations for their members. All of these bodies comprise constituent organizations that send members to these conferences. By contrast, Limmud functions only as an organizational platform and thus relies entirely on the "Limmudniks" to participate.

Andrew Gilbert transforms Limmud

Limmud's change in direction was precipitated by a crisis in 1989 resulting from a new UK Government policy requiring educators to undergo professional in-service training during their vacations. As a result, the educators who provided the core of the Limmud conference were unable to participate, and a change of direction was required. The change was led by Andrew Gilbert, a lay leader who became the chairperson of Limmud in 1990.[2] Gilbert set a goal of growth to five hundred participants and articulated a five-year plan to meet this goal. When retiring as chairman of Limmud in 1997, he had not only succeeded in leading Limmud to realizing its goal of growth, he had transformed the organization.

A key component of Gilbert's strategy was to recruit young adults to Limmud and particularly those who were graduates of the youth movements. He viewed the young adults as the key to the future of the organization. This vision ran contrary to the prevailing situation in which young adults had not shown major interest in Limmud. In 1989 there were perhaps only three participants who were under the age of thirty-five![3]

Having been a youth movement leader himself, Gilbert felt that there was a large reservoir of untapped talent that could be recruited for Limmud. This perception was informed by the frustration he

---

2   Thanks to Dr. John Boyde for this insight.

3   Interview with Andrew Gilbert.

noticed among young adult youth movement graduates, who lacked an avenue through which to apply the considerable skills they had accumulated in their previous leadership positions. While those who became formal educators had an easier task in finding meaningful challenges, those who chose other professions often felt underutilized in the Jewish community.

With this in mind Gilbert made a strategic decision to recruit these young adults. Initially he secured scholarships for their participation in the conference and invited them to give sessions. Later he entrusted them with organizing the program and running the conference. In transferring this responsibility to youth movement graduates, Limmud became a natural extension of the youth movement experience. Youth movements thrive on high energy, exuberance, creativity, commitment and peer learning, and Gilbert ensured that these assets of the movements would become the assets of Limmud as well. He understood the power of responsibility as a high motivating force, and therefore he granted it liberally. Mentoring these young graduates, Gilbert gave them the reins of leadership, and ever since, Limmud UK has benefited from the exuberance and leadership of youth movement graduates.

Limmud goes international and grows exponentially

Over the past decade Limmud has experienced exponential growth. In 1999 it offered its first conference outside the United Kingdom, in Australia. In 2016 there were eighty-three communities in forty-three countries that ran local Limmud conferences. This has resulted in Limmud achieving a global impact [Limmud].

In the United Kingdom, in addition to having an annual conference in the winter, a summer "Limmud in the Woods" attracts hundreds of participants. Multiple Limmuds are held in smaller communities, thereby providing local communities with access to the Limmud educational experience. As an organizational platform, Limmud has the flexibility to operate in diverse places and during different times of the year.

Limmud clearly demonstrates the potential of organizational platforms that harness the strengths of both the virtual platforms and the bricks and mortar platforms. An important strength of the virtual platform is its ability to stimulate conversation between large segments of diverse populations, cutting across multiple divides. A major strength of the bricks and mortar platform is the face-to-face interaction between the participants. At Limmud both of these advantages are realized. Cross-population conversations take place on a large scale around the clock, and they all take place face-to-face.

Organizational support platforms

Organizational support platforms are designed to support an entire field, and especially the organizations that operate within it. In the realm of Jewish education organizational support platforms can facilitate the following: growing the field by supporting the establishment of new educational organizations, increasing the number of students who enroll in the educational organizations, enhancing the sustainability of the organizations, offering increased opportunities for faculty development in the field, providing leadership training to improve the leadership skills of senior staff and providing programmatic resources for educational activities in the field.

An outstanding example of an organizational support platform is Foundation for Jewish Camp, which was discussed in detail in Chapter Six. Elssa and Robert Bildner's founding of this organization in 1998 transformed the field, making it a crucial vehicle for high-impact Jewish education.

Multiple Platform Organizations

In differentiating between the four platform types we have focused on organizations and programs that function as only one type. In reality, an organization could have multiple functions, thus operating as a "multiple platform organization."

An example of a high-impact educational organization that operates as a multiple platform organization is RAVSAK, the network for Jewish community day schools. RAVSAK's functions are twofold: It is a school network which operates as both a virtual platform and an organizational platform, and it supports the development of the field of community Jewish day schools, and in this capacity operates as an organizational support platform.

RAVSAK

RAVSAK is the Hebrew acronym for Reshet Vatei Sefer Kehilati'im, which means "network of Jewish day schools." The organization operated initially as a network for Jewish day schools in North America that defined themselves as "community schools," referring to their cross-denominational nature. These schools, developed outside of the denominational systems, relied on one another for mutual support. The chairperson of the network was a school director and the chair rotated between the different school directors.

A major change took place in the year 2000 with the appointment of Dr. Marc Kramer as CEO of RAVSAK. Under his leadership RAVSAK became an organizational support platform in addition to retaining its initial function of being a network.

Today, RAVSAK operates in the five following key areas, one as a network and four as an organizational support platform:

1. *Network: RAVSAK provides virtual platforms for communication between school directors and staff, and an annual conference.*
2. *Professional Development: RAVSAK is dedicated to enhancing the quality of community day schools, making a major investment in leadership training for senior staff and for Judaic studies faculty.*
3. *Programming: RAVSAK is engaged in Judaic curriculum development to ensure that the curriculum is intellectual, informative and engaging. In addition, it organizes national informal educational programs including shabbatonim.*

4. *Advocacy: RAVSAK plays a major role in highlighting the importance of community day schools. With fierce competition for both funding and students, advocacy is crucial to ensure that the strategic importance of local community day schools is understood.*
5. *Consultation: RAVSAK offers member schools consultation on complex issues, which are often unforeseen. This expert advice is often of critical importance given the myriad challenges schools face.*

Since the year 2000, RAVSAK has grown from a network of thirty schools to one of 135 schools, encompassing 35,000 students. This growth is indicative of a major vote of confidence both in the organization and in the field.

§

While the power of platforms for impacting the field of Jewish education is clearly evident, it is important to be mindful of two factors which may inhibit their growth.

First, since a major incentive for entering the field of education is direct interaction with students, there may be less motivation to design platforms for *others* to interact with them. This sentiment was expressed to me by a grants officer of a philanthropic fund, who commented on my good fortune to be "on the front line." When I remarked that his contribution was far greater than mine since it facilitated impacting so many others, he responded in frustration that he missed the interaction with the target population.

Second is the complexity in raising philanthropic funds for platforms, which by definition offer others the opportunity to impact the end users. Funders tend to favor organizations that give direct services and often do not fully appreciate the crucial role of platforms.

Hopefully, this chapter will make a contribution to changing these perceptions.

References

929.org.il (n.d.). "What is 929." Retrieved December 24, 2015. http://www.929.org.il/pages/aboutEN.html.

Bernstein, F. A. (2010, February 10). "The Four-Bedroom Kibbutz." The *New York Times*. Retrieved April 4, 2013. http://www.nytimes.com/2010/02/11/garden/11moishe.html.

Chazan, B., and D. Bryfman (2006, August). "Home Away from Home – a Research Study of the Shabbos Experience on Five University Campuses: An Informal Educational Model for Working with Young Jewish Adults." Chabad Campus International Foundation.

DesignCrowd (2010, October 28) "Crowdsourcing Is Not New: The History of Crowdsourcing, 1714 to 2010." Retrieved December 12, 2015. http://blog.designcrowd.com/article/202/crowdsourcing-is-not-new--the-history-of-crowdsourcing-1714-to-2010.

Deutsch, P. (former Florida congressman, founder of the Ben Gamla Charter Schools), in discussion with the author, November 15, 2012.

Dress for Success (n.d.). "What We Do." Retrieved January 26, 2013. http://www.dressforsuccess.org/whatwedo.aspx.

Fishkoff, S. (2001). *The Rebbe's Army.* New York: Schocken.

Foundation for Jewish Camp (n.d.). "What We Do." Retrieved December 28, 2015. http://www.jewishcamp.org/.

Harrison, H. (2000). "Childline: The First Twelve Years." *Arch Dis Child (Archives of Disease in Childhood)*: 283–285.

Hebrew Charter School Center (2013). Home page. Retrieved March 31, 2013. http://www.hebrewcharters.org/.

Hernandez, J. (2009, March 8). "Secular Education, Catholic Values." *The New York Times.*

Howe, J. (2006, June). "The Rise of Crowdsourcing." *Wired.*

JCC Association of North America (2014, January 6). "Jody Hirsh to Receive Morton L. Mandel Jewish Educational Leadership Award." Retrieved December 29, 2015. http://jcca.org/jody-hirsh-to-receive-morton-l-mandel-jewish-educational-leadership-award/.

Lanxon, N. (2011, January 13). "How the Oxford English Dictionary Started Out Like Wikipedia." Wired.co.uk. Retrieved December 12, 2015. http://www.wired.co.uk/news/archive/2011-01/13/the-oxford-english-wiktionary.

Limmud (n.d.). Home page. Retrieved December 29, 2015. http://limmud.org/.

Moishe House (n.d.). Home page. Retrieved April 4, 2013. http://www.moishehouse.org/.

National Public Radio (n.d.). "Nancy Lublin, Founder of Dress for Success." Retrieved January 26, 2013. http://www.npr.org/2010/10/21/130727578/nancy-lublin-founder-of-dress-for-success.

Shulzke, E. (2012, September 10). "Hebrew Charter School Founder Looks to 'Mormon School.'" Deseret News. Retrieved March 26, 2015. http://www.deseretnews.com/article/765603214/Hebrew-charter-school-founder-looks-to-Mormon-model.html?pg=all.

Sydney Opera House (n.d.). "Sydney Opera House History 1954–1958." Retrieved December 15, 2015. http://www.sydneyoperahouse.com/about/house_history/1954_1958.aspx.

TCC Group (2011). *Evaluation Report Moishe House.* New York: TCC Group.

Wiener, J. (2012, March 27). "A Charter Network's Emerging Imprint." *The Jewish Week.*

Wikipedia (n.d.). "Charter School." Retrieved April 1, 2013. http://en.wikipedia.org/wiki/Charter_school.

Wikipedia (n.d.). "Wikipedia." Retrieved December 24, 2015. https://en.wikipedia.org/wiki/Wikipedia.

Chapter Twelve

Changing the Rules

CENTRAL IDEA

WHEN RULES AND CONSTRAINTS HINDER THE ATTAINMENT OF EDUCATIONAL
VALUE, THE OPTIMAL STRATEGY IS TO BREAK OUT OF THE CONFINES OF THESE
LIMITATIONS AND TO OPERATE ACCORDING TO A NEW SET OF RULES.

Imagine the following situation. It is known that a valuable object
is to be found on the other side of a very high wall. Given its worth,
a number of creative individuals become obsessed with retrieving
it and devise a plan accordingly.

A first individual uses a long fishing rod and line, and with the aid
of mirrors tries to retrieve the object. A second drills a hole through
the wall and tries to maneuver the object through it. A third brings
a fire fighter ladder and tries to scale the wall. A fourth decides to
dismantle the wall.

What is the difference between the first three approaches and
the fourth?

The first three all creatively maneuvered within the limitations
of the constraint, i.e., the wall. The fourth decided to remove the
constraint. This had major implications both for him and for all who
resided in the area. Imagine the response! Whereas with regard to
the first three creative attempts at retrieval passersby would probably
be intrigued and perhaps even a little jealous, in the fourth situation
many would be delighted and celebrate their access to the other side
– although some might be irate and would probably protest against
this change in the status quo.

The implications of the fourth initiative as opposed to the first
three are significant. First, the beneficiary of any of the first three

initiatives would primarily be the individual who succeeded. In demolishing the wall, however, the fourth individual would provide access not only for himself but for everyone else as well. Moreover, theoretically, even though he was the one to remove the wall, others would benefit at his expense if they retrieved the object before he did.

A second implication relates to the short-term and long-term effects. If one of the first three individuals were to be successful the benefits of the successful action would be limited to the benefits accrued from the retrieval of the object. In dismantling the wall there could be benefits far beyond the retrieval of the object. With the area beyond the wall now accessible, there could be opportunities for the retrieval of other objects as well.

The fourth individual has deployed an important strategy of innovation. In removing the constraints he changed the rules of the game. Changing the rules is potent because it shifts the balance of power in any given "game" and opens up multiple new options. What was previously deemed to be impossible is now within reach, and new opportunities for growth and improvement emerge.

In this chapter we will explore three areas in which innovators have changed the rules, resulting in widespread impact on the field of Jewish education.

- *Changing the rules of access.* Groups that had no previous access to quality Jewish education are granted access, thereby adding to the social capital of the Jewish people.
- *Changing the rules within educational organizations.* This enables promising educational entities to reposition themselves and gain access to resources that were inaccessible under the former rules.
- *Changing the rules of the "game."* This refers to the policies and norms that define how the field is to operate. It includes the types of organizations that operate educational programs, quality control, funding policies, tuition policies and the like.

Changing the Rules of Access

In this section we will discuss changes in the rules that granted two major populations access to dimensions of Jewish education from which they had formerly been excluded. The first involved the changing of the rules within the area of women's learning in the Orthodox world, and the second was the inclusion in the *beit midrash* of populations that do not define themselves as Orthodox.

The revolution in women's Jewish learning within Orthodox circles

Within Orthodox circles in Eastern Europe at the end of the nineteenth century, boys and girls were treated in radically different ways with regard to their Jewish education. Boys studied in institutions and were steeped in Jewish learning, beginning with *cheder* and continuing with yeshiva. Girls received no formal Jewish education, though many attended non-Jewish public schools, receiving only a secular education. Girls had no access to a quality formal Jewish education, and this status quo continued until a seamstress named Sarah Schenirer changed the rules and pioneered a system of formal Jewish education for women [Chizhik-Goldschmidt].

Sarah Schenirer

Sarah Schenirer was born in Krakow, Poland, in 1883 to a family of Belzer Chassidim, and like her peers attended a Polish public school until the age of thirteen. She worked as a seamstress, yet her heart was in the study of Torah and its commentaries. Having received no religious education, Schenirer was self-taught. When she joined the youth movement Ruth, she was disturbed by the total ignorance of the young Jewish women in the group.

In 1913, with the outbreak of the First World War, her family moved briefly to Vienna. There she was exposed to the teachings of

Rabbi Samson Raphael Hirsch, who championed the duality of secular and religious learning. In Vienna Schenirer attended multiple Torah lectures and became totally committed both to the study of Torah personally and to providing girls with a religious Jewish education.

Schenirer returned to Poland in 1914 and received the blessing of the Belzer Rebbe to open a school for girls. In 1917 she opened the Bais Yaakov school for girls. Her first class consisted of seven students. Within five years there were seven schools, with a total of 1,040 students. In 1923, she founded a teacher's seminary in order to train teachers for her schools.

During the next decade the number of schools grew exponentially, and thus in 1933 there were 265 schools with 38,000 students. This network of schools evolved into the Bais Yaakov system, and was officially adopted by Agudath Israel, the ultra-Orthodox movement, as the official school system for Orthodox girls.

Schenirer passed away childless in 1935 at the age of fifty-two. While she did not have the joy of motherhood, multitudes of young women saw her as their spiritual mother.

Sarah Shenirer's extraordinary feat in "changing the rules" was first and foremost due to her personal passion for and commitment to women's learning. She had personally experienced the excitement of Torah study and wanted to enable other Jewish girls and women to have a similar experience. In addition, she was aided and abetted by a social need for a Jewish educational system for girls, which until then did not exist.

While this social need provided an impetus for establishing an educational system, the system that developed ultimately inhibited the fulfillment of Schenirer's original intentions. Schenirer's vision was to enable Jewish girls and women to have access to the traditional Jewish texts and to take part in the Jewish conversation. This was a quest for a "liberal arts" type of Jewish education, with a strong focus on Jewish literacy; an educational approach we described in Chapter Four.

The traditional establishment had a different educational agenda for Schenirer's fledgling system. In their ambivalence regarding Jewish education for girls and women, no system had been established. Given this void, Jewish girls spent a large part of the day in public school, absorbing the culture of the wider society. The establishment was highly concerned about the dangers of assimilation and sought an environment that would strengthen the traditional role of Jewish women. Emphasizing a woman's traditional role did not encourage involvement in serious text study.

In keeping with this goal, young women who studied in Bais Yaakov schools had limited access to the study of text. They studied Bible, Jewish law and moral codes, but the Talmud, which is the core text of rabbinic Judaism and which was at the heart of the boys' curriculum at the yeshiva, was out of bounds. Girls who studied at Bais Yaakov had the benefit of a traditional environment, and they studied literature that strengthened their commitment to Judaism, but their course of study also perpetuated their ignorance of the major classical Jewish texts.

This situation was prevalent not only in the ultra-Orthodox Bais Yaakov system, which ultimately spread to North America and Israel. A similar stance was adopted in the Modern Orthodox school systems. In Israel, in the state religious girls' high schools, Mishna, which is part of the Talmud, was included in the curriculum; Gemara, however, which is the lion's share of the Talmud, remained out of the students' reach.

It took a full sixty years until Orthodox women would be granted access to the study of Gemara in a systematic manner. This was facilitated by a number of educational entrepreneurs who established educational institutions that emphasized the importance of a comprehensive Jewish education for women, one that would be comparable to that which was offered to men.

Orthodox women are finally granted full access to Talmud study

The roots of this change can be traced to Rabbi Joseph B. Soloveitchik (1903–1993), *the* leading figure of the twentieth-century Modern Orthodox world in the Diaspora. He strongly endorsed granting access to all the Jewish texts, including Talmud, to women and girls. In 1948 the study of Talmud was introduced to girls at Maimonides School in Boston [Fuchs, 2014], the school that Rabbi Soloveitchik and his wife, Tanya, established in 1937.

However, it took another thirty years for an Orthodox post-high school institution to teach Talmud to women. In 1979 Rabbi David Silber founded the Drisha Institute for Women in New York and included Talmud in his curriculum. This was followed by Stern College for Women, a branch of Yeshiva University, which began offering Talmud courses to their students in the 1980s [Yeshiva University].

In Israel, Pelech girls' high school offered the study of Talmud in the 1960s, while the first women's post-high school institutions in Israel to offer Talmud study opened in the 1980s. Rabbi Chaim Brovender founded Michlelet Bruria, Rabbi Shlomo Riskin[1] founded Midreshet Lindenbaum and Malka Bina founded Matan. In addition, the Religious Kibbutz Movement established a Midrasha (the name adopted by post-high school Israeli women's seminaries) at Kibbutz Ein Hanatziv.

Today Modern Orthodox women who wish to study Talmud can choose from a variety of options, on both a high school and a post-high school level. The study of Talmud by women continues to be taboo, however, in ultra-Orthodox circles. Thus, while new rules now operate in some Orthodox circles, the old rules remain firmly in place in others.

---

1   Enabling Orthodox women to study the classic texts is only one of the multiple realms in which Rabbi Riskin has changed the rules. He pioneered women advocates in Israeli Rabbinic courts and more recently has championed a conversion process which could pave the way for hundreds of thousands of non-Jewish Israelis to undergo an Orthodox conversion.

New types of batei midrash (higher, non-academic institutions) are developed in Israel outside the Orthodox sector

In Israel prior to the 1970s, non-Orthodox post-high school students who wanted to pursue their studies in Bible and the classical rabbinic texts including Talmud were required to choose between academic studies offered by the universities and programs offered by Orthodox yeshivot.

The first institution to break the mold was Pardes Institute for Jewish Studies, which was established in Jerusalem in 1972 on the initiative of Michael Swersky. It was envisioned as a "nondenominational institute for learning Jewish texts in a coeducational *beit midrash*. It was designed to be a one-year program aimed at post-college young adults primarily from North America" [Pardes Institute of Jewish Studies].

Focusing on foreign students, the Pardes option remained outside the reach of Israeli students, and it was only sixteen years later that a nondenominational, Israeli *beit midrash* was established. Beit Midrash Elul was opened in Jerusalem in 1988 by Ruth Calderon, a secular educator, and Moti Bar Or, an Orthodox educator. At Elul a spirit of "open learning" evolved, which led to the opening of numerous other institutions, including Alma, the Home for Hebrew Culture founded by Calderon in 1995, and Kolot, the pluralistic *beit midrash* founded by Bar Or in 1997.

Pre-military mechinot

While the rules for post-college students were changed by Elul in 1988, it took another decade for pre-college students to gain access to *beit midrash* learning in a nondenominational setting. The catalyst for this development was the assassination of Prime Minister Yitzchak Rabin in 1995 by a former Orthodox yeshiva student. Rabin's assassination left a rip in the fabric of Israeli society and evoked a process of soul searching among different segments of the

Israeli population. Within secular spheres, there was a realization that the "Jewish bookshelf" had been neglected in non-Orthodox circles[2] and needed to be reclaimed by the wider segments of society.

This provided the impetus for the opening of Mechinat Nachshon in 1997, a non-Orthodox pre-military, yearlong study program. Based on the Orthodox model established by Rabbi Eli Sadan in 1988, Mechinat Nachshon offered comprehensive study of Jewish subjects for students who were willing to defer their military service for this purpose. Since their inception *mechinot* have flourished, and today there are twenty-four general, non-Orthodox *mechinot* spread around the country.

The establishment of secular yeshivot

An additional option developed in the past decade is the secular yeshiva. The Bina Center for Jewish Identity and Jewish Culture was the first secular yeshiva. It was established in 2006 by a group of scholars and educators from the kibbutz movement in the wake of the Rabin assassination. In 2011 a second yeshiva was established in Jerusalem, and in 2015 a third was established in Beersheba.

Egalitarian beit midrash study in North America

Until recently, non-Orthodox students in North America who wanted to pursue traditional text study on an advanced level also had to choose between studying in academic frameworks and Orthodox institutions.

The denominational institutions of higher learning, including the Jewish Theological Seminary (Conservative) and Hebrew Union College (Reform), are degree-granting institutions which focus

---

2   The term *mechina* is used to describe any preparatory program. In the academic realm *mechinot* prepare students for entry into faculties that require a certain academic level. In the context of this chapter, the *mechinot* are seen as institutions that prepare the students spiritually for their service in the Israeli military.

on the development of the movements' academic, spiritual and educational leadership. Their students comprise budding academics, rabbis, cantors and educators. Because of the academic bent of these institutions, lay students who have sought a non-academic *beit midrash* might not have been attracted to them and preferred studying in an Orthodox *beit midrash*. This situation changed with the opening of Mechon Hadar in New York in 2006.

Mechon Hadar, the egalitarian beit midrash

The roots of Mechon Hadar are to be found in the establishment of Kehilat Hadar in 2001 by Mara Benjamin and Rabbis Elie Kaunfer and Ethan Tucker [Kehilat Hadar].

Kehilat Hadar was founded on the Upper West Side of Manhattan as an independent, lay-lead minyan (community). It has become extremely popular with young adults, who frequent Hadar's services and events on a regular basis.

The minyan is traditional yet strictly egalitarian, and members are attracted by the strong synthesis which the minyan offers between egalitarianism, tradition and lay empowerment.

In the wake of Kehilat Hadar's success, Rabbis Shai Held, Elie Kaunfer and Ethan Tucker established Mechon Hadar in 2006. Mechon Hadar describes itself as "an educational institution that empowers Jews to create and sustain vibrant, practicing, egalitarian communities of Torah learning, prayer, and service" [Mechon Hadar].

Mechon Hadar operates in a traditional *beit midrash* format, offering *chavruta* study (in pairs) and lectures. It has a yearlong fellowship program which offers participants a year of intense study, as well as an intensive summer program. While Mechon Hadar has been in existence for only the past decade, its impact is widely felt by both the students who participate in the school's courses and others who listen avidly to their recorded *shiurim* (lessons).

In addition to its impacting the students, Mechon Hadar has become a major resource for independent *minyanim* as well as for established congregations who are interested in exploring ways to empower their members.

Only the future will tell to what extent Mechon Hadar has succeed in changing the rules and encouraging lay text study. Will sister institutions be established? Will there be Hadar high schools which follow Mechon Hadar's learning ethos?

Changing the Rules within Educational Organizations

A second realm of innovation in which "changing the rules" strategy can be used is that of organizational functioning. In this book we have focused mainly on entrepreneurs who have the liberty to establish new organizations. A great deal of social value, however, can also be attained by transforming existing organizations. If they possess important assets such as an experienced faculty, a large customer and donor base, and physical infrastructure, they may well be vital springboards for delivering future social value. In order to unleash the full potential of an organization, however, it may be necessary to significantly alter the internal and external norms and rules that have so far governed its operations.

An outstanding example of changing the rules within an organization is the Conservative congregation Chizuk Amuno in Baltimore, Maryland, which Rabbi Joel Zaiman transformed into a congregation that embraces the study of Torah.

Rabbi Joel Zaiman transforms Chizuk Amuno into the "education synagogue"

Rabbi Joel Zaiman is a second-generation rabbi. His father was an Orthodox rabbi, and during high school and his first two years of college, Joel studied at the Orthodox Chicago Hebrew Theological College. When he decided to follow a rabbinical career, his father suggested he study at the Conservative Jewish Theological Seminary in New York. The senior Rabbi Zaiman admired the Seminary's stellar faculty, which at the time included Professors Shaul Lieberman,

Abraham Joshua Heschel, Louis Ginsburg and Mordechai Kaplan. In addition, he admired the way in which the Seminary prepared its students for the rabbinate, and felt that his son would benefit greatly from this training.

Joel graduated from the Seminary in 1962. He served for eleven years as senior rabbi at Temple Emanu-El in Providence, Rhode Island, prior to his appointment in 1980 to the large Conservative congregation Chizuk Amuno in Baltimore.

The young Rabbi Zaiman had a deep love of Torah learning and a strong belief in the importance of quality Jewish education. A year after his appointment, he spearheaded the founding of the Krieger Schechter Day School. In addition, in order to ensure that those children who attended public school would also receive a quality Jewish education, Rabbi Zaiman appointed a full-time rabbi with outstanding educational skills to head Chizuk Amuno's supplementary school.

Rabbi Zaiman strongly believed that the vitality of the congregation needed to be fueled by a commitment to Jewish learning by his adult laity, and in 1996, with this in mind, he established the Stulman Center for Adult Learning.

It was within this context that Rabbi Zaiman requested to meet with me. He was visiting Jerusalem and we met in order to discuss strengthening adult education at Chizuk Amuno. He invited Lee Hendler, who was president of the congregation at that time, to join us. Rabbi Zaiman shared his vision with me. He described at length the strengths of Chizuk Amuno's educational faculty whom he had engaged in order to realize this vision.

He then made the pitch: he wanted to run a Florence Melton Adult Mini-School (which I headed) at the synagogue.

While I was totally taken by Rabbi Zaiman's sincerity, passion and vision, we were unable to accede to his request. Only a few months before, we had taken the policy decision to house mini-schools only within cross-community organizations such as Federations, central Jewish education agencies and JCC's.

*Our experience in working within synagogue frameworks
had not been favorable. The relationship was fraught with
clashes because invariably the congregational rabbis who taught
refused to be evaluated. Our policy was that prospective mini-
school faculty would be required to apply for the position and
to be evaluated at multiple intervals. Indeed, it would be an
untenable requirement if the rabbi had to apply to teach in his own
synagogue! Furthermore, synagogues were reluctant to employ
faculty outside of their denominations, thereby compromising the
cross-denominational ethos of the program.*

*I consulted at length with Dr. Betsy Katz, our North American
Director, and we decided to offer to write a tailor-made curriculum
that would meet the needs of the community, yet would operate
outside of the framework of the mini-school.*

*Rabbi Zaiman was incensed by this response and insisted that
Dr. Katz and I come to Baltimore in order to discuss the issue
face-to-face. We were caught off guard; we could not consent
to Chizuk Amuno's hosting the Mini-School, yet certainly could
not refuse!*

*We decided to go to Baltimore. We would stipulate conditions
for the housing of the mini-school that would meet our quality
requirements, but had a strong feeling that their chances of being
accepted were remote. These conditions were as follows:*

- *The congregation would appoint an outsider whom we
  would interview to direct the program.*
- *None of the congregation's rabbis would be permitted to
  teach in the program, since they could not be evaluated.*
- *The faculty would be chosen from all denominations and
  would be required to be evaluated.*

*We arrived at the meeting expecting it to end abruptly, and
it did; Rabbi Zaiman accepted the conditions wholeheartedly.*

Chizuk Amuno appointed Judy Meltzer, former dean of Baltimore Hebrew University, to head the program, and almost immediately it ranked among the highest quality mini-schools in the country.

Rabbi Zaiman's dedication to quality Jewish education was steadfast. While there is no doubt that this process was not easy, he was able to achieve the buy in of his board and community, thereby enabling Chizuk Amuno to achieve national status as the "education synagogue" [Chizuk Amuno Congregation].

The second example depicts a leader who changed the rules of a national organization, bringing change not only to the central organization but to its affiliates as well. A classic story of changing the rules, Richard Joel, CEO of National Hillel from 1988 through 2003, transformed the Hillel organization.

Richard Joel transforms the Hillel Foundation for Jewish Campus Life

It is not unusual for an outside appointee to an executive position of a central organization with local affiliates to encounter *one* of the following challenges:

- The legitimacy or authority of the appointee is challenged by insiders.
- The local organizations are not attractive to the target market and have very few "customers."
- The local organizations do not feel obliged to accept the authority of the central organization.
- The central organization is dependent on a "mother" institution for its core funding. Thus, if the organization is not a priority of the mother institution and/or the mother institution suffers a decrease in income, the organization's budget is cut irrespective of its performance.
- The central organization does not have a fundraising arm and has little access to outside funding.

- The mission of the central organization is a low on the community priority.
- The organization is perceived to be a failing one and consequently is not attractive to potential donors.

Each one of these challenges is formidable and complex, requiring a high level of leadership skills and creativity in order to change the rules. Richard Joel faced *every single one* of these challenges and met them successfully.

Richard Joel

Richard Joel grew up in up in Yonkers, New York, the only child of Modern Orthodox parents. He attended public elementary school, and for high school he studied at Yeshiva University High School.

Joel pursued a legal career and earned his B.A. and J.D. degrees from New York University, where he was a Root-Tilden Scholar. He also served as district attorney and deputy chief of appeals in the Bronx, and associate dean and professor of law at the Benjamin N. Cardozo School of Law.

At heart Joel wanted to serve the Jewish people. In his teens he was a popular youth leader, and during his college years he was asked to be the part-time director of a new leadership program for day school students.

At the age of thirty-seven, Joel was headhunted for the position of CEO of National Hillel. On being approached he was not interested, but at his wife's urging he agreed to go to the interview and ultimately was appointed.

Joel's was an out-of-the-box appointment. He was a Modern Orthodox Jew and a complete outsider to Hillel. The organization was primarily staffed by rabbis, and Joel was not a rabbi.

Joel served as CEO of Hillel until 2003, when he was appointed president of Yeshiva University. Avraham Infeld, who succeeded him in the position, became the head of an organization that was radically different from the one Richard Joel "inherited" in 1988. Joel had masterminded a radical change of the rules [3]. [Rosen and Sales, 2006].

Changing the rules at Hillel

The B'nai B'rith Organization founded the Hillel Foundation in 1923 in Illinois, and within a few years opened local Hillels on campuses throughout the United States. These were usually headed by rabbis, and while they were supported by the central office, each Hillel operated independently.

Within this *laissez-faire* situation the different Hillels varied widely with regard to the quality of services they provided to the Jewish students. In general, the perception was that only a small minority of Jewish students on campuses entered their local Hillel, and that Hillel was a low-impact organization.

Local Hillels were supported both by the national office and by the local Federations. Their local allocations were largely determined by the priority the Federations assigned to having a Jewish presence on campus, and by their perceptions of the local Hillel's effectiveness. When both were negative, the support given could barely cover the costs of creative quality programming.

Since the Hillel national office was operated by B'nai B'rith, its resources were a function of its priority within B'nai B'rith and B'nai B'rith's financial situation. Thus, while National Hillel enjoyed the luxury of not having to finance its own endeavors, it was severely limited in the resources it could offer the local Hillels.

Within seven years, Joel had completely transformed the organization in the following ways:

---

3   My analysis of Joel's achievements is based on my perceptions gleaned from Rosen and Sales' study

- Hillel formed an organization which was legally independent of B'nai B'rith.
- Investment in Jewish student life became a communal priority.
- The quality of local Hillels improved dramatically.
- The number of Jewish students touched by Hillel grew substantially.
- Both the national organization and the local Hillels raised significant sums for infrastructure and creative programming.
- The Federations agreed to cover 40 percent of National Hillel's annual budget.
- Hillel attracted a prestigious lay leadership, including a board of governors, each of whom made an annual $50,000 commitment in order to sit on the board.

How did Joel achieve this? Rosen and Sales deliberate on this question at length in their compelling study. They cite Joel's ingenuity, vision, creativity, passion and communication skills. Indeed, these attributes are indicative of commercial CEOs who transformed their companies, such as Louis Gerstner, who transformed IBM (1993–2002) after retiring from American Express, and Steve Jobs, who transformed Apple when he returned to the helm in 1997, until his death in 2011.

In social vision organizations additional attributes are necessary. In my view, in order to change the rules in these organizations one needs the following two attributes germane to this field in addition to the ones listed above:

- Total existential identification with the mission.
- Moral authority to change the rules.

These two attributes are interdependent, and Joel excelled in both. Joel's commitment to the future of the Jewish people commenced at a very young age. In his position at Hillel, he was "obsessed" with the importance of creating quality Jewish educational experiences for Jewish students on campus.

One of his first innovations was the introduction of the accreditation system, which comprised an outside evaluation of each Hillel. This was considered to be a radical idea, with the prospect of a rebellion by the local Hillels. Yet Joel insisted that the Hillel network could justify its existence only if it could deliver quality programming. In moving quickly in this direction his entire future at Hillel was at risk. Yet because of his unswerving existential dedication to Hillel's mission, he was unwilling to compromise.

It was his deep concern that Hillel was catering only to "insiders" that landed Joel his first major gift, from Michael Steinhardt. Joel believed that the challenge was not to bring Jewish students to Hillel but rather to bring Hillel to the students. In the early years of his tenure, when the central organization was severely strapped for cash to cover its current liabilities, Joel convinced Michael Steinhardt to give a matching grant for the recruitment of twenty-five fellows who would be trained to engage Jewish students on campus who had never contemplated involvement in Hillel activities.

While the position required Joel to interact with lay leaders, philanthropists and the like, his primary love was interacting with the students on campus. He believed strongly that their commitment to a Jewish future was crucial for the future of the Jewish people, and he never missed an opportunity to espouse this cause.

While Joel was not an ordained rabbi, de facto he became the "chief rabbi" of Hillel and college campuses. His love of text study and commitment to Jewish learning were important contributors to his growing moral authority. Because he reached out to the disengaged, nobody questioned his commitment to empower the insiders as well. By replacing rabbis with excellent educators, his commitment to Torah study could not be questioned. Through his passion and proven existential commitment to the cause, he had acquired the moral authority to change the rules.

Moral authority is crucial for winning support when controversial decisions are taken. Former Israeli prime minister Menachem Begin's history as a political hawk gave him the moral authority to sign a peace treaty with Egypt's president, Anwar Sadat. It is hard to imagine that a Labor Party prime minister would have had the public support to return every inch of the Sinai Peninsula to Egypt.

Changing the Rules of the "Game"

In this chapter we have explored the norms and practices of an organization and its affiliates, and how the strategy of changing the rules serves to reposition the organization.

The broader field of Jewish education operates within certain norms and paradigms, and in extreme situations entrepreneurs will resort to changing the rules of an entire field in order to gain social value. These changes have an effect on the field at large and will require organizations to make a decision as to whether they will play according to the new rules or whether they prefer to play according to the traditional rules.

This level of changing of the rules is reflected in the commercial field with the rapid growth of e-commerce. Bricks and mortar platforms, which play according to the traditional rules, are being forced to respond to these new rules. Many stores are now being reduced to "showrooms," as consumers visit these stores yet ultimately decide to purchase the same item on the Internet for a lower price.

Changing the rules that govern the modi operandi of the Jewish education field

Since the turn of the century there have been entrepreneurial attempts to change the rules of how Jewish education is operated, and these new rules provide a series of opportunities for the growth of the Jewish education field as a whole.

The prime innovator of these new rules has been Taglit–Birthright Israel. In Chapter Six we discussed Taglit–Birthright's evolution and its success in navigating within "blue oceans." In this section we will highlight the rules that Taglit–Birthright changed, turning it into a beacon of success that enrolled and impacted half a million noncustomers over a period of fifteen years.

Taglit–Birthright's modi operandi
Taglit–Birthright comprises a number of components:

a. ## The Birthright Israel Foundation
    In the original agreement with the Israeli government, the government was to cover a third of the costs of the free trips while the remaining two-thirds would be covered by philanthropists and local Federations. In order to raise these funds the Birthright Israel Foundation was established in the United States. This organization, which at the time of this writing is headed by David Stern, is responsible for financially supporting the program.

b. ## Taglit–Birthright Israel
    Taglit–Birthright Israel was established in Israel as a supervisory organization that would outsource the trips to trip organizers. In its early days, Shimshon Shoshani, former director general of the Israel Ministry of Education and director general of the Jewish Agency, was appointed CEO of Taglit–Birthright Israel, and under his leadership the "founding fathers" decided that it would not operate the trips but rather outsource them to other organizations. This was a seminal decision, as Taglit–Birthright immediately became a catalyst for growing an existing field instead of being a competing "player" in the field.
    Shoshani's operational model was based on the prevailing model of the Israeli Ministry of Education whereby the ministry provides educational guidelines, supervision and

budget to Israeli schools, yet does not operate the schools themselves. With regard to Taglit–Birthright trips, various educational organizations apply to operate the trips. In order to ensure that trips meet the quality standards, trips are awarded on the basis of strict educational, logistical and security criteria.

c.   The trip organizers

The trip organizers are both nonprofit and for-profit local organizations which are given a budget from Taglit–Birthright Israel to recruit participants and organize the trips. If they themselves are tour operators they will also operate the trip. If not, which is generally the case, they will contract with Israeli tour operators.

d.   The tour operators

The tour operators are Israeli companies that are licensed to offer tourist services. They employ the tour educator and other Israeli staff, and are responsible for the logistics.

e.   Evaluation

Every trip is evaluated by an outside company. Evaluation takes place by participant observation in some trips, interviews with participants and surveys. In addition, the Cohen Center at Brandeis University evaluates the impact of the trip. This is done on the basis of a multiyear study of Jewish identity trends among Taglit–Birthright participants and a control group of those who applied to Taglit–Birthright but did not go on the trip.

Birthright changes the rules
An analysis of Taglit–Birthright reflects that it changed the following rules:

1.   *Quality Jewish education is a birthright.*
     This represents a change from the former rule according to which quality Jewish education is a privilege reserved for those willing to pay for it. In accordance with this new rule, Taglit–Birthright covers the entire costs of the ten-day educational trip to Israel.
     The difference between these two approaches relates to the onus of responsibility. According to the "old" rule the onus rests on the participants. As Jewish education is perceived to be a privilege, it is the participants' responsibility to cover costs. According to the new rule, a quality Jewish education is a right, and the onus of responsibility rests on the community.

2.   *Those who deliver education do not engage in fundraising.*
     In the Birthright model, the educational organizations, i.e., the trip organizers and tour operators, are paid in order to "deliver" the trip and its educational contents. As a result, they are singularly focused on the logistics and educational components of the experience without needing to engage in fundraising. In the old paradigm, the CEO of an educational organization is constantly engaged in fundraising for the organization. This change removes a great deal of pressure from those engaged in educational endeavors, and may alleviate the high level of executive burnout which is the result of the constant need to raise funds for the cause.

3.   *There are no territorial issues regarding Jewish education.*
     Taglit–Birthright has given legitimacy to nonprofit as well as for-profit organizations to organize its educational programs.

Their decision to award the trip is contingent on the organization meeting quality criteria. According to traditional rules, Jewish education is territorial, and thus even if an organization has educational expertise, if they offer a Jewish educational program that "invades" the territorial space of another organization they face major political pressure. This rule, for example, has led to JCCs refraining from offering Jewish educational programs for the pre-bar mitzvah age if there is opposition from the congregational Hebrew schools.

4. *Quality control: all educational activities are evaluated by an independent third party.*
All Taglit–Birthright trips are evaluated by an outside organization and the operators receive these evaluations. These evaluations are acted upon and steps are taken in response to weak performance. In the traditional model, it is rare that organizations are penalized for weak performance, and as a result standards are not necessarily maintained.

5. *The Israeli government funds Jewish educational programs that strengthen Jewish identity, unconnected to encouraging aliyah.*
Taglit–Birthright made a major breakthrough in convincing the Israeli government to be a major supporter of the project even though Birthright's primary intention was to strengthen members of Jewish communities who would continue to reside in the Diaspora. This presented a major policy shift, and in its wake the Israeli government is now prepared to invest major resources in Jewish education in the Diaspora.

Operating in accordance with the New Rules

If these new rules are adopted universally they will have large-scale ramifications.

The antagonists protest that we cannot afford the costs incurred by these new rules, and secondly that they have led to a sense of entitlement by the participants and a reticence for taking personal financial responsibility for their Jewish future.

The protagonists believe that we cannot afford *not* to adopt these new rules, since they have ensured our ability to succeed with these crucial noncustomers. In order to counterbalance the feeling of entitlement, we need to stress the importance of giving back to the community as an integral part of the educational process.

Similar to other strategies of innovation, changing the rules requires a high level of ingenuity and creativity. However, it needs a great deal of courage as well. A change of rules leads to a shift in the balance of power, and accordingly those who stand to lose their advantage may apply a great deal of pressure on the innovator to prevent the change.

We are highly fortunate to have innovators who are not only brilliant and creative but who are blessed with courage and resilience as well.

References

Chizhik-Goldschmidt, A. (2013, October 22). "The Ultra-Orthodox Seamstress Who Determined the Fate of Jewish Women ." *Haaretz*.

Chizuk Amuno Congregation (n.d.). "Meet the Clergy." Retrieved January 17, 2016. http://www.chizukamuno.org/about/meet-the-clergy/.

Fuchs, I. (2014). *Jewish Women's Torah Study: Orthodox Religious Education and Modernity.* New York: Routledge.

Kehilat Hadar (n.d.). "History." Retrieved March 15, 2016. https://www.kehilathadar.org/about/history.

Mechon Hadar (n.d.). "About US." Retrieved January 7, 2016. http://www. mechonhadar.org/about.

Pardes Insitute of Jewish Studies (n.d.). "About Pardes." Retrieved March 14, 2016. http://www.pardes.org.il/about/pardes/.

Pardes Institute for Jewish Studies (n.d.). "History." Retrieved March 15, 2016. http://www.pardes.org.il/about/history/.

Rosen, M. I., and A. I. Sales (2006). *The Remaking of Hillel: A Case of Leadership and Organizational Transformation.* Boston: Brandeis University Press.

Yeshiva University (n.d.). "Stern College for Women: History and Mission." Retrieved January 11, 2016. https://www.yu.edu/stern/about/mission-history/.

Chapter Thirteen

Investing in Innovation and the Challenge of Sustainability

CENTRAL IDEA

WE NEED A SYSTEMATIC APPROACH TO SUSTAINABILITY IN ORDER TO ENCOURAGE INNOVATION AND REAP THE BENEFITS FROM ITS SUCCESS.

In this book we have discussed key concepts of social entrepreneurship in the context of Jewish education and have highlighted them with examples from the field. Here in the final chapter we will discuss two outstanding initiatives that have achieved global impact. Highlighting them will give us the opportunity to apply some of the key concepts mentioned in earlier chapters and to focus on the major financial challenges facing entrepreneurs in the field of Jewish education

The first description focuses on TaL AM, the Judaic curricula for the lower grades in Jewish day schools.

TaL AM

TaL AM[1] the brainchild of Tova Shimon. Shimon was born in Rumania and came to Israel at the age of ten. After completing her undergraduate studies she moved to Montreal, Canada, and embarked on an illustrious career in Jewish Education.

Shimon's first major curriculum breakthrough was the design of Tal Sela, a Hebrew language arts curriculum for Grades 2–6 in

---

1   The name "TaL AM" is a Hebrew acronym for *Tochnit Limudim Ivrit Moreshet* ("Hebrew and Heritage Curriculum"). The first letter "a" is written in lower case as it is not the abbreviation of a word. The word *am* means "nation."

Jewish day schools which began being developed in 1979. With major funding from the Canadian government as well as support from the L. A. Pincus Jewish Fund for the Diaspora and the Jewish Community Foundation of Greater Montreal, Tal Sela became the standard Hebrew language curriculum in many day schools in North America; by 1989 it was being taught in 176 schools. Shimon's development of Tal Sela was recognized by the Covenant Foundation in 1992 when she received the coveted Covenant Award [the Covenant Foundation].

In 1989 Shimon put together a think tank to design a second-generation curriculum which would add a Jewish heritage component to the curriculum. In 1990 the TaL AM curriculum project commenced work, with funding from the Canadian government, The Pincus Fund, The Heinish Foundation and the local Jewish Federation, CJA. In 1995 the first grade curriculum was disseminated in schools.

The curriculum was a major success, and in 1999 Shimon sent in a proposal to the AVI CHAI Foundation in New York seeking funding for the development of a second grade curriculum.

AVI CHAI granted TaL AM a two-year initial grant and the second grade curriculum was successfully implemented. Given the daunting challenges that curriculum developers face, TaL AM's achievement should not be taken lightly.

Shimon shared her vision with AVI CHAI to develop a curriculum all the way through elementary school. The foundation had monitored the impact of the project, noting its success in multiple ideological and geographical environments. It awarded Shimon and her team a generous, multiyear grant, which enabled her to tap the best minds in Canada and Israel to develop the curriculum. TaL AM was ultimately developed up to fifth grade, delivering a spiral curriculum of the highest quality.

At the time of this writing, the project has been implemented globally in 350 schools, with over 30,000 students, in thirty-eight countries, using the curriculum on an annual basis [the AVI CHAI

Foundation, "TaL AM"]. The curriculum is now being redeveloped for the digital world, complete with a learning management system to enable more personalized learning (iTalAm, in partnership with Compendia, an Israeli educational gaming company). These new developments are taking full advantage of prevailing teaching and learning styles as well as the technological advances that can enhance the pedagogical experience.

This success would not have been possible without the major funding and support that the AVI CHAI Foundation will have invested in the project over seventeen years by the end of 2019.

The AVI CHAI Foundation

The AVI CHAI Foundation was established by Zalman Bernstein in 1984. Bernstein founded Sanford C. Bernstein and Co. in 1967 and developed it into one of the largest privately owned investment firms in the United States. In the 1980s be began to move toward tradition, and in 1989 he came on aliyah, settling in Jerusalem.

The mission of the AVI CHAI Foundation is the following:

- *To encourage those of the Jewish faith toward greater commitment to Jewish observance and lifestyle by increasing their understanding, appreciation and practice of Jewish traditions, customs and laws.*
- *To encourage mutual understanding and sensitivity among Jews of different religious backgrounds and observances.*

In order to fulfill this mission the foundation initially adopted a broad approach, but in the mid-1990s it made the strategic decision to focus on investing in Jewish day schools. Alarmed by the findings of the 1990 National Population Study in North America, which showed an increase in intermarriage and a weakening of the Jewish community, AVI CHAI commissioned a study from the Guttman Israel Institute in 1993.

The Guttmann Institute studied different types of Jewish education and the subsequent adult Jewish involvement of the graduates. The findings were unequivocal: "Jewish day schools are the only type of Jewish education that stands against the very rapidly growing rate of intermarriage." As a result of the Guttmann Institute's findings, the foundation commissioned sociologist Marvin Schick to do an in-depth study of Jewish day schools and to report on areas which needed to be strengthened in order to enhance the impact of Jewish day school education [the AVI CHAI Foundation, 1998].

Spearheaded by Yossi Prager, the director of AVI CHAI in North America, the foundation adopted a proactive approach to the strengthening of Jewish day schools in North America, particularly those schools willing to adopt AVI CHAI's core mission with a commitment to "encourage mutual understanding and sensitivity among Jews of different religious backgrounds."

AVI CHAI thus examined different areas within the day school milieu and sought opportunities to strengthen the schools. When it identified organizations that advanced this mission, such as TaL AM, it invested heavily in their growth. In situations in which there was a void, the foundation sought talented individuals and commissioned their services in order to develop solutions. An example of this is Neta, an organization that develops curriculum for high schools. AVI CHAI commissioned its founding.

In operating in this manner, AVI CHAI is impact-driven. It has formed genuine partnerships and long-term relationships with its grantees, constantly mentoring and challenging them. It has always had a long-term view and consequently is able to see the fruits of its investments, which by nature are long-term.

In 2004, AVI CHAI added overnight Jewish camping as its second area of strategic support. For a few years the foundation sought to impact segments of the population not attending Jewish day schools. They commissioned a study from the Cohen Center at Brandeis University on the impact of sleepaway summer camps, and the study, titled "Limud on the Lake," undertaken by Len Saxe and Amy Sales, emphasized the potential of these camps for impacting teens [the AVI CHAI Foundation, Annual Report 2004].

Here too AVI CHAI adopted a strategic approach, with a view to strengthening the Jewish content of the camps. Working in the same way they worked with the Jewish day schools, the foundation focused on areas that needed to be strengthened, and supported them on a multiyear basis.

TaL AM is an outstanding example of a bridging strategy that enables teachers to connect with their students in a meaningful way, leveraging the motivation of the students to learn and the ability and commitment of the faculty to teach. In those schools where there is no standard curriculum, the teachers need to design their own bridge, which can be highly time-consuming and without a guarantee of success.

TaL AM's macro theory of change is that it is possible to design an elementary school curriculum and associated teacher training that will have the buy in of faculty and students alike across geographical and denominational divides. The macro theory is very ambitious and has few precedents, particularly in the field of Jewish education. TaL AM's strength is its innovative micro theory that draws on the five senses, on song, art and text, and on highly engaging themes. The curriculum requires teacher orientation seminars, which are central to the micro theory.

The return on investment is very high given the global reach of the program. In focusing on developing curriculum across the entire day school spectrum, TaL AM operated in a blue ocean. Until its launch, curriculum initiatives had been denominational, limited to the schools that were part of the different denomination networks.

Moishe House

A second outstanding initiative is Moishe House, which focuses on post-college young adults.

Moishe House is the brainchild of David Cygielman who opened the first Moishe House in Oakland, California, in January 2006, and a second in San Francisco three weeks later [Bernstein, 2010]. Cygielman, who was in his early twenties at the time, worked for philanthropist, Morris Squire. He wanted to do something for those young Jewish adults who were too old for college organizations but had not yet settled down and joined synagogues and other communal organizations. He convinced a few friends to turn their rented house into a place where they would dedicate themselves to offering Jewish programming for their peers, using the home to house these Jewish activities.

He secured the support of Morris Squire to establish the first houses and, as requested by the donor, called them "Moishe Houses," naming them after Morris's Yiddish name, Moishe. Morris was the sole supporter of the project through 2008, after which Cygielman successfully secured widespread philanthropic support.

Despite the recession of 2008, Cygielman was able to grow the project, increasing the number of Moishe Houses annually. His success received widespread attention, and in 2011 the TCC Group conducted an evaluation with very positive results [TCC Group, 2011].

This evaluation culminated in Moishe House receiving $6 million in funding in 2012 from the Jim Joseph Foundation, the Charles and Lynn Schusterman Family Foundation, The Leichtag Foundation, Genesis Philanthropy Group and the Maimonides Fund in order to grow the project [The Algemeiner, 2012].

Moishe House's growth

Between 2011 and the beginning of 2016, the number of Moishe Houses had almost doubled, reaching out to 105,000 young adults in 2015. Located in twenty countries, eighty-five Moishe Houses provided these young adults with a Jewish home environment, which hopefully will encourage them to build their own Jewish home in the future.

The impact of Moishe House

In 2015 an independent evaluation of the impact of Moishe House was published. Its key findings are as follows:

Moishe House

- Remains a high-quality, compelling opportunity for Jewish young adults to engage in active Jewish lives, which is particularly significant given its rapid growth, nearly doubling in size and reach since 2011.
- Uses a unique approach of providing peer-based programs in a home-based setting, which continues to appeal to young adults as a model for building Jewish community.
- Deepens participants' connection to Judaism and Jewish life.
- Is a hub of Jewish life for Jewish young adults.
- Helps people connect with Jewish life outside (in the larger realm).
- Helps young adults become stronger leaders in the greater Jewish community. [Moishe House, 2015]

Necessary factors for achieving success

Cygielman's success is no doubt due to his personal creativity, passion, commitment and leadership skills which have enabled him to take full advantage of a ripe marketplace. He has the DNA of an entrepreneur, as do many others whose stories I have discussed in this book. This DNA, while necessary, is not sufficient, however. Many educational entrepreneurs who have it may still require support in two key areas:

- The practice of entrepreneurship. If they have never built an organization from scratch they quickly discover there is a gap between their ambitions and the complex reality.
- Access to funding to enable them to develop their entrepreneurial models.

In both realms Cygielman had strong support. He benefited from his membership in the ROI Communities, which is supported by the Charles and Lynn Schusterman Family Foundation, and the support of UpStart Bay Area. Cygielman received funding from the major philanthropies we have mentioned and many others, and benefited from strong lay leadership support through his board and other mentors.

UpStart Bay Area

UpStart Bay Area is part of the growing startup and innovation support sector, which commenced in 1998. The impetus for this new sector was the realization that with technological and cultural changes, as well as the "changing of the rules" which was sweeping the world, the Jewish community needed both to be innovative and to absorb innovation.

The major organizations that comprise this sector are Joshua Venture Group (established in 1998), Bikkurim (in 2000), ROI Communities (in 2005), UpStart Bay Area (in 2006), PresenTense (in 2007), Jumpstart (in 2008), and JHub, which was established in the United Kingdom in 2008.

Barry Camson enumerated the following activities of these organizations: To Incubate or accelerate the actual ventures, to support connections and the sharing of knowledge among people working on startup ventures, to educate or train people to prepare them for working in this area, to develop leadership competencies and to Sensitize people to the potential to be innovative in responding to contemporary Jewish challenges [Camson, 2014].

The emergence of this sector is quite remarkable. In the commercial sector, startup and innovation support centers have a strong financial base. They are sponsored by either public funds or commercial companies. Governments who support these centers believe that the startups will strengthen their economies, attracting new investments and increased employment. Commercial companies nurture startups in return for a stake in the new company.

In the Jewish nonprofit world, which does not receive government and commercial support, startup and innovation support sectors are part of the entrepreneurial startup field they are endeavoring to support. The support organizations are startups themselves, and consequently those founded through individual initiative as opposed to foundation initiative may need to compete for funding with the startup fledglings they wish to support.

The above challenges notwithstanding, these support organizations have had a remarkable impact on the Jewish community at large, and specifically on Jewish education. Over fifty new organizations and hundreds of entrepreneurs have benefited from their support. These include Moishe House, Mechon Hadar, Hazon and G-dcast, all of which are playing a vital role in the community at large.

Innovation is not limited to the startup sector. There is a growing trend among the large, established organizations including Federations and Bureaus of Jewish Education to build in-house innovation support departments to benefit them and their affiliates.

A leader in this field is the Jewish Education Project in New York City, which was previously the Board of Jewish Education. This organization was extremely fortunate to attract Dr. David Bryfman to its ranks in 2008 in the newly created post of chief learning officer. Bryfman is a leader in the field of educational innovation and firmly believes in the importance of innovation within established organizations.

An analysis of Moishe House's success
The development of Moishe House reflects many of the themes we have discussed in this book. Moishe House's strategy of innovation was to build a physical platform that would provide creative programming for post-college Jewish adults in the community. The target audience is a blue ocean, with too few Jewish organizations competing for their attention.

For these participants, Moishe House is successful in providing them with a "jobs to be done" within a Jewish context. Young, single adults appreciate an open, welcoming home environment that enables them to interact socially and meaningfully with their peers.

The macro theory of change is very creative and highly plausible, and the simple micro theory is easily replicable. According to the macro theory, if young, enthusiastic adults volunteer to offer programming for their peers in exchange for a rental subsidy, they will succeed in creating a meaningful connection with their "customers" and thereby will attract them to their activities. The micro theory, which has been replicated successfully around the globe, includes the application and selection process of prospective "personnel," orientation and training, and the support they receive from the central organization.

The return on investment is significant on two levels. First, with a minimum of resources there is a major impact on the participants. Second, and no less important, is the leadership development of the personnel. In order to succeed, Moishe House hosts need to develop leadership skills and learn how the Jewish community operates. In the wake of their experience at Moishe House the personnel may naturally transition themselves into leadership positions in the future, whether in lay or in professional capacities.

Comparing TaL AM with Moishe House

TaL AM and Moishe House are both significant success stories that have impacted many Jewish populations around the globe. Moreover, both organizations are driven by the passion and vision of extremely capable entrepreneurs. In comparing the endeavors, it is evident that they operate on opposite sides of the innovation spectrum. TaL AM is an excellent example of sustaining innovation, while Moishe House is an excellent example of disruptive innovation.

TaL AM: Sustaining Innovation

TaL AM was established in order to strengthen the "high-end" consumer market of Jewish education, i.e., the Jewish day schools. Parents of day school children pay high tuition fees and they expect a high-quality Judaic curriculum for their children.

In order to produce its high-quality curriculum, TaL AM needed to make a major investment in research and development, at times engaging a team of seventy. Moreover, TaL AM makes a major investment in staff education and in ensuring the materials are kept up to date.

Moishe House: Disruptive Innovation

Moishe House is a disruptive innovation of the highest level designed to serve a wide group of noncustomers. The house residents are the "personnel." These passionate individuals do not view themselves as professionals. Rather, they perceive themselves as peers who understand the needs of the target population and who are committed to meeting these needs. The model allows young adults to fully engage in building Jewish community on the nights and weekends, allowing them to pursue many different professional careers while still leading their peers.

Similarities

Despite the differences between TaL AM and Moishe House, there is a striking similarity in their success in scaling up. In year six of its development phase, TaL AM had completed the first grade pilot curriculum and demonstrated that it had a successful design model, which could be scaled through to sixth grade. Four years later, the AVI CHAI Foundation made a multiyear investment to ensure the program would reach its full potential.

Similarly, it was in year six that Moishe House demonstrated it had an effective educational model. At this stage the Jim Joseph Foundation, together with its partners, made a major investment, thereby allowing the program to grow exponentially.

Regretfully, these success stories are exceptions to the rule. In the main, when organizations move from startup mode to post-startup mode, as did these two organizations, there is often a *drop* in available funding. This finding was published in the landmark study of Jewish community startups [Herman, Mazor, Landres and Weinmen Stienberg, 2012] and reflects the major difference between startups in the commercial world and those in the area of Jewish education.

Startups in the Commercial World Compared with Startups in the Field of Jewish Education

Commercial startups and Jewish education startups will go through similar phases during the initial, "seed" stage. In order to begin the process, both types of entrepreneurs will need to take financial and career risks, often requiring a level of personal sacrifice. They will work hard to find initial funders who will enable them to build a first prototype of their product or system. These funders, who are called "seed investors" or "angel investors," will be taking a major risk with their pre-launch investment, since they are investing in an idea and little more.

A seed investment in the world of Jewish education is motivated by the funder's deep commitment to the vision and willingness to invest in an endeavor that shows a potential for fulfilling this vision. In the commercial world, seed funders may be motivated by the prospect of making a major profit should the endeavor prosper. Thus they may request equity in the fledgling business, which ultimately could result in major profits. This is illustrated by the seed investment in the cosmetics and skin care company, the Body Shop.

The Body Shop

In 1976 Anita Roddick opened a store, the Body Shop, in Brighton, United Kingdom, creating and selling personal products. Her store, which was modeled on a similar one she had seen in Berkeley,

California, was successful, and she decided to open a second one in Chichester, seeking a loan of £4000 for this purpose.

The banks refused to give her a loan, and in desperation she turned to a friend, Ian McGlinn, who offered her a loan on condition she would grant him 50 percent equity in the company [Quarter, 2000].

The Body Shop grew exponentially, opening stores across the globe. It was floated on the London Stock Exchange in 1984. At this point McGlinn's share in the business was now worth 4 million pounds. In 1991 his stock in the company grew to £150 million. Over the years he sold some stock, and in 2007 sold the rest to L'Oréal for £137 million [Financial Times].

Within thirty years, following a £4000 loan to a fledglings company, McGlinn had become one of the richest individuals in the United Kingdom!

Angel funding

Using angel funding, the entrepreneur will be able to develop a prototype which can be tested in the field. If the model proves to be successful the entrepreneur is ready to embark on a second phase, which comprises completing the model and enhancing its capabilities. In this phase, entrepreneurs from both worlds will embark on fundraising in order to finance these developments. They will need to personally engage with potential funders in order to convince them that the prototypes are highly promising. Their "human touch" in raising funds will also be critical.

While both commercial and educational endeavors will "go out of business" if they fail, when they are successful there is generally a radical difference in their developmental path.

In the commercial sector the company should be on its way to profitability. At last the founders are able to enjoy the fruits of their labors, and if they are highly successful they will contemplate an exit or a buyout. By contrast, in the Jewish educational realm the endgame of sustainability is much more elusive. Foundations that are vested in innovation prefer investing in organizations in the startup phase and as a result finances are tight during the second phase of development. Thus fundraising needs to continue in earnest. In the worst case scenario, even if the initiative is educationally successful the organization could close [Herman, Mazor, Landres and Weinmen Steinberg, 2012).

This is what highlights the radical difference between the two realms. In the commercial world the rules of the game offer the possibility of a happy financial end, thereby *encouraging* entrepreneurship. In Jewish education entrepreneurship the rules of the game point to an uncertain future, thereby *discouraging* entrepreneurship.

The implications of these rules were brought home to me when in one of my interviews with a highly creative entrepreneurial thinker I discovered that he had elected to work for a traditional Jewish educational organization rather than an innovative one. When I suggested that he could make a major contribution to the field if he were to spearhead an educational startup, his response said it all. He had a family and could not afford a financially insecure future.

Can We Change the Rules?

In this discussion we have compared the incentive of commercial entrepreneurship with the financial disincentive of entrepreneurship within the realm of Jewish education. Do these disincentives prevail within the general area of nonprofits?

In the general nonprofit field, there is a critical third source of income not accessible to Jewish education in the United States because of the church-state divide: government support and contracts. This is a major source of funding, and gives general nonprofits a third primary avenue for possible funding in addition to earned income and philanthropy. In the realm of Jewish education, however, only the two latter avenues are available.

Philanthropy and the state can work hand in hand in order to enhance social value. In areas in which the state is prepared to fund an endeavor's operations, philanthropists will invest in program and infrastructure development in order to enable the organization to reach larger audiences. Likewise, when the state is prepared to invest in enhancing the capabilities of the product or service, philanthropists will invest in sustainability. Given this third avenue of funding in the general nonprofit sector, sustainability is within reach. This encourages nonprofit entrepreneurs to develop new organizations.

In Jewish education, the absence of a major third stream of funding leads to an overburdening of the other two. Philanthropy is double-mined for both developing new programs and sustainability, and when funds are not available, excessive financial demands are made on the customers in order to increase the source of earned income.

Is it possible to establish a third avenue of funding for Jewish education? If the answer to this question is yes, the system will resemble the general nonprofit sector and the prospect of sustainability will be in reach.

Since state funding for religious education in the United States will not happen in the foreseeable future, a third tier will need to be artificially developed as a priority of the Jewish community.

Possible sources of a third income stream

In order to ensure that current philanthropy is not double-mined, a third avenue of income needs to comprise new sources currently out of reach. There are a number of potential sources:

a. *The government of Israel.*
    In light of its investment in Taglit–Birthright Israel and Masa, the government of Israel has committed to investing in Jewish education in the Diaspora. In a Cabinet decision taken in June 2014, ILS 187 million (approximately $47 million) was allocated for this purpose [Sokol, 2014]. Investing this

255

sum in sustaining quality Jewish education would certainly be an effective use of these funds.

b. *The Jewish National Fund.*

The Jewish National Fund (JNF) has become a major funder of community education projects. In its financial report for 2014, the JNF reported an investment of ILS 81 million (approximately $20 million) in education [Boso, 2015]. Given Diaspora support for this important agency, it would not be unreasonable for a sizable amount of funding to be invested in sustaining quality Jewish education in the Diaspora.

In addition to the two possible sources mentioned above, there are two relatively new initiatives which have thus far generated limited funds. However, both sources have huge potential given their access to blue ocean funds.

c. *Equity from startups.*

In 2002 Yedid Kaufman, an Israeli investor, founded Tmura, a nonprofit organization that has thus far generated $12.8 million for education and social welfare projects [Tmura]. Kaufman believed that successful commercial startups should make a financial contribution to society, and he devised a creative mechanism for achieving this goal.

As we saw from the Body Shop, when startups are in their first stages they sell equity in order to raise capital. At this early stage, Tmura invites entrepreneurs to donate 1 percent of their equity to the organization, which at the time of the donation is practically worthless yet potentially could be worth a substantive amount if the startup becomes successful.

Tmura's successes include $1.5 million they received for their equity in Waze, which was sold to Google in 2013 for $1.03 billion (Shamah, 2013). To date 465 companies have donated equity to Tmura, and thus the organization's income should grow dramatically in the future.

Tmura's model is highly replicable across the globe and has a huge potential given the high number of Jewish entrepreneurs who are in the process of developing startups. If entrepreneurial graduates of Taglit–Birthright Israel could commit themselves to pledge 1 percent of their future equity to quality Jewish education, this could be an important source of future income.

d.   *Social impact bonds.*
Social impact bonds (SIBs) have become a major vehicle for raising funds from the private sector to ensure the sustainability of projects with measurable impact in the nonprofit sector. Their global champion is Sir Ronald Cohen, the British Jewish financier who pioneered the development of Social Finance UK in 2010, Social Finance US in 2011 and Social Finance Israel in 2013.

Social impact bonds explained
Social impact bonds are non-tradable bonds that operate as follows:

The private sector puts up funds for the operation of a social program, with a commitment from a third party that if certain outcomes are achieved it will repay the investors the principal of their investment plus interest. The third party enters into a "pay-for-success" contract with the investors, and it is the investors who bear the financial risk if the social objectives are not met.

The investors assess the social project's probability of success. Because of their commitment to the cause and their belief that the project has a reasonable chance of success, they are willing to risk their funds. They bring not only their financial investment, they also invest their professional expertise to ensure the project's success.

The third party plays a critical role in this transaction by undertaking to pay for the endeavor should it be successful in achieving the projected outcomes. In order to alleviate any possible difference of opinion at the end of the process, an independent evaluator is appointed and this individual or company is empowered to determine if the projected outcomes have indeed been met.

The motivations for a third party coming to the table could be multiple, whether related to their own mission, their financial interests or their ideology. Third parties are guaranteed success, and if they are motivated and have financial capabilities their role becomes a natural fit. Thus local municipalities, whose mission is to provide services to their constituents, may be prepared to be the third party if the project serves its mission. Governments that are shown how a project could save them future costs may be willing to be the third party for an endeavor of this nature. Likewise, ideologically motivated foundations may be willing to be the third party should the project's objective realize the foundation's ideological goals.

This three-sided partnership carries distinct advantages over the traditional two-sided partnership. In the latter, when there is a government department or a philanthropic organization that pays for a project operated by a nonprofit organization, the donor has no guarantee of success. Should the donor insist on a pay-for-success contract, the organization would be foolhardy to enter into the contract. It will be risking its precious resources on projected outcomes, which may prove beyond reach. Thus the social impact bond provides a mechanism which sets up a dream situation for both donor and operator. The donor pays only if the endeavor is successful and the nonprofit organization is able to operate in a stable financial setting, which guarantees its sustainability.

Investing social impact bonds in general educational programs

Following are two examples of SIB investments in general educational programs, the first in the United States and the second in Israel. In both situations these were the first educational SIBs to be issued in these respective countries.

Investment in early childhood school readiness programs in Utah

In August 2013, investment bank Goldman Sachs, together with J. B. Pritzker, partnered to create a social impact bond financing early childhood education [Goldman Sachs].

This $7 million bond invested in expanding the Utah High Quality Preschool Program. This program had an impressive track record of radically increasing school readiness among disadvantaged children who otherwise would have required special education support in their schooling years. The third party in this transaction was the United Way of Salt Lake City and other public authorities, which committed themselves to repaying the investors annually.

In July 2015, the United Way paid the investors $267,000 from its own funds as a result of the initial success of the program [Walsh, 2015].

Investment in retention among college computer science students in Israel

In November 2015, Social Finance Israel facilitated its first SIB. A coalition comprising the Rothschild Caesarea Foundation, Bank Leumi and the Beyond Impact Investment Company committed ILS 8 million over eight years for a program to radically reduce attrition among college students who study computer science at Haifa University and Tel Aviv–Jaffa Academic College. With a 30 percent attrition rate among computer science students Israel is no different from other OECD countries, and the program's objective is to reduce this figure by 35 percent. Aluma, a nonprofit organization specializing in making higher education accessible to weaker populations, was chosen to implement the project.

In this pay-for-success contract, the third party will be the two academic institutions. They receive per-student funding from the government, and if they retain their students this funding will be increased substantially. In receipt of these funds the academic institutions will have a source of funding which will enable them to run the program at a surplus. This surplus will then be channeled back to the investor [Social Finance Israel, 2015].

Issuing social impact bonds for sustaining quality Jewish education

Given the effectiveness of utilizing private market expertise and funding in the form of SIBs for the above general educational endeavors, it is worth exploring their use within the field of Jewish education. While they are an enticing option, several key questions need to be addressed first:

- Will investors be prepared to purchase social impact bonds for investment in Jewish education?

  This is an open question worth pursuing. Within a Jewish community context the mixing of philanthropy with commercial gain may seem a little strange. However, on closer observation we find a highly successful organization that combines these two motivations.

  Israel Bonds is an investment program that pays interest for long-term investments, thereby guaranteeing a financial return. Furthermore, in marketing the bonds there is a distinct appeal to support Israel. The call for financial support is no different from the calls which raise philanthropic funds for Israel, and the individual who invests in Israel Bonds may be motivated both ideologically and financially. As this "double bottom line" appeal has been very successful in promoting investment in the Jewish state, perhaps similar success could be achieved with a call to invest in the Jewish people.

- Which third party will be prepared to ultimately pay for the investment?
  Hopefully the Jewish Agency and the local Jewish Federations will consider this option seriously. If they are committed to sustaining quality Jewish education, SIBs might be a tempting option, enabling fundraising organizations raise funds for success – not as mere rhetoric, but backed up by the independent, outside evaluation of the educational projects.

- Will a pay-for-success model succeed in growing the field of quality Jewish education?
  In keeping with our concerns for sustainability, pay-for-success models would herald a change in the rules which could enable us to leverage the power of entrepreneurship. They would focus the efforts of entrepreneurs on accomplishing the task with less reliance on fundraising. Pay-for-success models would reward and effect growth and quality, encouraging creative entrepreneurs to meet *our* challenge of making quality Jewish education accessible to all.

Utilization of the resources mentioned above for sustaining quality Jewish education will certainly serve as a catalyst for the development of the field. However, if we are to enjoy dramatic growth we will need far greater financial resources. Fortunately, these resources do exist and the challenge we have is how to build bridges to them.

This is a major challenge; it's our challenge!

References

The Algemeiner (2012, August 8). "Moishe House Given $6 Million to Expand." Retrieved February 3, 2016. http://www.algemeiner.com/2012/08/08/moishe-house-given-6-million-to-expand/.

The AVI CHAI Foundation (2004). *2004 Annual Report.*

The AVI CHAI FOUNDATION (1998). "AVI CHAI 1995–1997." JERUSALEM.

THE AVI CHAI FOUNDATION (N.D.). "TAL AM." RETRIEVED FEBRUARY 9, 2016. HTTP://AVICHAI.ORG/PROGRAM-LISTINGS/TAL-AM/.

Bernstein, F. A. (2010, February 10). "The Four-Bedroom Kibbutz." The *New York Times.* Retrieved April 4, 2013. http://www.nytimes.com/2010/02/11/garden/11moishe.html.

Boso, N. (2015, July 7). "Nadlan." The Marker. Retrieved February 21, 2016. http://www.themarker.com/realestate/1.2678467.

The Covenant Foundation (n.d.). "Tova Shimon." Retrieved February 9, 2016. http://www.covenantfn.org/awards/past-recipients/awards-1992/tova-shimon.

Camson, B. (2014, April 24). "A Panorama of Jewish Venture-Based Organizations." eJewish Philanthropy. Retrieved February 10, 2016. http://ejewishphilanthropy.com/a-panorama-of-jewish-venture-based-organizations/.

Goldman Sachs (n.d.). "Impact Investing." Retrieved February 23, 2016. http://www.goldmansachs.com/what-we-do/investing-and-lending/impact-investing/case-studies/salt-lake-social-impact-bond.html.

Herman, F., A. Mazor, S. Landres, and D. Weinmen Stienberg, eds. (2012). *From First Fruits to Abundant Harvest: Maximizing the Potential of Innovative Jewish Start Ups.* New York: Bikkurim, Wellspring Consultants.

Moishe House (2015, April). "Moishe House 2015 Evaluation." Retrieved February 8, 2016. https://www.moishehouse.org/2015eval.

Quarter, J. (2000). *Beyond the Bottom Line: Socially Innovative Business Owners*. Westport, CT: Quorum Books, 135–150.

Shamah, D. (2013, September 11). "With an Options Donation, Waze Spreads the Wealth." Times of Israel. Retrieved February 23, 2016. http://www.timesofisrael.com/with-an-options-donation-waze-spreads-the-wealth/.

Social Finance Israel (2015, November 5). "Israel's First Social Impact Bond Gets Underway." Retrieved February 23, 2016. http://www.socialfinance.org.il/news-item/97/israel%EF%BF%BDs-first-social-impact-bond-gets-underway.

Sokol, S. (2014, June 1). "Cabinet Approves Budget for Diaspora Outreach." The Jerusalem Post. Retrieved February 21, 2016. http://www.jpost.com/Jewish-World/Jewish-Features/Cabinet-approves-budget-for-diaspora-outreach-355044.

TCC Group (2011). *Evaluation Report Moishe House.* New York: TCC Group.

Tmura (n.d.). "About Us." Retrieved February 23, 2016. http://www.tmura.org/.

UpStart (n.d.). "The UpStart Story." Retrieved February 3, 2016. http://www.upstartbayarea.org/about/our-story.

Walsh, B. (2015, August 10). "Why This Preschool just Wrote Goldman Sachs a Check." The Huffington Post. Retrieved February 23, 2016. http://www.huffingtonpost.com/entry/goldman-sachs-social-impact-bond-preschool_us_5616810fe4b0082030a15169.

Postscript

This book is my own social entrepreneurial endeavor. Now that we have reached the end I'd like to take the concepts and paradigms developed, to apply them to this book and to look ahead at its potential impact. Since in social entrepreneurship the most important question that needs to be addressed refers to the social value of the endeavor, let us explore the social value of this book.

Social Value

The social value that I have endeavored to achieve is the enhancement of social vision entrepreneurship in general, and the advancement of quality Jewish education in particular.

The current literature in social entrepreneurship focuses on meeting social needs and articulates strategies that have alleviated or could alleviate social problems and suffering. To the best of my knowledge, this book is the first comprehensive theoretical work in the field to focus on strategies for the implementation of a social vision.

In order to go about this task systematically, it was necessary for me to develop a common language for use by the different stakeholders – the professionals, the policymakers, the funders and the academics. The text comprises the theories, paradigms and concepts that are applicable to all social vision-driven initiatives. The context is Jewish education, and I have demonstrated the application of the theories, paradigms and concepts with regard to the advancement of quality Jewish education.

While the focus of this book has been on social vision entrepreneurship, those involved in social needs entrepreneurship may also find sections of this book of use. The chapters on theory of change and disruptive innovation are both pertinent to social needs entrepreneurship. Social needs entrepreneurs aim to intervene in society, and in order to succeed they need a plausible theory of change. Moreover, they seek to make goods and services accessible to those who currently lack access to them, and disruptive innovation is a crucial vehicle for achieving this objective. Similarly, the four strategies of innovation we have discussed: developing new products and processes, designing platforms, bridging and changing the rules, are all pertinent for social needs innovation in the quest to develop solutions to social ills.

Theory of Change

Our theory of change for this book starts with the assumption that those who are invested in social entrepreneurial initiatives come from different fields and different disciplines and thus speak different "languages." Educators focus on the acquisition of knowledge and values, and frame their discussions in these terms. Funders, who come from the private sector, may focus on the financial aspects of the endeavor, and their discussions will be framed in economic terms. Policymakers may be sensitive to the political and institutional implications of the endeavor, and concepts from these fields may inform the discussion. Finally, academics may engage in discussions emphasizing theory and research.

The lack of a common language often leads to discussion at cross purposes, a lack of mutual understanding and different priorities among the different stakeholders. In extreme circumstances, the endeavor's chances of success may be seriously hampered.

Our *macro theory of change* suggests that if we are able to develop a common language among all the stakeholders, this will enhance the field of Jewish education in general and individual endeavors in particular.

Our *micro theory of change* suggests that if we draw our theories, paradigms and concepts from multiple disciplines and particularly from the commercial literature, and present them in a stimulating and engaging manner, the different stakeholders will be encouraged to adopt this common language.

Extending the Boundaries

Traditionally, books about Jewish education are read by a small band of dedicated professionals, lay leaders and funders. The intention of this book is to reach out to a broad base and to challenge all who are concerned about our Jewish future to become familiar with social vision entrepreneurship in the context of Jewish education. The field needs blue oceans of entrepreneurs, funders and policymakers in order to succeed. This book thus endeavors to connect with new audiences and tempt them to further their interest in the field.

Strategies of Innovation

In embarking upon strategies of innovation in this book, I have adopted those of "developing new products and processes" and "bridging."

Developing new Products and Processes

In this work I have designed a common language for social vision entrepreneurship. The theories and concepts "blue ocean," "disruptive innovation" and "jobs to be done," as well as "return on investment," were all borrowed from the commercial literature. I myself developed the "macro theory of change" and the four strategies of innovation.

Bridging

A prime objective of this work is to build a conceptual bridge between the different stakeholders in Jewish education. As discussed, it is crucial that the entrepreneurs, funders, policymakers and academics are all able to communicate with each other in a meaningful and purposeful manner.

In addition, I have aspired to do the following:

Changing the Rules

I hope this book will encourage policymakers and funders to change the rules of the game. In order for social vision entrepreneurship to succeed in the realm of quality Jewish education, the latter needs to become a community responsibility and a funding priority. These objectives are of critical importance and will largely influence the future of the field.

Designing a Platform

It is my intention to develop a web platform in order for readers to make their contribution to this important field. This book is merely a starting point, and through crowdsourcing, i.e., the contribution of insights and experience from the "crowd," the theoretical field could be greatly enhanced.

Success of the Endeavor

Ultimately, all of us together will determine the degree to which this social entrepreneurial endeavor will succeed in the field of Jewish education.

In order to maximize the chances of our success, I invite you to send me your thoughts, reactions, questions and insights. I am hopeful that the next phase of this work will indeed be a joint endeavor.

Jonathan Mirvis
msmirvis@gmail.com

CPSIA information can be obtained at www.ICGtesting.com
Printed in the USA
BVOW06s0240230616

453176BV00011B/88/P